# Roots in the Sawdust

# Roots in the Sawdust

Writing to Learn across the Disciplines

Edited by

Anne Ruggles Gere
University of Washington, Seattle

National Council of Teachers of English
1111 Kenyon Road, Urbana, Illinois 61801

NCTE Editorial Board: Candy Carter, Julie Jensen, Delores Lipscomb, John S. Mayher, Elisabeth McPherson, John C. Maxwell, *ex officio*, Paul O'Dea, *ex officio*

Book Design: Tom Kovacs for TGK Design

NCTE Stock Number 41986

**Library of Congress Cataloging-in-Publication Data**
Main entry under title:

Roots in the sawdust.

    Bibliography: p.
    1. English language—Composition and exercises—
Study and teaching (Secondary)—United States—
Addresses, essays, lectures.   2. Education, Secondary—
United States—Curricula—Addresses, essays, lectures.
3. Study, Method of—Addresses, essays, lectures.
I. Gere, Anne Ruggles, 1944–
PE1404.R66   1985        808'.042'071273        85–21573
ISBN 0-8141-4198-6

# Contents

## The Long Waters

In time when the trout and young salmon leap for the low-flying
insects,
And the ivy-branch, cast to the ground, puts down roots into the
sawdust,
And the pine, whole with its roots, sinks into the estuary,
Where it leans, tilted east, a perch for the osprey,
And a fisherman dawdles over a wooden bridge,
These waves, in the sun, remind me of flowers:
The lily's piercing white,
The mottled tiger, best in the corner of a damp place,
The heliotrope, veined like a fish, the persistent morning-glory,
And the bronze of a dead burdock at the edge of a prairie lake,
Down by the muck shrinking to the alkaline center.

I have come here without courting silence,
Blessed by the lips of a low wind,
To a rich desolation of wind and water,
To a landlocked bay, where the salt water is freshened
By small streams running down under fallen fir trees.

—Theodore Roethke

# Introduction

Anne Ruggles Gere
University of Washington, Seattle

Terry, the student across from me, had failed junior social studies the previous year and was taking the course again in order to get enough credits to graduate from high school. I was interviewing him because his teacher had participated in the National Endowment for the Humanities-sponsored "Writing-to-Learn" workshop the previous summer, and I wanted to find out what he thought about writing to learn. Terry spoke haltingly, searching for words. I asked whether he liked to write, and he shook his head, but when I asked about his journal, Terry's face brightened, and he said that he liked this daily writing. When I asked why, he responded, "Writing makes more thoughts in my head."

Writing as Terry defined it was not the writing that had always been his enemy, the writing asking him to show what he knew (or more often didn't know). It was not the kind of writing to which a teacher could respond with "right" or "wrong." Writing in his journal was something Terry did for himself, to "get more thoughts" about what he was reading. If I had tried to explain the difference between transactional and expressive writing or had tried to distinguish between reflexive and extensive writing or contrasted heuristic and explicative uses of prose, Terry would have stared with glazed eyes (Britton, et al. 1975; Emig 1971; Nystrand 1977; Flower and Hayes 1977). Yet, he demonstrated comprehension of these distinctions by his claim that the writing he did in his journal was different from the other writing he did; Terry had discovered the difference between writing to show learning and writing to learn.

Writing to show learning has been a standard part of the curriculum for many years. We teachers have routinely asked students for written evidence that they have mastered such things as the difference between mitosis and meiosis, the causes of the Civil War, and the symbolism of *The Scarlet Letter.* While this kind of writing has been helpful

1

to those who must evaluate (sort and place) students, there is some question of how writing to show learning has helped students. In fact, in recent years many educators have deplored the dominance of writing to show learning because it has been accompanied by neglect of writing to learn.

According to this line of thinking, writing is a powerful means of learning, and students should be given opportunities to use writing to get course material "right with themselves" (Britton 1975), to create their own "webs of meaning" (Vygotsky 1962). One of the strongest statements of the need for emphasizing writing to learn comes from Randall Freisinger, who makes a direct connection between documented student inability to handle formal operations and schools' general lack of attention to the value of writing to learn. Freisinger states that the "cognitive impairment of a significant number of our students" is due to schools' neglect of the learning function of writing (1979).

The cognitive impairment to which Freisinger refers is best described in terms of Piaget's description of intellectual development. In Piaget's terminology the transition from concrete to formal operations is marked by the ability to think abstractly. Societal claims that schools do not teach students to think are validated by research. Some studies show that by the time students enter college only one-third of them have made the transition from concrete operations to formal operations. The National Assessment of Educational Progress found that students were able to make statements about what they read but less than 50 percent of them could offer any explanation or justification for these statements. Despite considerable effort on the part of many teachers, students are not getting as much from school as they could, and many of us see evidence of this problem in our own classes.

When students cannot function at the level of formal operations, they have difficulty discerning cause-and-effect relationships—for example, explaining or understanding how to solve a word problem in math. These students have difficulty forming and comprehending propositional statements; they may not be able to write a convincing argument about the causes of the Civil War. These students have difficulty discriminating between observations and inferences, which means that they may not be able to distinguish plot from theme in a novel. These students have difficulty drawing inferences from evidence, which means that they may not be able to explain the significance of a scientific experiment even if they conduct the experiment flawlessly. These students have difficulty analyzing a line of reasoning; they would probably not be able to make sense of a statement such as "I think, therefore I am." These students have difficulty visualizing outcomes; they may not be able to see how a series of events could lead to conflict. These students have difficulty drawing analogies, which means that their capacity for learning is limited because they cannot see what one set of information has in common with another.

Many of the teachers I know shared my concern with the quality of students' learning, but they felt the need for a bridge between accepting writing to learn in theory and implementing it in their classes. Our work in the Puget Sound Writing Program (a site of the National Writing Project) demonstrated the power of collaborative work and simultaneously provided an opportunity for an initial exploration of writing-to-learn strategies that could be used in the classroom. A generous grant from the National Endowment for the Humanities enabled us to move from these initial stages to full-scale implementation.

We feel that our account is worth sharing, not only because it is a success story, but because we assume there are many secondary teachers who face the same quandary we did three years ago, teachers who are convinced that writing can aid learning but who are uncertain of how to begin—or, more likely, are jaded by the succession of gimmicks that have flashed and fizzled. Accordingly, this is not simply a collection of "things to do on Monday," although many practical classroom activities are offered. Rather, individual chapters in this book provide an excursion into the mind and classroom of a secondary teacher, a teacher harrassed by such conflicting demands as coaching, participating in professional organizations, grading papers, advising students, handling administrative tasks, and serving on committees: A teacher who speaks with the authority of several years of using writing as a way of learning.

These teachers will take you into their classes to see how writing fosters learning in math, science, English, social studies, foreign language, philosophy, psychology, and art. They are not teachers who have special facilities or unusually able students. Their classes—in urban, suburban, and rural schools—are crowded, and they have the usual mixture of problem, average, and gifted students. Before you enter their classes and see for yourself how these teachers use writing to help their students learn, I would like to provide some background about the assumptions and experiences from which these teachers operate.

## A Way of Thinking, Not a Set of Facts

Secondary education should provide students a way of thinking, not a set of facts. In our complex and ever-changing world, teachers cannot hope to give students all the information they will need for their life-times. Much of what students learn in schools will be obsolete in a few years; therefore, teachers need to give attention to learning that goes beyond assimilation of information. The measure of success in education should be how well students can think rather than how much of the teacher's knowledge they take with them as they leave class. Put another way, the secondary teacher aims to make students independent thinkers.

Recognizing the preeminence of thinking over facts means changing ideas about "covering" material in a course. Many of the teachers involved in the Writing-to-Learn project came to the conclusion that reading a specific number of chapters was less important than working with a small number of chapters in a way that enables students to make connections with the material.

## Writing to Foster Abstract Thought

Writing is uniquely suited to foster abstract thought. As cognitive psychologists and composition theorists have noted, writing is an extremely focused activity which simultaneously involves hand, eye, and brain. The linearity of writing, one word after the other, leads to more coherent and sustained thought than thinking or speaking. The physical limitations imposed on writers make writing a slow process (slow relative to thinking or talking), and this slowness seems to free some parts of the brain for the discoveries so common among writers.

## The Value of Unfinished Writing

Unfinished writing has value, just as finished writing does. Education that emphasizes writing to show learning assumes all writing must reach a final stage, one which can be "graded" or examined for form and content. However, writing to learn means accepting the value of writing that does not lead to a finished product, writing that evinces thought but does not merit the careful scrutiny which a finished piece of writing deserves. Another way of saying the same thing is to say that writing to learn is not the same as prewriting. Many of the strategies described in this book may resemble activities used in the early stages of writing a finished selection; while some writing to learn does indeed lead to finished writing, that is not its essential purpose. Writing to learn is not "pre" anything; it has value in and for itself.

## More Than Merely Writing

The fact of writing does not itself constitute writing to learn. While fluency in writing is an important goal, one essential to writing to learn, the mere act of writing does not guarantee that learning is occurring. It is possible for writing, like any other school activity, to be done mechanically so that students learn nothing. The implication of this is that teachers need to consider which writing-to-learn strategies will accomplish their goals and to monitor their students' writing to be sure that learning is occurring.

## Differs from Writing across the Curriculum

Writing to learn has different goals from writing across the curriculum. Although writing to learn, like writing across the curriculum, emphasizes writing in all disciplines, its goal is different. Writing across the curriculum aims to improve the quality of writing, while writing to learn focuses on better thinking and learning. To be sure, students who use writing as a way of learning often produce better written products, but this is a side benefit, not the chief purpose.

## Not a Formal Approach

As the diverse approaches in this book indicate, there is no "right way" to use writing to learn. Although the general approach is solidly grounded in theory, there are no quick fixes or rigid systems for implementing writing to learn. Rather, as is true of all good teaching, it is the responsibility of the individual instructor to select from a wide range of approaches those which seem best suited to accomplish course goals.

## Changes in Teacher Behavior

Writing to learn requires changes in teacher behavior. When writing-to-learn strategies are introduced in a class, the teacher's role changes. Instead of being the source of knowledge, she or he becomes a guide who helps students find their own knowledge. In practical terms this often means adopting a more student-centered teaching style. However, the shift toward student-centered teaching does not relieve the teacher of any responsibility. In fact, it becomes even more important for the teacher to exert leadership and control: without firm guidance students who write to learn will flounder.

## No New Course Content

Adopting writing to learn does not mean changing course content. The writing-to-learn strategies discussed in this book are not intended to change the substance of courses in any discipline. Rather, they are to be incorporated into existing courses as a way of enhancing learning. Some teachers have found that extensive use of writing to learn meant that they did not "cover" the same amount of material as they had in past years, but these teachers were convinced that the increased quality of learning more than compensated for the slight decrease in quantity.

While these assumptions are common to all the authors represented in this collection, each chapter takes a slightly different angle on writing to learn. Chapter One provides a comprehensive overview of a writing-to-learn classroom as Steve Pearse explains how he sets his class up at the beginning of the year, integrates course goals with writing-to-learn strategies, and evaluates his students' progress.

In Chapter Two Priscilla Zimmerman explains how writing helps her students learn to make connections between art appreciation and art production. She also used writing to develop the perceptual skills, aesthetic criteria, and specialized vocabulary that facilitate informed appreciation. This connection between specific course goals and writing to learn is maintained in Chapter Three. Deborah Peterson explains how her students write to develop insight into cultural and historical phenomena and to learn more about the grammar of the German language.

In Chapter Four Bruce Beaman shows how he uses writing to ensure that his students understand historical reasons for today's headlines, develop self-esteem, and broaden their concept of phenomena such as suicide, apartheid, and religious differences.

Chapter Five demonstrates that writing to learn can be used effectively with a wide range of students. Ray Marik explains how his special education students use writing to learn more about U.S. history. Ray's "touchstone" concept allows students to deal thoroughly with a few topics rather than rush through many superficially. Writing fosters engagement with what they study.

Patricia Johnston, in Chapter Six, demonstrates how writing helps students learn scientific vocabulary, develop more insight into organisms they study, and understand their lab experiments more completely. In Chapter Seven Don Schmidt shows how students can write to overcome their anxieties about math and to enrich their understandings of mathematicians and tools of math. Schmidt assumes, as do most teachers who use writing to learn, that affective learning is as important as cognitive development.

Sophisticated concepts of philosophy can be made accessible to students through writing, and in Chapter Eight Jessie Yoshida explains how writing brings her students closer to works by authors such as Plato, Sartre, and Niebuhr. Tom Watson explains in Chapter Nine how Washington State History (or any history course) comes alive for students when they use writing to project themselves into the material being studied.

The last six chapters consider more encompassing issues of writing to learn. Both Steve Arkle and Syrene Forsman explore the relationship between writing and thinking by looking at the kinds of tasks students accomplish in their literature classes. Janet West explains how writing to learn can liberate rather than imprison instructors because it enables students to take responsibility for more of their own learning. In Chapter Twelve Patricia Juell presents ways of initiating and using course journals to get the most effective learning from writing. The two concluding chapters consider writing to learn from a more objective perspective. Barbara Bronson recounts her visits to writing-to-learn classes in Chapter Fourteen, and in Chapter Fifteen Ralph Stevens reports on the responses of the ultimate judges, the students.

A glossary and an annotated bibliography appear after the final chapter. The bibliography suggests further reading, and the glossary explains the bold-faced terms used throughout the book. Although some of the terms used here are novel, they represent "naming" rather than "inventing." The approaches they describe are based in existing theory and research, and the authors included here have merely identified what already existed.

The process of writing and rewriting this book has been a learning experience for all involved. Our hope is that it will fulfill one of the mandates articulated by Arthur N. Applebee in *Writing in the Secondary School*, the research report that chronicles the limitations and meager quantity of writing in schools across the country. In concluding his report, Applebee writes:

> As a first step in improving the writing of secondary school students, then, we need more situations in which writing can serve as a tool for learning rather than as a means to display acquired

knowledge. Bringing this about will take further work in [provid-
ing] . . . practical descriptions of specific techniques and activities
that can be successfully incorporated into the various content areas
(including English)—descriptions of "good practice" that will
make sense of the subject-area teachers involved (Urbana, Ill.:
NCTE, 1982).

We invite you to enter individual classrooms and minds in the hope
that our work will help you see ways of using writing to give life to the
roots in the sawdust of your classes.

*[handwritten: Descriptions of writing activities in Glossary.]*

# Writing to Learn: The Nurse-Log Classroom

Steve Pearse
Shorewood High School, Seattle, Washington

> The nurse log, an ancient fallen tree out of which new and some-times different varieties of trees grow, along with all manner of mosses, fungi, and other plant life, is an ideal metaphor for writ-ing-to-learn strategies.

Imagine this scene: It is four o'clock on a Friday afternoon, and five weary teachers wander into what passes for a faculty workroom. One seems preoccupied or just plain tired, while a second complains to the librarian that a film she ordered for fourth period never arrived. Still another teacher simply walks toward the door, rolls his eyes heavenward, and lugs a box of what are evidently student notebooks in the direction of the faculty parking lot. Yet, in a vacant corner, just to the left of the world's balkiest copier, you overhear what appears to be a lively con-versation. And what is more, the participants are talking, of all things, about *school*.

*[handwritten marginal note: ponderous ending tone]*

*A:* So what's this writing to learn all about?

*B:* Well, the idea is that students can and should take responsibility for their own learning. They have to care about what they write simply by definition of the kind of writing they're asked to do.

*A:* You mean back to the old feelings and thoughts journals, right?

*B:* Not really. Students must stay on task, even though writing to learn is student-centered learning.

*A:* That sounds great, but what about grading all that stuff? I barely have time to prepare study questions and tests, never mind read thirty or more student notebooks every week. Look at poor old Johnson over there. I don't see how he lifts that box, much less grades all those notebooks.

*B:* With a well-designed writing-to-learn program, you can be freed from at least some of that and concentrate instead on working along with the students as they learn. Study questions and tests, when you and your students feel a need for them, can be generated by writing-to-learn strategies.

*A:* This sounds pretty complex. If you don't grade all that writing, what keeps the kids on track? You must have some sort of system.

*B:* I do. But it's taken a good deal of experimenting, and I'm still fine-tuning it. The best brief answer I can give you is this: Because writing to learn is student-centered, expressive, and exploratory, evaluation comes in many forms and is used for a number of purposes. Much of it is carried out by the students themselves.

*A:* I'm interested, but I need to know more.

*B:* Maybe we could sit down and discuss what I do.

*A:* Okay, but later, huh? Right now I'm swamped with papers to grade and tests to prepare. In fact, let's hold off till next quarter. I've got five days' worth of lectures to write.

Teacher A is a composite of the many dedicated, conscientious teachers I know. She is a fastidious organizer, she sets high standards for her students, she works hard. Too hard. Most of the work she finds herself doing is tied to directing, monitoring, and evaluating her students. She spends an enormous amount of time assigning and grading papers, constructing and scoring tests, reading and responding to student journals. Yet despite her hard work and good intentions, she has been cheating herself and her students. Herself, because she rarely has time to reflect on course materials and sequence and misses the pleasure of becoming personally involved with her students' work. Her students, because they have not been given the opportunity—and responsibility—of helping to determine and monitor their own learning.

Writing-to-learn strategies have made a real difference for my students and me in four distinct but related ways. A writing-to-learn emphasis in my literature classes has:

1. Helped me make the transition from sage-on-the-stage dispenser and director to class coordinator and contributor, thereby placing more learning in students' hands;

2. Created an environment where students can express their feelings about and reactions to their learning, the subject's value for them;

3. Provided students and me with ongoing reviews or checks of their understanding and application of course concepts and material, along with their thinking processes and capacity for self-expression; and

4. Served as a springboard or incubator for activities and projects that demonstrate the extent and quality of student learning and involve students personally with class work.

Two years ago, following the first three weeks of my initial attempt to implement writing-to-learn strategies in my sophomore literature survey class, a girl who had been reticent to participate at best and downright negative at worst tossed a note in the general direction of my desk just as the bell rang:

> Mr. Pearce
>
> I just wanted you to know that I think I'm changing my mind about you. That first week when you told us we had to teach ourselves I thought you were going to be one of those teachers who lets kids do all the work while he does football plays or something. Now I see I was wrong. You wanted us to help each other do a good job, even if we don't like to read and write. I'm not promising anything, but I'll try.

I remember how hard it was for this girl—and many other students— to figure out "what the teacher wanted," even though I thought I had made myself and the program clear. Just taking the reins of her own learning spooked her, I guess. She was used to receiving a course syllabus that included a timetable for readings, films, quizzes, tests, and long-term research projects, then settling back and waiting for the usual things to happen: that first lecture, followed by discussion questions or a study sheet to be filled out and turned in the following day. In short, she was well schooled in passive learning. Occasional excursions into action, studying for tests or completing prescribed research, were tolerable because they were the exception, not the rule. For her, the teacher's job was to dole out the information; hers was to absorb and recite it.

To move students away from that traditional classroom model, I invest much of the first ten days of both my freshman honors English and sophomore literature classes in community-building activities. Whether a small-group exercise ("Write a sentence that makes only a little sense, using the first letter of each group member's name as beginning letters for five of your sentence's words. Each member should contribute his or her own word and offer a reason, if any, for choosing it"), or one involving the entire class ("List the first name of every person in the room as roll is called. Next to each name, write a complimentary comment about the person"), the emphasis is on establishing a positive, supportive atmosphere that invites open questioning and sharing.

As part of this series of small and large group community-building strategies, I ask students to consider my role as a member of the total group. By the end of the first week, students have had a chance to gain at least some sense of belonging; a class identity has begun to surface.

EVERYONE WRITES —

BUILD RAPPORT

Personalities emerge as most students move from apprehensions about one another, the course, and my expectations to an anticipation that good things are going to happen. Just as the teacher's attitudes toward the subject and his or her students have always been central to student feeling and response, writing-to-learn strategies have to be presented in an atmosphere of mutual respect and trust, along with a clear sense of who will be responsible for what. This is no easy environment to establish, yet a fairly simple one to maintain.

Nothing new here; every successful teacher tries to set a positive tone, particularly at the onset of a school year or semester. And when I think of positive relationships between teachers and students, qualities like evenhandedness, enthusiasm, and high (but reasonable) expectations come to mind.

Such student-teacher rapport is especially critical to a writing-to-learn program's success, for both teacher and student must take greater risks, including moving into and out of one another's traditional roles. Risk taking has been centrally important to the students in my classes who have made the program work well for them. Those basic principles of direct and personal involvement with and creative application of subject apply to every learner.

Following the first several days that have been given to a course overview and community-building activities, along with an introduction to a number of writing-to-learn strategies, students are ready to consider the responsibilities and opportunities the program will place on all of us. They are primed, then, for a discussion of their views of teaching and learning, including how they and I perceive my role, now that they have an idea as to how the class will be conducted and what our goals will be. I begin by asking students to complete an **admit slip** anonymously during the first ten minutes of the period:

> Your admit slip today concerns teaching. Please write what you believe are qualities or characteristics of good teachers and effective teaching.

On teachers, such comments as "listens to my ideas," "explains things well," "makes me want to learn," and "cares but isn't pushy" come up repeatedly. On teaching, I get less-than-serious comments such as "films shown daily," "no tests or grades," and "time out for donut runs," but I also receive responses including "having a reason for everything we do," "letting us do some things on our own," "giving students choices."

That last comment, as students soon discover, is the most telling. Many fifteen-year-olds have begun to see beyond black-and-white solutions to complex problems; some have grown to the realization that life is a series of difficult choices in an increasingly challenging, even confusing, world. This matters very much, since a major goal of my literature classes is for students to develop the ability to read with discrimination and insight as they recognize relevance for their own lives. And the shifting of many teacher responsibilities to students is vital to writing to learn; the student-centered curriculum reinforces such larger themes of transition as child to adult, taker to giver, consumer to producer.

As I read their admit slips aloud, a volunteer records key points on the board while others jot them down in course **journals.** The board writing leads to the next activity; the journal recording establishes a reference that students can return to if I (or they) feel they are not following through on their commitments to themselves and the class at some later time.

At that point we write a **biopoem** that fits the prevailing class view of "Good Teacher." As the poem begins to take shape, I remind students to keep the traits and descriptive phrases listed on the board in mind. The resulting product is less than aesthetically pleasing, but it helps students focus on key characteristics.

> Open-minded, friendly, patient, and caring
> Sister of Justice, Daughter of Wisdom
> Lover of learning, good books, and her students
> Who feels important, respected, and loved
> Who needs lots of support, help, and praise
> Who fears too many papers to grade, fire drills, and PA
> announcements
> Who gives time, energy, and compliments
> Who would like to see all students pass, everyone in their seats,
> nobody absent
> Resident of Shorewood High School
> Goodteach.

In the discussion that follows, students notice the complex nature of the teacher's job. While she may be open-minded and patient, she also needs support and help. And although she brings energy and wisdom to the job, a number of factors work against her ("too many papers to grade," for example). The next step is to steer students into considering the duties and skills that mark the traditional divisions of labor between teachers and students. My goal is to point out how the writing-to-learn emphasis has implications for all of us, and we develop a list such as the one that follows:

> Introducing new material and topics,
>
> Taking attendance,

Planning use of class time,

Assigning papers and other projects,

Collecting and grading completed assignments,

Helping students who are having problems or are behind,

Giving lectures,

Leading discussions,

Keeping everybody busy,

Making up tests,

Preventing and stopping disturbances, distractions, and

Giving advice on schoolwork and other things.

This listing helps students see how complex and demanding the total teaching act—and by extension, learning—really is. Students have always noticed from time to time the pressures of teaching; now an entire class has focused its attention on the subject. In addition, students invariably comment that, now that they have taken the time to consider all that is expected of teachers, it is difficult for them to see how any one person can do all those jobs, fulfill all those responsibilities and expectations.

And with that, I've sprung my trap: The only workable alternative to one person taking on so much must be found in some sort of division of labor, of shared responsibilities. Now we are ready to consider who might be expected to help out, and in what ways. Someone begins by offering up group leaders as glorified teacher aides, but others worry about how those five or six people might react to being singled out in this way, and how the class might respond to them. Another student volunteers one or two people who seem born to direct others, and that suggestion unleashes a few guffaws and several groans. Finally someone makes the sort of comment I've been waiting for: "It's not fair for only a few people to do the work! Everybody has to be treated the same."

Although I'll make my case for special group leader responsibilities, I'm gratified that this student has raised the need for everyone to take an active role in at least some of those duties and responsibilities we identified earlier. Now we are ready to chart the major tasks according to the four basic types of membership in our class: the teacher, all the students, the five or six group leaders, and the individual writing groups.

I draw a chart on the board on which these four "populations" are represented, and we discuss which tasks are best suited for each, not-

| Learning/Teaching Tasks | Teacher | All Students | Group Leaders | Writing Groups |
|---|---|---|---|---|
| Introducing new material | X | | X | |
| Taking attendance | X | | X | |
| Planning use of class time | X | X | X | X |
| Assigning papers and other projects | X | X | X | X |
| Evaluating student work | X | X | | X |
| Helping students with learning problems | X | | X | X |
| Giving presentations | X | X | X | X |
| Leading discussions | X | | X | |
| Keeping everyone involved, on task | X | X | X | |
| Designing quizzes and tests | X | | | X |
| Preventing disturbances, derailing distractions | X | X | X | X |
| Giving advice | X | X | X | X |

ing that some tasks might be shared. As we begin to fill in the chart, students think of other teaching tasks ("keeping everybody busy" is divided into "keeping students from working on other teachers' assignments" and "not letting anybody just sit there"). I tell them to keep major categories or tasks intact for the time being; we'll have chances to return to our chart if we find something has been overlooked or is imprecisely worded. Completing the chart and discussing its implications helps students view the next eighteen weeks as a process of establishing a personal motive for success, discovering and practicing learning strategies, and evaluating and sharing their work with one another. Certainly, the chart's categories do not touch upon all of my course's action strategies for learning (where is "sharing and responding to written work," for example?). Yet even though the chart focuses on teaching as opposed to an integrated view of teaching and learning, we have begun to consider all of our obligations to one another. Students know that I have designed the program and established its objectives, yet they realize that the learning process requires everyone's involvement and commitment. I point out that even those tasks most often associated with the teacher (assigning papers and projects, helping students with learning problems, and giving presentations) will be shared with them in a number of ways. I stress that being able to recognize one's own understanding of and ability to apply course material is the course's ultimate objective, its purpose.

Students know, of course, that I will be exercising a good deal of authority in the room, no matter what sort of program or emphasis I establish. They expect me, for example, to decide which literary concepts should be included in our study of the short story or of contemporary poetry. But if students are going to be asked to connect personal experiences and observations with course material in an honest and direct way, it is appropriate to involve them in designing, presenting, and evaluating (after responding to) individual and group assignments, projects, even tests.

Students in my writing-to-learn classrooms are more involved and clearer about our purposes than students I have taught in more traditional ways. Writing to learn plays a significant role as students move more actively and meaningfully through course activities and units. Actively, because they are obliged to "talk through" mental blocks and misunderstandings that occur in group discussion and individual writing exercises; meaningfully, because the affective mode naturally emerges and in many ways takes precedence over students' cognitive development. The need to express their reactions to and feelings about literature is met by writing to learn.

As an introduction to writing to learn and to our first unit (the short story), I ask freshman honors students to complete a focused write in response to the question, "What makes or constitutes a good short story for you?" Comments usually include references to personal likes and dislikes—the right starting point for the reading, discussing, and writing to follow. I want students to use their own experiences, beliefs, and attitudes as points of departure, as frames of reference; in this way an environment encouraging personal connections begins to take shape.

Sheila's response to this opening question was as follows:

> A good short story is very difficult to determine because many people have different ideas about what a good story is. In my opinion a good story is one that you can get involved in, and that will make you feel some emotions, such as sad, happy, mad, or anything else. The story should have a good setting that makes you feel like you were really there and that this event could very easily be happening to you. I like stories that have an interesting full-bodied plot, full of adventure and excitement. The story should have some sort of theme that could be put across to the reader in a very subtle manner, or in a way that is easily distinguishable to the reader. Stories must make you feel a part of them, and let you get so caught up in them that you lose track of time. Of course, this is just my opinion of what constitutes a good story, but most "good" stories I know are this way. Characters are very important to a story because these characters should be so real, that by the end of the

USE JOURNALS TO DISCOVER
ST. IDENTITY AS WRITERS

story you would feel like they were your best friends. The characters often help depict the mood of the story.

Sheila's first writing-to-learn journal entry is a telling one. She demonstrates her reluctance to express her thoughts and feelings; "Many people have different ideas about what a good short story is" and "Of course this is just my opinion" are forms of apology. But her comments also indicate a working knowledge of a number of literary concepts. "A good setting that makes you feel like you were really there" is a reference to verisimilitude; her use of setting is definite and direct. "A good story is one that you can get involved in, and that will make you feel some emotions" points to Sheila's understanding of mood and atmosphere and their contributions to fiction. Finally, her statement, "Stories . . . let you get so caught up in them that you lose track of time" demonstrates her awareness that unity of impression, a term I will soon introduce, is a key component of the successful short story.

Admittedly, Sheila's focused write is self-conscious rather than self-revelatory. Before long, though, she discovers that I really mean it when I announce that only sharing and suggesting—not evaluating—will be applied to this sort of writing to learn. Sheila's writing will become more exploratory, less tentative. Further, Sheila will be able to use this piece as a springboard for a major essay she will be writing in the coming weeks, and I can use it now as an indicator of her innate understanding of the short story.

At the cognitive level, then, Sheila's focused write is a kind of pretest, and she has done remarkably well, as have many other students. But from the perspective of her role in the class and her obligations to herself, including her need to express reactions and opinions freely, we have work to do. In the affective domain, writing to learn helps me assess students' attitudes, inhibitions, and growth.

By the midpoint of the first quarter, nearly all students are writing (and discussing) more freely. Sheila's journal entries become less restricted, more wide-ranging and representative of, as she puts it, her "true feelings." Her response to metaphorical questions ("Imagine this work of art as a medicine. What is the disease? What are the symptoms? How does the medicine cure it?") in connection with Jean Stafford's seriocomic short story "Bad Characters" is still a bit restrained yet is also more forthright, less qualified:

> The disease would be inability to get along with people—Insecurity around others—insecurity about yourself. The symptoms are, not getting along with people, blurting things out and hurting people, not being able to communicate very well with people. The medicine would have to help them realize how they are acting, and

> how they really are hurting other people. This story would help
> them realize about themselves, and that they are selfish and a little
> bit spoiled. When people see themselves acting they are taken
> aback because of the realizations of their actions!

Not all writing-to-learn activities need to refer directly to personal experience; the group readings and discussion that follow give Sheila and the others a chance to move from the generalizations included in their metaphorical question responses to a listing of experiences (a kind of group write). The purpose of this sequence of activities is to gain insight from one another's comments and suggestions, not to ascribe a value to individual written responses. Simply observing the dynamics and listening to class presentations of each group served as informal evaluation for me.

Students have opportunities to discuss and otherwise share journal writing throughout the semester, yet in keeping with the class concept and organization agreed to by all of us, some writing-to-learn exercises are purely expressive (Britton 1970). That is, they are written to and for the writer. When writing is shared, the nature and purpose of that sharing needs to be communicated clearly (springboard for an in-class essay, grist for discussion, search for concepts) before the writing begins. Writing to learn is, as I have been suggesting, flexible and adaptable. But if it is to be used to "free up" students who might not otherwise participate wholeheartedly in class activities in their own learning, students need to be let in on the purpose and potential use of their writing. To shroud assignments in mystery is to deny real student involvement and to undermine the very atmosphere that is essential if students are to develop a personal stake in the process as well as in the subject.

Writing-to-learn strategies that lend themselves well to small and large group sharing in my classes include dialogues, unsent letters, scenarios, metaphorical questions, free writing, and brainstorming. All can be seen and used as divergent, exploratory, writer-based exercises that help students make connections. Yet although most such activities are writer-based as opposed to reader-based, most students are willing, and even eager, to share their work in writing groups and welcome other students' ideas and reactions. Once I have explained what they are about to do and why, students relax at least enough to tell the truth. As Ken Macrorie says about writers, "Perhaps when they're telling truths (as they see and feel them, not as superhumans with absolute truthtelling powers), they concentrate first on what they're saying and second on what others will think of it" (*Uptaught*. New Rochelle: Hayden, 1970).

Most of us remember a time when the anticipation of tackling a new skill or task was fraught with worry and even dread; the thought of learning to swim or ride a bike, for example, may have been far more threatening than the experience itself. And those kids who always seemed so self-assured did nothing to help us to feel better, to be more optimistic about our own chances for success.

When I announce the first major test or to-be-evaluated (summative) writing assignment, I ask students to write about an experience or responsibility that was traumatic for them. But before they begin to write to and about themselves, I break the cathartic ice by relating a personal anecdote that speaks to the need and value of rehearsal, of writing for oneself in preparation for and in anticipation of an assignment or other obligation. This anecdote is significant to me; students recognize this importance and are able to identify or classify it with an experience of their own.

> I was twelve when our family moved from upstate New York to a Detroit suburb. Adjusting to new situations had always been difficult for me, but one incident was particularly unnerving. It was in gym class, in the days when boys' gym teachers either actually had been Army drill sergeants or played convincing interpretations of them.
>
> This one always wore a tight crew-neck T-shirt, regulation gym shorts, a brass whistle and an authentic military-issue scowl. Everything we did included lining up, counting off, and competing with one another. I could deal with ropeclimbing, long-jumping and even balance-beam running, but the prospect of moving hand-over-head from one end of a ten-foot-high horizontal ladder to the other was too much. We never knew what we were going to be doing from one day to the next, and finding myself third in line to leap from an unsteady metal chair at what seemed a ridiculously distant first rung violated every principle of self-preservation.
>
> The only chance I had to prepare was watching the kid in front of me nearly miss, just manage to white-knuckle rung number one, then flail his way to the end of the ladder. Meanwhile, the coach blew his whistle from a distance of two feet as the kid behind me jabbed his thumb into my back, just in case I hadn't noticed that I was next. In that brief moment, I decided that I would certainly miss the rung, then succumb if not to a broken back, most assuredly to terminal embarrassment.

I tell students that I believe I did in fact slip and fall not because I couldn't reach the ladder, but because I had not had a chance to persuade myself that I could. If only I could have walked up to that chair, reached for the rung from a position of safety, then seen myself firmly grasping each successive rung, hesitation and panic almost certainly would never have occurred. What I needed was a chance to rehearse, to see myself dealing positively and confidently with a new experience.

So too for students who are asked to write about literature (or history or science). Writing-to-learn activities allow students to express their feelings about literary works and concepts that they may be uncomfortable or just unfamiliar with. Rather than begin a survey of contemporary poetry by defining or otherwise describing it, I ask students in my Introduction to Literature class to respond to the question, "What are your feelings about or experiences with poetry?" in the form of a focused write.

Many students say that they have no feelings about or reactions to poetry, that in fact they do their best to avoid it. (Of course that gives me an opportunity to return to their claims of disinterest!) Others point out that poetry is either serious business or senseless play, and that in either event, they have never cared for it. A few refer to past experiences with poetry that were enjoyable and meaningful. But whatever the response, being given the chance to write open-endedly about their thoughts and reactions goes a long way toward creating a positive, accepting environment for the work to come, especially after students have a chance to discuss and share their ideas and experiences in groups.

Because this is the first subject-related writing-to-learn exercise I ask these students to complete, it helps me gauge their attitudes, voices, and perspectives. Peter's comments, for example, point to his need for reassurance and support, as well as my need to convince him that I really do want him to write to and for himself when he is asked to write freely:

> How should I know what poetry is—I guess I just don't have feeling about it, except I don't like it. I hope we're not gonna write any poems, I had to do that in junior high. Ugh.

Peter doesn't seem to trust me or himself when it comes to something as alien and suspect as poetry. And as I decide who will work with whom in writing groups, I consider Peter's reticence. I want him to work with students who will accept him but who will, I hope, be a bit more receptive to the idea that poetry has value for everyone. But what bothers me most about Peter's comments is that they are other-centered; he is complaining to me rather than speaking to and for himself.

Wendy, on the other hand, evidently accepts poetry. I appreciate her comments, but I worry about her purpose for writing, too:

> I like poetry! In fact I write it all the time. My mom encourages me and my friends say I'm a good rhymer. My all-time favorite poems are inspirational, even though I like fun poems, too, like limericks and haiku. Well, that's why I like poetry.

I want Wendy to write to and for herself also, but this first focused write is obviously written for me. Wendy's apparent enthusiasm is refreshing, but her response is too controlled, too orderly to be an example of spontaneous (if focused) expression. That last line ("Well, that's why I like poetry") is the clincher. In my first conference with her, I tell Wendy that I value her comments, but that she needs to become her own audience for this kind of writing.

After students are convinced that I really do want them to write expressively for themselves, they usually respond more freely. For example here is John's focused writing response to the question, "What sort of person must or should a poet be?"

> I guess I have trouble thinking about poets, probably because I don't know any. They're serious people I guess that go home at night and think beautiful thoughts or something. No, I know that's not true. I suppose they get up, eat breakfast and go to work like everybody else, but they might smile more or something. Unless they write death poems. I know I can't be a poet because I don't like words that much, but it's good somebody does it, I guess.

John's response rambles, even though it focuses on the topic. It moves from point to point almost at random; the voice I hear is unrehearsed, disordered, spontaneous. It is John speaking to and for John, even though we all know he is completing a required assignment. The teacher is surely nearby; otherwise, John would probably never indulge in this sort of expressive writing. But providing the opportunity and the impetus is, I think, where my influence ends and John's own interests and needs begin.

And that's when I know students are ready to use writing to learn as a guidepost for their own learning. Once they are fairly comfortable with writing to learn and sharing much of it with others, students learn to use a variety of written responses as checks for understanding course material. In this and other ways, students are making writing to learn work for them.

Students make previous journal entries work for them as they study for tests, prepare for group and individual oral presentations, and generate topics and constructs for end-of-unit projects. The writing groups also adjust, as students are expected to find and share key ideas and information found in one another's writing, devise tests and discussion questions for themselves and other groups, and contribute suggestions for individual members' project proposals or essays. Writing groups move from sounding boards to critical readers to synthesizers and back again as they support, encourage, and prod writers who are reluctant to participate and are in turn inspired and helped by those who lead best by sharing with others.

To illustrate how writing to learn helps students recognize and apply their understanding of course material, I'll explain the purpose and sequence of activities in a unit on poetry. My major goals for these students are (1) to become involved (through reading, writing, and discussing) with representative examples of contemporary poetry, (2) to recognize how a variety of poetic devices (such as imagery and figurative language, for example) contribute to a poem's effects on the reader, and (3) to develop critical skills that lead to analysis, evaluation, and application of those devices.

A tall order, to say the least. And not all of my students learn to read critically to the extent that I intend for them. But no student has ever completed the series of activities dealing, for example, with distinctions between prose and poetry without demonstrating both affective and cognitive growth. I know this to be true because students' writing-to-learn responses illustrate and underscore it.

I chose Andrew Grossbardt's "Fifty Below," a poem that graphically depicts the effects extreme cold has on anyone caught in it. Grossbardt's poem works on other levels and suggests other meanings, of course, and because it uses so many devices so effectively, it is an excellent poem for students to read and respond to.

Back to my sequence of assignments. I begin by telling students that my objective is for them to recognize and explain distinctions between language that is typically prosaic and language that is poetic. I also mention that I want them to become aware of language's richness and diversity and its tendency to combine prosaic and poetic elements.

Before they read the poem, I ask students to complete a personal scenario: "Describe an experience in which weather conditions made you very uncomfortable or even frightened." Tracy's response is more formal than most, but her message and incorporation of poetic devices are typical:

> As I stepped off the plane, the heat caught me as a gale would overcome a lone tree. The warmth was almost nauseating as I had been accustomed to the fragile hum of an air conditioner. The effort to make it in to the airport terminal seemed to strain every nuance of energy from my body. The 150 feet I had to walk seemed a mile. I not only had myself, but my luggage as well. My companions, as I could see through the streams of sweat stinging my eyes, also seemed reluctant to launch one of their two feet forward. This did not happen to us once, but it happened three times. My clean hair had been transformed to strings of wet masses clinging to my head. It took me a month to finally get used to the hot, humid weather which I had succumbed to.

"Streams of sweat," "caught me as a gale would overcome a lone tree," "strings . . . clinging to my head"; I point out to Tracy and others who volunteer to share their work with the class that their prose contains elements of poetic language. Then students return to their **writing groups** in order to find and categorize those phrases and lines that seem to fit our definitions of poetic expression. I also ask the groups to be prepared to offer their explanations of how and why each selected phrase works to create mental pictures for the reader or to draw striking yet fitting comparisons and associations. Students who may have had trouble identifying metaphors or similes—and especially finding and being able to explain the comparisons involved, for instance, on objective tests without such writing-to-learn preliminaries—become more conscious of figurative language and its effects on them. As a result, poetic concepts and techniques make the transition from isolated facts to be studied to real-world strategies to be practiced.

At this point, students are ready to read and respond to the poem. I ask them to circle any phrases or lines that seem particularly poetic and to look for references or details that carry a graphic picture of coldness. Students recognize that the most telling (dramatic, according to several students) lines and phrases were also those that incorporate one or more poetic techniques or features. Like their own scenarios, the poem's most strikingly realistic lines create pictures for the reader; they are image-based. A recent list of circled phrases included:

> the sky turns clear, brittle / as glass
> you scrape the ice from your breath
> the only tremor is silence too dense to dream moonlight burns
> the hills.
> A dull ache squats behind
> both eyes and stays
> You hear an underground river thud
> through some dense artery beneath the earth

We spend some time discussing why these particular phrases and lines are chosen by so many people. Nearly everyone says something about these selections being "colorful," "unusual," or even "strange," and "haunting." Students call attention to similes ("brittle as glass") and images ("moonlight burns the hills").

Aside from earlier discussion of how such poetic devices pervade even casual conversation, I had not prompted the students' next response to an assignment that asks them to list language that seems prosaic in one column and poetic in another (taken from "Fifty Below"). Jane's columns show her ability to make a workable distinction:

| Prose | Poetry |
|-------|--------|
| at first there is no sense of | hear your frail breath catch in throat |
| cold, the first hard fact | the air crackles every step |
| Three feet of snow give way | dull ache squats behind both |
| your skin begins to turn | eyes and stays |
| | even the soul can start to freeze |

Jane is not the most incisive thinker or prolific writer in her class, but she has succeeded in the basic distinction and awareness I had hoped for. And what is even more important, she now has a personalized study guide for any future quiz, writing assignment or project. And along the way, she has realized that just as elements of prosaic language are to be found in poetry, poetic devices are often characteristic of prose. Hers is an unstated but quite well-understood awareness of the fluidity and flexibility of language.

Following these activities, I have students complete a focused write that will be shared in groups and used to help each group arrive at a definitive statement that members must be able to defend and illustrate at a later time. In her response to "What are the differences between poetry and prose?" Wendy writes:

> The main difference between poetry and prose is that poetry is thought over more until you come up with a finished product. Prose is using more common words. Physically, poetry lines are in stanzas instead of paragraphs and the lines don't always end in sentences. Sometimes poems rhyme and poems have a deeper meaning than what you read when you first read it. Prose is not as original and it usually has only one meaning. Poems sound almost musical but prose doesn't. Poetry suggests, prose tells. Words do more in poetry.

Wendy was asked to generalize, and she certainly has. Also, I asked students to respond to this question as if "poetry" meant the exclusive use of poetic language (or nearly so). Yet the attitudes underlying Wendy's comments hit the mark. Wendy clearly recognizes poetic language's tendency to be complex, to operate on a number of levels ("Words do more in poetry"). She is able to discuss a number of poetic devices (stanza, rhyme, rhythm), and she is aware of the demands poetry often makes on the reader: "Poems have a deeper meaning than what you read when you first read it." Wendy's writing-to-learn response demonstrates both cognitive and affective growth, and she has something of value to share with her writing group as well as with the entire class. And finally, she has provided the kind of evidence that surpasses any objective test of her learning.

As every teacher knows, finding time to teach all the concepts and skills students need to feel and be successful requires careful planning and a commitment to an integrated curriculum. No English teacher can afford to think in terms of discrete, unrelated units. Students need to see how such seemingly diverse topics and skills as editing, literature study, vocabulary development, sentence structure, and research are related and complementary. And even more important, all such skills and experiences contribute to the image we want most for our students: that of the confident, articulate, informed yet inquisitive learner and producer.

Perhaps writing-to-learn's most significant quality is its power of integration, the incorporation of many skills within a meaning web whose center is the student. Its adaptability to process just naturally encourages my own tendency to include convergent as well as divergent class activities. Since keeping up with the latest information in even the narrowest of subjects has become nearly impossible for any one person, to be able to integrate new information with old experience and use that knowledge in innovative, creative ways is critical to the student's long-term success or real progress.

I ask students to read less material than is usually assigned in comparable courses taught in my school district and in nearby districts. While students taking traditionally taught courses most certainly read more selections, a writing-to-learn focus makes each literary contact in my class count for more. Asking students to work toward higher levels of cognition means providing quality time and opportunity. Few students—whether motivated or reluctant learners—are disciplined enough to engage in synthesis and evaluation in the absence of teacher guidance and classroom time and emphasis. And simply plugging into the writing process for five days before the essay is due, following two or more weeks of subject-centered instruction, is not the equal of a consistent writing-to-learn program. We may tell students that we are interested in their personal responses to literature or history or science, but if we have time for writing only when it's essay-writing time, we are sending them a different message.

I wish I had a nickel for every uninspired, impersonal, dry student essay I received before I implemented a writing-to-learn program. Even the best thinkers who wrote nearly error-free, five-paragraph themes impressed me more with their powers of regurgitation than their ability to speak truly. Yes, a few student writers did incorporate personal experience in appropriate ways and arrive at striking yet well-supported conclusions, but these were young people who, as a result of innate ability or previous experience, would have done so in any case. Most students simply do not write freely unless they have been allowed and encouraged to draw the newly encountered into the circle of their experience.

In order to prove to students that their writing-to-learn responses
are as important or even more important than recall of information and
summative arguments, I begin each semester by explaining the
course's grading system. In the introduction to literature class, every
assignment and test successfully completed is awarded a set number of
points, usually ranging from ten to fifty. Course journals—containing
expressive writing, focused revisions, writing-to-learn activity sequences leading to major projects—account for 60 percent of the course
grade. And because direct involvement in writing groups (meeting at
least twice weekly) is critical to everyone's success, class participation/
attendance is valued at another 20 percent. Quizzes and tests, then, are
relegated to a secondary and subservient role. I want students to view
tests as useful benchmarks for immediate feedback, not as measures of
their success according to the teacher. And even though test scores are
added in to the total grade, most students are not threatened by them
and as a result don't allow themselves to become preoccupied with test
taking. Some students may do poorly on objective tests, but their written responses to literary selections often demonstrate the ability to use
concepts and strategies. More often than not, this ability surpasses
their capacity for memorization or recognition. This is a distinction
very much like, for example, the case of the student who couldn't
underline all the adverbs in a sentence to save his life, but rarely if ever
misused adverbs in his writing.

The 60 percent journal grade includes three entries that students
choose to revise and share in writing groups, then earmark for my evaluation. My only restriction is that they work toward three distinctly different types of summative, transactional products. For example,
although each topic/project might be inspired by previously completed
focused writes, the writer might complete revisions leading to a biopoem, or a dialogue.

Now students are moving from expressive to transactional writing,
from divergent to convergent thinking, from writing to learn to writing
to demonstrate learning. I do not want them to think that all those journal entries serve the cause of show-and-tell writing, but both they and
I know that real-world operations invariably include the ability to communicate clearly what one knows to others. Additionally, students who
see themselves as demonstrators and sharers are more confident and
less hesitant to help themselves and others learn. Finally I benefit as a
teacher; students who recognize a pattern or hierarchical order ending
in a clearly defined goal stay involved. They stay interested.

Class time is provided for students to select earlier writings and to
revise or build on them, with advice from writing groups at two or

more stages from initial entry to product evaluation. I provide criteria for each major project type, metaphorical question, focused writes, scenarios, monologues, unsent letters.

For example, if students choose the focused write as a product, I ask them to work toward the following guidelines:

1. Do you incorporate personal opinion in your remarks?
2. Do you analyze some aspects of the selection or passage, then make clearly worded judgments about it?
3. Do you refer to your own knowledge and/or experiences as part of your response to the passage or feature of the literature?

The revised focused write reprinted below was selected by Linda as one of the three entries she wished me to evaluate. Prior to submitting her notebook, she met with her writing group in order to get suggestions for improving her original ten-minute write.

> When one lives off the land, in harmony with the land, and be-lieves to know the secrets and tricks of it, one would believe he's going to get the sweetest part of life, the sweet, rich nectar. In a small town in India, though, that is not the case. The farming fam-ilies are left with virtually nothing, like nectar flowing straight through a sieve and leaving only minute signs of the product's passage.
>
> Rukmani, one of the villagers, and her family live as poverty-stricken peasants. They have too much pride and faith in their tra-ditional beliefs to discontinue turning their soil and go to work in a modern tannery built by foreigners. Their farming is on a bare sub-sisitence level because the land is so barren and the weather so poor, especially during the monsoon season when the crops are destroyed. When one lives in these hardships it seems that it would be easy to lose faith in one's gods and reject the land and seek refuge in another form of work which would be more prom-ising. However, these Indians did no such thing.
>
> Living, even according to Mother Nature's laws is not as sweet and rich as the fruit she bears but can rather leave one nothing, through natural disasters. When these people thought they have under-stood how to successfully harvest in the end was to be contained with a sieve.

This represents Linda's third product grown out of earlier journal writ-ing. What follows is characteristic of the kind of response I generally make to students' summative writing:

> Linda:
>
> This is a successful piece of writing! You have followed the rules for effective focused responses here. I noticed references to the novel's major themes and concepts with regard to the importance of the

land, the agonies of change, the contradictions of life—in short, interpretation. You analyzed the significance of the title ("like nectar flowing straight through a sieve and leaving only minute signs of the product's passage").

I wonder, though, if you could have incorporated references to your own experiences, knowledge and/or beliefs with respect to human pride and sacrifice, hope and despair? Perhaps this entry has moved from focused write to a kind of miniature essay; that's okay, because I know that you did seek the advice and suggestions of your writing group, and I recognize evidence of your ability to connect the plot, characterizations, and atmosphere of the novel with issues that concern all of us (especially those references to man at the mercy of Nature). Overall, you've done well. Where might this revision lead, in terms of your choice of an even more detailed essay?

The revision has moved in many ways from the expressive to the transactional. One purpose has led to another. This writer's journal writing and discussions have contributed to a clearer, more integrated and perceptive view of the literature and its implications than might otherwise have resulted. My comments to Linda are added to her cumulative anecdotal evaluation record, and she has the opportunity to indicate the letter grade she feels her work deserves along with a brief explanation or "defense." I determine letter grades only for major student projects.

Toward the beginning of this chapter, I referred to writing to learn as a springboard or incubator for student projects that involve students personally in course work. It is in my freshman honors English class that projects work best for me, largely because these students are highly motivated, and my emphasis is on blending instruction in writing with a study of literature.

During this course, students see many correlations and applications of subject matter as well as of process. When, for instance, I introduce them to drama in general and *Macbeth* in particular, students have developed confidence in literary interpretation, writing-to-learn activities, research and documentation, and the seeking of creative solutions to problems.

During the literature/writing strand of the course, I let students know by the second week that all of their notes, reading, discussions, and journal writing will serve as resources for a major writing project dealing with a theme, characterization, or other feature of *Macbeth*. When I discuss the role of their preliminary work with them, I use such metaphoric associations as incubator, nurse log, springboard, and seed packet. That which is about to emerge and bear fruit will evolve from raw material with which it may appear to have little in common. I tell students not to anticipate too far in advance the nature or scope of the project they will eventually complete, for to do so would stifle, limit, or even eliminate possibility.

Jackie writes a series of newspaper articles that might have appeared in a Glasgow daily. Initial accounts of Macbeth's grab for power are objectively reported, but successive articles become increasingly subjective, even condemnatory as the facts and motivations of the play's events come to light. Jackie's project explores the connections between writing style and purpose and between tone and perspective as she implies the enormity of Macbeth's crimes, particularly as they effect and nearly destroy the sense of order that preceded his deeds. Representative headlines include:

> Scotland Victorious at War! Cawdor Commits Treason
>
> King Duncan Murdered!
>
> King Macbeth a Traitor!

Cary tries her hand with a soliloquy; her project captures her view of Macbeth's self-deception.

> I, Macbeth,
> at the pinnacle of power,
> looking down at the human steps over which
> I clawed, on which I climbed to the summit!
> Rejoice! Celebrate!
> It is my world!
> . . . . . . . . . . . . . . . . . . . . . . . . . . . . . . . . . . . . . . . . . . . . . . . . . . . . . . . . . . . . . . . .
> My eyes have warned me.
> They have seen the dagger, stained with blood,
> a weapon tantalyzing, offering itself to me,
> Yet I cannot grasp it.
> I am distressed; deceptive visions appear
> before my eyes.
> I have seen the fearsome ghost of Banquo,
> a friend whom I came to fear—his shadowy
> apparition, returning to haunt me, reminding
> me of my evil ways.
> My ears resound at the ringing of a bell,
> compelling me to proceed with my plan.
> The signal of doom!
> My ears echo with the knocking,
> the knocking at the gate.
> Macduff has arrived for the gracious
> Duncan. Oh, could they but arouse the
> King with their clamour!
> If it were possible . . . !
> I taste the bitter truth of false friendships,
> My lips recoil from the cowardly lies

that have stung my soul.
The sweetness of my lady is poisoned
by the distorted words that she speaks.
I feel love for her, my wife, my strength.
On her I lean, without her I am less.
I feel the craving for power, control, reign,
to fulfill my total ambition.
Yet I am reluctant, as if it were not
intended by nature, as if evil controls,
my soul destined for the devil.
I sense my doom;
   it shrieks and I quiver
     seeing,
       hearing,
         touching,
          feeling,
            smelling
              the perverse truth.

Another student writes a children's story ("Mack and Beth") based upon characterizations and events of the play, but twisted and manipulated in such a way that a fitting moral for children (helpful, gentle people were and are appreciated by others) surfaces.

Ken writes a powerful political commentary in his version of "Macbeth: Soviet's New Leader" as published in a special edition of *Time* magazine. Ken drew upon his earlier response to the question, "Describe Macbeth as a modern-day politician."

Each of these students, along with their twenty-six classmates, followed a sequence of writing-to-learn activities; read them in writing groups; and generated potential formats and themes through brainstorming, unsent letters, and metaphorical questions. Each one produced a project worthy of the name, and most—especially when they shared their work with the class—contributed to the learning of everyone. And even though each project could have benefited from further revision, editing, and even proofing, writing to learn has worked. All but a few students who entered the honors program as freshmen are currently enrolled in the junior honors section, and many students who are taking standard classes have requested that they be considered for admission. Introduction to Literature via writing to learn enjoys a positive reputation among students who are usually lukewarm in their responses to any class that seems even a little bit like work. Evidently, this is work students are willing to do. As Bill, a terrible test-taker who earned a C in the Introduction to Literature class last year, said as we recently passed in the hall, "Hey, I still don't like all that writing, but I never filled a whole notebook before. When can I have my journal back?"

# Writing for Art Appreciation

Priscilla Zimmerman
Spanaway Lake High School, Spanaway, Washington

Art production, art appreciation—do they always occur together? Most art curricula aim toward these two equally important goals: to involve students in the act of self-expression through the production of art, and to provide opportunities for students to acquire an appreciation of art. However, most programs accomplish only the first goal by placing undue emphasis on art production.

The teaching of art production usually focuses entirely on composition, artistic procedure, and skill development. There is no evidence that studying art production provides students with an appreciation for art. If art classes teach only the knowledge and skills necessary for self-expression and do not prepare the student for reflection on and discussion about art, they do nothing more than teach a trade. By itself, the artist model cannot lead a student to an appreciation of art. In other words, art appreciation does not always occur with art production.

As a secondary art teacher with eight years of experience, I am concerned with increasing art appreciation as well as developing skills in art production. I have found that many students skilled in using several art media were able to make only superficial responses to the work of other artists. This indicated that I needed to place more emphasis on developing perceptual skills, aesthetic criteria, and specialized vocabulary, all of which would aid my students in making knowledgeable responses to art. This led me to find alternative strategies that would teach students to describe, analyze, interpret, and judge art.

Aesthetic education, commonly known as art appreciation, aims to sensitize viewers to aesthetic elements (line, shape, color, and such) so that the viewers may place value on art and aesthetic experience. For example, the plight of the Jews during WWII can be felt through the design elements of Ben Shahn's *Warsaw 1943*. Sharp pointed lines, stinging in feeling, make up the tortured hands in this print reminding the viewer of the many acts of barbarism. It is hard to remain unaffected by this dramatic representation of human pain and suffering. The degree of sensitivity to these elements directly affects the quality of the viewer's response. This sensitivity is determined by the viewer's conscious perceptual awareness of the design elements. What remains on the unconscious level is lost in the experience. Because language is a tool of the conscious mind, it is the vehicle through which awareness and sensitivity can be developed. Through writing-to-learn strategies, verbal responses to art can be provoked, and sensitivity to design elements can be increased. In this chapter, I will first discuss oral and written responses to art and then share specific strategies for increasing art appreciation through writing.

## Responding to Art

In general, works of art have a complex range of aesthetic qualities. Because of the perceptual complexities inherent in works of art, formal instruction in perceptual skills and writing plays a major part in the development of art appreciation.

### Perceptual Skills

A technique useful in forming verbal responses to situations with perceptual complexity is **listing** concrete descriptions of visual properties. I direct my students to describe the subject matter of a work or particular design elements. For example, I used the painting *Crucifixion* by Salvador Dali and asked students to list subjects or objects within the work. Jane, a sophomore in my basic design class, made the following list of subjects:

> female figure
>
> male figure
>
> square
>
> platform
>
> cross
>
> loincloth
>
> shadow of arms on cross
>
> cubes
>
> checkered floor pattern
>
> cloth in lady's arms
>
> mountains in background
>
> sun setting

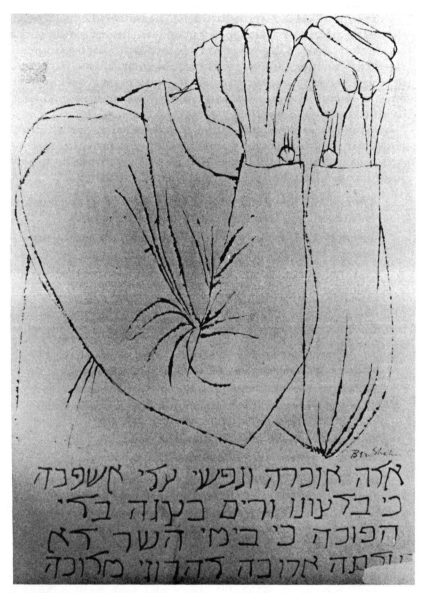

Figure 1. *Warsaw 1943* by Ben Shahn 1963, Poster 36¾" × 28⅛"

This exercise helped Jane realize that it takes time to actually see the richness of subject and detail in a work of art. The act of listing made her account for what she was perceiving, provoking her to go beyond a superficial summing up of the picture. In essence, Jane has learned that to get something out of a work of art, she must take over where the artist has left off. That is, she must give the work the time and thought the artist's effort deserves.

As students become more astute at understanding aesthetic qualities, descriptive listing can become broader, encompassing many aspects of one work of art. I used the following activities to broaden students' understanding of space and linear perspective:

> Taking notes to acquire the vocabulary necessary to discuss and write about how artists use space and perspective,
>
> Viewing slides of art to identify the ways in which artists use space,
>
> Drawing to incorporate the principles of linear perspective into their own art project.

I then used *Crucifixion* again and asked the same students to list ways in which the artist used space and perspective. Jane added the following to her list:

> Cross and floor pattern are done in one point perspective.
>
> Male figure is free floating against the cross.
>
> Lady figure is standing on a platform with her hand on her shoulder, and she is looking up at the male figure and cross.
>
> Much space between foreground and mountains.
>
> Male figure's head is turned away from the viewer.

This listing exercise enabled students to postpone their interpreting and judging the art long enough to collect the perceptual data necessary to make a sensitive response. Because of the activities mentioned previously, Jane had a sense of what to look for in her analysis of Dali's use of space and perspective. This is evident in her use of such terms as "one point perspective" and "foreground." Through writing she was able to get a more complete picture of Dali's complex use of these elements. Students agreed that they saw a lot more detail in the work after doing this exercise.

*Specialized Vocabulary*

Critical language about art determines to a great extent the possibilities for writing. Perceptions which invite the use of previously learned words or phrases generally surface while important observations which strain the individual's vocabulary may remain unexamined. My students' level and depth of visual perceptions are related to their existing language resources. I teach my students a vocabulary through which the description, analysis and interpretation of aesthetic qualities is possible. This vocabulary is built gradually throughout my basic art course. I begin by introducing my students to the element of line in art. Line is defined and then examined in terms of its variation (changes in width, curvature, and so on) and analyzed in terms of how artists use it (to create pattern and texture). By the end of the course, my students are familiar with the elements of line, shape, color, space, value, and texture as well as with the principles of unity, contrast, pattern, rhythm proportion, balance, and emphasis. As they acquire the ability to understand, respond to, talk, and write about visual images, they become, in the most complete sense, visually literate. Accordingly, I try to stimulate spoken and written language about visual images.

Language is also a practical tool through which students can actively respond to art. In order to have meaning for students, art appreciation programs need to provide experiences in which the student is an active participant. The value of art is not learned by listening to someone else talk about it. My students want to talk about what they see, not be told what it is that they are looking at. We gain satisfaction from talking about what we like and dislike and in turn comparing reactions with others. This collaboration often uncovers details that were missed and furthers the enjoyment and understanding of the total experience. If the purpose of art appreciation is to increase the student's ability to share aesthetic experiences, the student must be asked to respond rather than passively view slides and films on art.

Writing-to-learn art appreciation places the student in an active role. The students' verbal abilities are exercised when those students are asked to give written responses to art. They use recently acquired vocabulary as well as personal experiences and perceptions. Mike, one of my basic design students, wrote the following when asked to respond to the shape, color, and texture of Claes Oldenburg's *7-up*.

> The colors consist of green, orange, and blue. The shape is that of a 7-up beverage container slightly crunched in the middle. Its texture is rough with mountains and valleys. The 7-up can symbolizes the waste problem which the world has.

In order to make this statement, Mike isolated the elements of color, shape, and texture in the work. His description of each element was created according to his present perceptions. As my students acquire a greater vocabulary, they perceive more qualities in each of the elements. Their first thoughts then include analysis of the elements as well as descriptions. For example, orange and blue are complementary colors. After studying color order and characteristics, which I teach toward the middle of the course, students are likely to observe complementary colors while viewing *7-up*. Also, Mike's statements reflect his knowledge of the world's waste problem and give a description of the design elements. It is this integration of the students' newly acquired knowledge with their past experiences that enhances their appreciation of art, because the most fulfilling interpretation of art reveals a commonality between the viewer's personality and the actual contents of the work itself.

Art criticism is any spoken or written discussion of art. To criticize art knowledgeably is to appreciate it in a meaningful way. Writing techniques are excellent vehicles with which students can practice art criticism in the form of description, analysis, interpretation, or judgment concerning art. Prior to analyzing and interpreting art, students must acquire skills for describing art.

Describing art is simply holding back all judgments and objectively listing concrete features in the work. Any artwork could be the focus for this exercise. If the lesson centers on the elements of art, students would list descriptions of specific shapes, textures, and colors in the work. If the intention is to give an interpretation of a representational work, students would list descriptions of objects and details in the work. I asked students to interpret the painting *My Gem* by William Harnett. In *My Gem* Harnett has juxtaposed related still life material that provides a comfortable set of practical associations. He has placed every object in sharp focus, as if each were under a magnifying glass, thereby fooling the viewer into accepting them as real instead of painted. The objects are all commonplace. For example, a feather pen, a book, and a wood table could all have been found in many homes during Harnett's lifetime. In order to lead my students to an eventual interpretation, I first asked them to make a list of all the objects they could see in *My Gem*. This painting was a good choice because it contains so many different objects. Jane listed the following items:

wood table
old tablecloth
thick books
feather pen
black ink
sheet of music

pipe

blue wrinkled piece of paper

burned matches

old-fashioned lamp

artistic pitcher

words

chain

flute

ashes

I then asked her to give an interpretation of the painting by writing a description of the owner of these objects. I directed students this way in their interpretations because of the title Harnett gave his work. I assumed the objects in the painting were of personal value to the artist, functioning as a kind of self-portrait. Jane's response follows:

> I think he would be a rather old guy, with white hair, wearing a grey suit. I think he would be a writer of music and books. He's not real organized. He's probably a loving person. It looks as though he were a lonely kind of man.

Listing the objects in the painting helped Jane get a feeling for the personality behind the painting. She has used her imagination in associating these objects with the artist. In her interpretation the artist is characterized as not very organized, loving, and lonely. Juxtaposing the many objects in the picture elicited these ideas and feelings, making her interpretation a personal one. After this exercise I asked students if this helped them get more out of viewing the work, and they responded positively. Here are a few of their comments:

> It showed me how to read a painting, not only to see the objects in the painting, but to feel the painter's expressions.
>
> It helped me understand why he painted what he painted.
>
> It helped me to use my imagination.

My students enjoyed making their lists and sharing them with the entire class. Usually I ask my students to share what they have written when I sense they are eager to do so and when time allows. Group interaction provides students with perceptions they might otherwise have missed. They also enjoy hearing their peers express ideas and feelings which are similar to as well as different from their own.

After students have gathered visual data through listing, an exercise in analysis can easily follow. An exercise in analysis works best when it is kept down to a few specific concepts. Adequate preparation is vital at this stage. Students must understand the meaning behind each concept to be analyzed. For example, if the students can define the principles of contrast and identify several ways artists use contrast, they are ready to analyze how contrast is used in a variety of situations. I help my students accomplish this by giving them specific examples of six or seven isolated uses of contrast. Then the students view slides of a variety of works of art and are asked to identify which situation previously seen in the example is closest to the present situation. At this point students begin to depart from the rigid list of kinds of contrast and see new situations or ways artists use it. True analysis has begun. Students put together their own explanations of how contrast was used by relating new situations to those previously learned.

## Strategies for Increasing Art Appreciation

One particular writing technique, the **dialogue**, is an excellent means of getting students not only to analyze the use of specific concepts in art but also utilize their imagination, sense of humor, and ability to see the opposing sides of a situation. To write a meaningful dialogue, students need clear guidelines and should be provided with exercises which lead up to the final written work. Students gain a clearer understanding of the concepts they are using if they are allowed to rework their first attempt into a final written work.

It is important to take time to introduce and discuss aspects that make up a good dialogue. Specifics need to be stated such as what concepts are to be analyzed, how many lines each voice should have, how much class time is to be spent writing the first draft, and perhaps how to get started. Students can be given individual reproductions, art out of magazines, or the entire class can focus on one reproduction. An exercise listing elements in the reproduction helps the students begin an analysis, for description is a major part of the dialogue.

After creating a geometric design, using the elements of line and shape and the principles of unity, contrast, and variation, I asked my students to write a dialogue incorporating these new concepts. The assignment was broken into the following units: (1) Students made a list describing the elements in a reproduction; (2) Students did a **focused write** analyzing how contrast, unity, and variation were utilized by the artist in the work; (3) Students wrote a dialogue incorporating information about the work from their list and focused write, and (4) Students reworked the first draft of the dialogue into a final product considering clarity and continuity. They were required to use two voices, one a gallery owner's, the other a visitor's. I instructed everyone to open the dialogue with the visitor saying, "How on earth can this be worth $100,000?" and to define the work in terms of the concepts recently covered in class. Here is a sampling of student responses to this exercise.

## Example One

*Visitor:* How on earth can this be worth $100,000?

*Owner:* You have to realize that it is very difficult for an artist to create effective variation and contrast in a picture. The value of this painting is based on the use of variation and contrast. If you look at this picture closely, you will discover that there is a lot of variation in the colors.

*Visitor:* Oh! Now that you mention it, I do notice the beige against the blue. The light blue sure gives variety in the blue too.

*Owner:* Another good point is the contrast of the shapes. Take the triangles and the rectangles for example.

*Visitor:* The arcs against the rectangles are a pretty interesting contrast in themselves. Also, the lines sure are a contrast to the other two shapes, triangles and rectangles.

*Owner:* I wonder if you noticed the lines are red and dark blue, not black as one would guess at first glance.

*Visitor:* Hey! I didn't even notice that. But, now that you mention it, I do notice. You're pretty observant.

*Owner:* Well, that is my job. Speaking of observance, did you notice the red specks in the black rectangular area?

*Visitor:* No, I didn't. Wow, when you look at a picture you really look! Know what, though? I sure wouldn't spend that much on one painting.

## Example Two

*Visitor:* How on earth can this be worth $100,000?

*Owner:* Now sir, please don't be so irrational, note its extraordinary qualities.

*Visitor:* What qualities? You mean a few multiple colored oil paints slapped on this piece of canvas?

*Owner:* Sir, please note the artist's use of contrast, repetition, and variation.

*Visitor:* What do you mean? What's contrast?

*Owner:* Contrast is just one of the three principles of art I just mentioned. Contrast is defined as a strong difference, for example, dark versus light or big versus small.

*Visitor:* Okay, I see, the darker colors of the painting are contrasting with the light ones as are the large triangles and squares to the smaller ones.

*Owner:* That's right, now you're catching on. Shapes can contrast as well as color and shades of value.

*Visitor:* And what do those other two principles mean that you mentioned? Repetition and variation.

*Owner:* Repetition means to repeat the same shape over and over, but the artist doesn't just stop there, he also uses variation in the shapes. Variation means a slight difference, a slight change from shape to shape. The two combined create unity. Otherwise the painting would be very dull.

*Visitor:* I see, so without repetition and variation working together, the design would be missing something, right?

*Owner:* Right, because unity brings together all principles and elements of art to create a sense of oneness to make the perfect design.

*Visitor:* Boy, without contrast, repetition, variation, and especially unity, art would be worthless. I can see how designs are valued at such high prices.

*Owner:* By Jove, I think you've got it. So would you like to purchase this particular painting?

*Visitor:* Are you kidding me? A painting with such caliber as this is priceless, it should be put in a museum of fine art.

*Owner:* Why, I never!

*Visitor:* Yeah, and you probably never will either, but thanks for the lecture.

*Owner:* @#:!!%

In both examples students used the previously learned concepts of unity, contrast, and variation to analyze the reproduction in their dialogues. But, there is an obvious difference between them in terms of the learning demonstrated. In the first example, the owner points out how the artist used variation and contrast but fails to mention how the artist unified the work. On the other hand, the owner in the second example not only points out how variation, contrast, and unity were utilized by the artist but also clearly defines each concept for the visitor and explains how they function together to make the design successful. Both dialogues indicate that the students have learned to make close observations as evidenced in their descriptions of each work. Although both examples are successful in achieving a conversational tone, the second is more interesting because of tension created between the gallery owner and visitor. Using these concepts to talk about design was a hard bridge for some to make. It helped a great deal to analyze the reproductions first in terms of how each concept was used by the artist in a focused write before the dialogue was begun. All agreed this experience taught a more critical way of seeing.

The best interpretation of art is one that makes a connection between the personality of the viewer and what is seen in the work. Once my students understand and accept this, they are eager to give meaning to what they have observed. I found a sequence of writing exercises to be very effective in helping students to uncover particular personal ideas and experiences needed in making the connection with art. **Clustering** works well for drawing out ideas and experiences. Participating in a directed **free write** for several minutes after doing a cluster can be effective preparation for a meaningful interpretation. I used Imogene Cunningham's photograph entitled "My Father" for an exercise in interpretation. Students were first asked to create a word cluster around the words "my father." Here is an example by Ray, a sophomore design student.

gets along with my friends        shy        fishing
       caring

               funny

              **my father**

retired            beer drinking       watches television

The class was then asked to describe a visual portrait of their father that would communicate their feelings toward him.

> "In the portrait my dad would be sitting down in front of the TV with a big smile on his face. He's sitting on the couch kind of bent over. In the background there's a picture of him with a fishing pole in his hand."

Ray has taken his ideas and feelings about his father and transformed them into a written visual portrait. For example, the word fishing appears in his word cluster and later in the portrait is visually translated into a hanging picture of his father holding a fishing pole. This thinking process is significant for communicating ideas and feelings in a visual way. Cunningham's portrait of her father is indeed more than just a snapshot; it is a statement about her feelings toward him.

Finally, I asked students to examine Imogene Cunningham's photograph, taking its title into consideration. They were asked to list qualities of the man in the photo which they felt stated what Cunningham felt and thought about her father. Ray listed the following qualities:

> outdoors type
> loves nature

wears striped overalls

splits own wood

uses cane

old, has white hair

At this point in the exercise, students began to appreciate and understand in a sensitive manner what Imogene Cunningham was saying about her father. Because of their earlier reflections of their own fathers, they were able to make personal connections between themselves and the work of art. Listing these qualities served as an interpretation of Cunningham's statement about her father. The key to success with this sequence is care in choosing one idea or word from the work with which to create a word cluster and develop an interpretation.

I also used the sequence of writing exercises with a reproduction of a drawing entitled *Burden* by Paul Klee. The title again was used for the word cluster. Students put everything in their word cluster from money pressures to problems in relationships. They enjoyed writing about their feelings; it was a cathartic experience for some. Here is an example of the complete sequence by a student in my basic design class:

*Word Cluster*

<pre>
                         (health)
                         sickness
                 friends      no job
      news                house         not going home
        brother                 boyfriend  staying out too late
      people      **burden**        car
    smoking     (trouble)       parent's pressures
          alcohol                school
                 drugs    law
                 no money
</pre>

The student is making a personal connection with the word "burden."

*Written Response to Idea in Word Cluster*

> I have a lot of trouble with my parents and it creates a great burden on my peace of mind. Like, for instance, my car. I have had my car for about 2 years now and up until 7 months ago it was in perfect working condition. Then, I listened to my friends and burned rubber and raced it and took it four-wheeling when it's only a two-wheel drive and eventually I screwed it up. Now, the brakes need

Figure 2. *Burden* by Paul Klee 1939, Drawing 11½″ × 8¼″

fixing, and it needs a new radiator, the front axle is bent and it needs a tune-up. I have $200 to have most of it fixed but, my parents keep telling me, "We'll fix it." So far, they haven't done a single thing for it. My boyfriend keeps asking me when it's going to get fixed, and I can't even tell him. I have to have my car so that I can get a job. When I had my car, I got drunk and drove, and skipped school with it, sometimes. I can see why they wouldn't want me to have it. But, every day that I can't drive my car, there is a burden. A burden that maybe I'll never get to drive it again. And I want to have it.

In this selection the student has elaborated on a current personal burden. The feeling which surfaced was used to make a personal connection with Paul Klee's drawing. The student has related to Klee's visual statement more so than before reflecting on what it felt like to be burdened. The reasons for the feeling are insignificant. It was the reflection on the feeling of being burdened that became the student's interpretation for Klee's drawing.

## List of Aspects Relating to Word "Burden"

As a class we listed five aspects of the drawing that related to the title. The purpose of this list was to help the students recognize how Klee symbolized the feeling of being burdened into visual form and to help them associate their present personal connotations with "burden" to Klee's depiction of it. Here is the list:

> His head is hung down.
>
> His arms are between his legs; no hands.
>
> The objects above his head are on him.
>
> His legs are crossed; he's skinny.
>
> Arrows point downward.

In addition to using writing-to-learn techniques for the description, analysis, and interpretation of art, I have employed writing to encourage students' learning in other ways. Writing to learn works well in any art class when students write summary statements on the process they went through to arrive at a finished artwork. This provides closure for specific projects and helps students to reflect on what they have learned. I gave students questions to answer in their summary. Here are a few examples of questions I most often ask.

> In what ways did you transform your original idea to fit the medium?
>
> What problems in technique did you encounter?

What new aspects did you learn about the medium?

Did you enjoy doing the artwork?

What would you do differently if you were to do this same project again?

Here is an excerpt from a summary written by one of my ceramics students after she completed the construction of a coil pot.

> I had a little problem with making my coils round. Instead of round, they tended to be a little flat. To solve that problem I slowed down my process and made small rolling motions with the tip of my fingers. Coiling then went smoothly. I thought the project was fun. I learned a lot about coiling and different things I could do with it.

Aesthetic education increases a student's sensitivity to art. The vast majority of students will go on to become art consumers, responding to rather than creating art. Aesthetic education prepares students to make knowledgeable responses to art, primarily through teaching students to understand and use the specialized language of art, enabling them to describe, analyze, interpret, and judge art. Since language is the vehicle through which awareness and sensitivity to art can be developed, writing-to-learn strategies play a vital role in the aesthetic education program.

Using writing-to-learn strategies aimed at increasing art appreciation yields many new possibilities. The strategies already discussed by no means represent all possibilities. Much more experimentation is needed with these strategies. It is important to remember that, in order to find what works, a risk must be taken. This is where the real challenge of curriculum development begins. If you are the type of teacher who delights in revamping teaching strategies until they provide you with satisfactory outcomes, you will love using writing-to-learn art appreciation strategies in a creative way.

# Writing to Learn German

Deborah Peterson
Bethel High School, Bethel, Washington

The ultimate goal of foreign language instruction is to teach students the skills needed to communicate in the foreign language. For this, students need insight into cultural and historical phenomena, as well as knowledge of grammatical functions. They need to trust their teacher and classmates before they will be willing to speak another language and make the mistakes that nonnative speakers are bound to make. And speaking in the foreign language is essential because students must move from acquisition to application of skills.

Writing-to-learn techniques help students begin to communicate successfully in the foreign language, reducing students' fears of making errors and looking dumb. In addition, writing to learn helped students understand grammatical functions, historical events, and cultural phenomena. In this chapter I will describe how my students write to improve speaking, to learn grammar, to simulate real-life situations, and to understand cultural concepts.

## Organizing

The foundation for use of writing-to-learn techniques in my classes was the **journal.** The journal, a three-ring binder, was a student log of activities as well as a place to record thought processes. Students also kept handouts such as song sheets and news articles in the journal. The journal organized students physically, an obvious advantage. It also organized students mentally; if they were unable to record their thoughts on paper, they knew their understanding was weak, and they would seek help. Students knew they would write on a daily basis and came to realize that daily writing projects would help them reach the goal of a lesson. I used a partner system so that students would share their work on a regular basis and get feedback on it. For many, consistent use of the journal provided tangible evidence that each day was important and that each activity was a stepping stone toward mastery of the unit.

Students dated and labeled each entry and kept work in chronological order. If we were working on command forms on Monday and Friday's assignment involved commands, students would often refresh their memories by going through their journals to review the week's notes and exercises. Before they began using journals, such a review would have been more difficult.

Since the journal contained expressive language, which tends to be personal, students preferred to review their own notes, rather than ask me to review material in class. Considering the number of interactions teachers have with students each hour, students and teachers can both benefit from a procedure that enables students to help themselves by relying on their own knowledge and records. The journals also helped the students who missed class; they could find out from classmates what the assignment was and ask me for additional help if necessary.

That the students valued the journal was especially clear to me the last week of school. As I collected the journals to review their content one last time, I mentioned that I might not be ready to give them back until the afternoon of the last day of school. Many concerned students came to me after class and during lunch to tell me how much they needed the journal and to ask if they could pick it up earlier. They genuinely desired to have and use the journal the following year, and some ambitious students wanted to use it over the summer vacation. Even graduating seniors came back to get their journals.

## Speaking Skills

Speaking skills receive the greatest emphasis in the foreign language classroom because achieving communicative competence requires making the transition from "skill-getting" to "skill-using." I want my students to control the German language, not have it control them. I often used writing-to-learn techniques in my classes to help students improve their oral German. These writing projects usually involved visual cues that the speaker and listener could use to increase understanding. These techniques provided "stepping stones" for the speaker reducing anxiety and assuring success.

One assignment in the beginning German class asked students to introduce themselves and each other. The chapter in our text introduced the vocabulary and provided a dialogue for using it. It also covered possessive pronouns and their endings. As we read various dialogues in the text, we made **lists** of characteristics we would need to describe people. They were divided according to categories: eye color, hair color, favorite sport, favorite class, and so on. Students wrote all the possibilities, not just those that applied to them. The listing exercise helped reinforce what they had previously learned: spellings and meanings of words. After finishing the lists, students circled those items that applied to them. This allowed them to focus on the vocabulary they would need to introduce themselves.

We then began to produce cards that would be visual aids for speaking exercises. Students brought pictures of themselves from home; these were glued to five-by-seven-inch cards. They recorded on their cards what they perceived as the most important information about themselves. They were not allowed to write full sentences, only skeletal information, for example:

| | |
|---|---|
| Name: | Konrad R. Whitney |
| Alter: | 17 Jahre alt |
| Wohnort: | Tacoma, Washington, USA |
| Haarfarbe: | blond |
| Augenfarbe: | blau |
| Hobbies: | Malen, Wandern, Essen, Camping, Lesen, Sport |
| Lieblingssport: | Fussball, Korbball, Schwimmen, Football |
| Lieblingsfach: | Sport |
| Lieblingsgruppe: | Blue Oyster Cult |

Translation

| | |
|---|---|
| Name: | Konrad R. Whitney |
| Age: | 17 years old |
| Residence: | Tacoma, Washington, USA |
| Hair color: | blond |
| Eye color: | blue |
| Hobbies: | drawing, hiking, eating, camping, reading, sports |
| Favorite sport: | soccer, basketball, swimming, football |
| Favorite subject: | sports |
| Favorite group: | Blue Oyster Cult |

Before beginning the exercise, we reviewed subject-verb agreement with the verb "to like." And I reminded the students that the listeners also had visual cues for comprehension, since the pictures and the person matched the vocabulary. They saw the word *fussball* on Konrad's card at the same time they saw his blond hair and blue eyes.

Before students spoke to the class, they were given a few minutes to practice introducing themselves, with their partners as the audience. Students now had been led through all the steps to get to the goal of introducing themselves fluently and confidently.

During the introductions to the class, speakers were encouraged to use the cards as cues. Listeners were encouraged to ask questions of the speakers, just as would happen in real-life conversations. Students interacted very well; they were interested in learning about each other and in telling about themselves. The cue cards and the listmaking that led to the production of the cue cards fostered confidence.

When writing the cards, students had time to think through the project. They knew the goal, and they wanted to communicate accurate information. Their knowledge of the words and grammatical functions was reinforced as they made their lists and used the lists to make their own cards. As they moved to higher levels of thinking (the comprehension and application levels), students were able to depend on their writing to help them communicate orally with their peers. The speaking activity was not spontaneous, but it gave them practice for speaking in real-life situations.

Writing-to-learn techniques such as **brainstorming, clustering, lists,** and **first thoughts** can be used to assure successful communication. These techniques can help students complete the following traditional assignments.

| Topic | Material |
|---|---|
| Traveling | Make a travel brochure of a place you've visited in Germany, Austria, Switzerland, or the United States. Use pictures and cue words, but not full sentences. You'll use your brochure to introduce the travel destination to the class. |
| Breakfast Foods | Bring in pictures of your favorite German breakfast foods. Write an advertisement and use it to make an oral presentation to the class. |

| | |
|---|---|
| Sports | Bring in a picture of your favorite athlete. Write her or his biography and make an oral report to the class. |
| Party | Make invitations to a party. Include the following on the card: What the occasion is, When the party is, Where, and Who is invited to the party. |

The advantage of writing-to-learn speaking is clear: students are communicating once when writing the information and again when speaking. The cue cards provide visual cues and are produced by students. Furthermore, they incorporate students' diverse interests. Materials can be used repeatedly by varying the actual speaking exercises to fit the goal of the specific lesson. For example, the cards students used to introduce themselves were used later in the year to discuss clothes, colors, and fashions. Students enjoyed seeing their classmates' cards and discussing them.

## Learning Grammar

Learning grammar is another goal in foreign language class. Many students get their first taste of grammar rules in the foreign language classroom. Some students apply grammatical concepts easily; others struggle continually with terms and concepts. Often students can repeat from memory how a given part of the sentence is defined, yet they cannot identify that part of the sentence or explain why one would need to know what part of the sentence a word is.

In German the speaker must know what part of the sentence each phrase is because the definite articles change to reflect the function of the nouns they precede. For example, in English the definite article remains the same regardless of the noun's function. While in German there are six choices of definite articles (*der, die, das, den, dem,* and *des*). Writing-to-learn exercises can help students understand this and other grammatical functions.

My favorite exercises for teaching grammar are **dictation** and vary-the-audience. For example, when I introduced students to the conversational past tense, I asked them to copy my definition of the tense. After they copied it, I explained it to them in greater detail and answered their questions. To confirm their understanding, I asked them to write in their journals how they would explain the conversational past tense to a grade school child. Students occasionally explain concepts to classmates who have been absent, but to explain a concept to a young child, they need to use simple language with clear examples that reflect a thorough understanding of the concepts involved. This variation in audience made some students realize that they did not understand the concepts well enough to explain them to their peers, let alone to younger kids. Others realized how well they did comprehend tense, and they were able to help students who were having difficulty.

The dictation and vary-the-audience exercises were my favorite because I could monitor the students as they worked and get immediate feedback on their understanding and ability to apply concepts. Students did not have to flunk a test before they or I realized they needed help. The writing exercises helped them process the information and eventually master the concepts.

All of the work was done in the journal, and many students referred back to their grammar dictation and vary-the-audience exercises when working on composition assignments. They preferred to use their own work when they had questions rather than the textbook. In most situations, students were able to rely on themselves and on their partners when they needed to review previously covered material.

### Writing in German

Ultimately, of course, students should be able to complete real-life writing tasks in the foreign language. The following is an assignment I give to more advanced students who have developed speaking and grammar skills.

> Write a letter (using the German format) to a person who does not know much about the landscape of northern Germany. Compare and contrast the landscape of the North with that of southern Germany. Convince your reader that the landscape of the North is as beautiful as that of the South. Use the conversational past tense where possible.

This assignment requires the ability to compare and contrast, as well as basic knowledge of vocabulary and application of grammar rules. Because of their inability to diagnose and analyze their thoughts, students found such an assignment very difficult to complete.

Writing-to-learn activities, however, gave them stepping stones toward it. These activities took place during two class periods and involved some homework.

1. Because of the organization of our textbook, we had viewed a movie on a town in northern Germany two months before the letter-writing project was assigned. At that time students had listed in their journals characteristics of the architecture, landscape, food, outdoor activities, and such. We reviewed those lists for the letters.
2. I then showed a movie on the Swabian Alps in southern Germany. Students were encouraged to note characteristics of the landscape.
3. After the movie, we listed what we had seen using clustering. (See figures 1 and 2.)This organized the ideas generated from watching the movie. Students did not have to spend time looking up previous chapters' vocabulary; the cluster that we composed as a class served as a vocabulary review.
4. The next assignment was to use clustering for northern Germany. (See figures 3 and 4.)Although most students were able to recall the characteristics of the landscape, some students needed to re-

Figure 1.

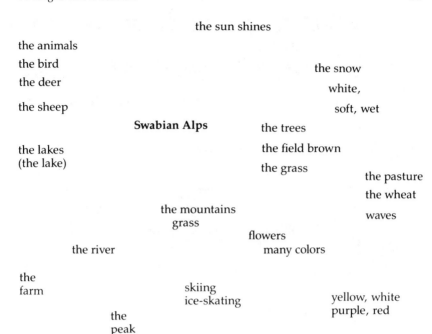

Figure 2.

fer back to their lists from two months earlier. (Since the lists were in the journal, this was no problem.) After we finished this map, students had two loosely organized outlines of the characteristics of northern and southern Germany. These outlines would be crucial for comparing and contrasting northern and southern Germany.

5. The final preparation for the assignment was to review letter format and application of the conversational past tense. Students now had several stepping stones for the assignment: knowledge of the landscapes and outdoor activities; vocabulary; a loose organization of information; a review of the conversational past tense; and a review of the letter format. I then asked students to write the previously described letter, convincing the reader of the beauty of northern Germany. Since many American students know only the beauty of the south of Germany, I hoped the letter would give them a different perspective on northern Germany. The writing-to-learn techniques that I used for this assignment greatly reduced students' anxiety, and letters were organized, clear and grammatically correct.

das Wetter (weather)         der Wolke (n)—cloud

die Blumen

es regnet viel      flach    der Sonnenaufgang

(sunrise)

meadow

die Wiese

Gras (sehr grun)      **Nord Deutschland**     der See

der Nordsee

(beach) der Strand     Hoch See Angeln    der Ostee

schwimmen    die kuh

angeln    braun werden    die Milch

straw roof    ist frisch

das Strohdach (-er)    die Butter

danisch   Hauser

mild, sanft: gentle    die Landschaft

Figure 3.

the weather      the cloud

the flowers

it rains a lot    flat    the sunrise

the meadow

**North Germany**    the ocean

the beach      the North Sea

high seas fishing    the Baltic

swimming

straw roof    fishing    to get a tan    the cow

the straw roof(s)    the milk is

danish   houses    fresh, the

butter

mild, soft: gentle    the landscape

Figure 4.

23 Januar

Liebe Elke,

Iche mochte Dir ein bischen von meiner Reise in Nord Deutschland erzahlen. Die Landschaft ist ja herrlich. Die Wiesen sind sehr grun und alles ist sehr flach. Alles ist einfach aber schon. Die verschiedene Farben—grun, braun, orange, und rot im Herbst—sind beruhigend. an den Alpen ist es auch schon und uberall sind prachtige Aussichten aber in Nord Deutschland kann man den Sonnenaufgang und Sonnenuntergang Meilen weit umher sehen.

Ich schlage Dir vor, Nord Deutschland zu besuchen. Ich weiss, dass die Alpen herrlich sind, aber Nord Deutschland ist wieder etwas ganz anderes. Auf den Seen kann man segeln und schwimmen; und Hoch See Anglen kann man auch. Am Strande kann man sich sonnen. Ich glaube Nord Deutschland wird Dir gefallen und du wirst eine sehr schone Zeit hier haben. Bitte, komme hierher und ich werde Dir alles zeigen.

Deine
Natalie

Translation

Dear Elke,

I'd like to tell you a little about my trip in northern Germany. The landscape is gorgeous. The pastures are very green and everything is very flat. Everything is simple but beautiful. The different colors—green, brown, orange, and red in the fall—are soothing. In the Alps it is also beautiful, and all over there are magnificent views, but in northern Germany you can see the sunrise and sunset for miles.

I recommend you visit northern Germany. I know that the Alps are gorgeous, but northern Germany is something else. You can sail and swim in the ocean, and you can also go high-sea-angling! On the beach you can lie in the sun. I think you'll like northern Germany and you'll have a very beautiful time here. Please, come and visit me, and I'll show you everything.

Yours,
Natalie

Natalie used the vocabulary and the organization that the clustering activity provided to successfully point out the beauty of northern Germany as compared to southern Germany. Although she chose not to use the conversational past tense, she did use two-verb construction and the future tense properly. The review of the conversational past tense helped her to remember the rules for constructing those sentences.

One student was absent for the clustering assignments and later came in to get help. We worked on his clusters together. I asked him when he would need to come in again. "I've got everything I need. I can do it on my own," he stated confidently. (This student was unable to complete even the most elementary assignment the previous year.) Many students felt the same way; anxiety about the assignment was minimal, yet the quality of their work was high. The stepping stones we used to produce the letter enabled students to complete the assignment by organizing their thoughts on paper. The use of writing-to-learn techniques was crucial to their success on this assignment.

## Cultural Activities

Integrating diverse cultural activities into regular classroom activities is a major goal in my German classes. A mere tolerance of a different way of doing things is not enough. I want my students to know enough about the German people to understand why things might be different and eventually to accept these differences.

I used writing-to-learn methods in a brief unit on dancing, because I felt my students would have the "we're-too-cool" syndrome and would automatically close their minds to this aspect of Germans' social interactions. I wanted students to think about the value of the unit and, through various writing assignments, convince themselves to participate. Writing about the proposed dance unit was also a way to get their anxieties out in the open.

To begin, I asked my students to record first thoughts on why it might be important to study the role of dancing in German society. Some were aware of the value of the unit, but responses varied tremendously.

Sally
### Why learn a dance from another country?

1. To get a taste of one of their pastimes
2. Because it would be fun (sort of)
3. To learn a custom and the reasons for their dance
4. To feel familiar with a dance so if you visit you can do it comfortably
5. To make a fool of ourselves and hopefully have fun doing it

Ron
### Why learn a dance from another country?

To learn different traditions, because it looks and is fun, and there's nothing else to do!

Chris
### Why should we learn a dance?

I believe we should learn a German dance simply because we requested that our class be taught as much as possible about German culture and tradition. Not only did we want to learn their language but we wanted to know about them as people.

After they shared their writing with the class, and it became clear that they were interested in the unit but concerned about their images, I gave a brief explanation of the role of dancing in the German teenager's life. In addition, I talked about my own experiences with dancing as a seventeen-year-old exchange student in Germany. Of course, background information was not enough to convince them of the value of the unit. Students need to understand why they should learn about a behavior before they will be receptive to information. I wanted students to understand why we were doing the unit, but I also wanted them to be comfortable with the activities.

Our next writing project was a **dialogue.** I asked students to describe a conversation between themselves (as reluctant students) and a German youth who really wants to attend dancing school. The German youth served as an "alter ego." My looking silly while dancing also gave them insight into the role of dancing in Germany. Students scribbled furiously; after all, their reputations were at stake. many students expressed their fears; some expressed slight interest in the unit. Others went one step further: they convinced themselves that the unit was important.

Anthony

*American:* What do you mean you're going to a dance school? Dancing is boring when learning it in school. I can't stand it.

*German:* Dancing is not boring, it's fun, exciting. You should learn something different for a change.

*American:* Why? It's only a waste of time. When could I use such a stupid dance?

*German:* Well, when you're invited to dances or parties.

*American:* I'm never invited to dances or parties.

*German:* Well, you could go to the one at school.

*American:* I have no one to go with and I don't know how to dance.

*German:* Well, that's why you should learn how to.

*American:* I have two left feet.

*German:* With practice you can be good at it. I'm excited about learning a new dance.

Sally

*American:* We're learning dancing in German class and I don't want to.

*German:* You're kidding! I would love to be taking dance classes. It's such an important part of our society, and I don't want to be left out.

*American:* Really? I didn't know it meant so much to you guys, but I don't think I need to learn them.

*German:* You would be surprised! If you ever come over to visit, you might feel pretty uncomfortable sitting down while everyone is dancing. Seriously, dancing could be considered a major pastime!

*American:* Mmmm, well, I guess I better pay attention then and learn the dance.

Fran

*American:* Shoot! I really think dancing lessons are stupid! I don't want to dance.

*German:* What was that? You don't want to dance? But dancing is fun and healthy. You get to know people and to be involved.

*American:* Yeah, but dancing just isn't the thing for me. I don't think I can do it.

*German:* Oh, but you can. If you look at it openmindedly you can really enjoy yourself.

*American:* Well . . . .

*German:* Come on—give it a try—it's a lot of fun!

After sharing dialogues and laughing and joking nervously, students were more sensitive to the importance of the German social situations that call for dancing. At the end of three days of instruction on actual dance steps, types of music typical to a region or age, and dance etiquette, students were asking questions related to the unit and were eager to learn more dances. Not a single student had asked to be excused from the lessons.

The writing assignments gave students a chance to think about and publicize their insecurities about looking like fools. The dialogue with the "alter ego" convinced many students that the unit was important and motivated them to actively participate. The success of the unit could well be attributed to the attitude change that occurred as students wrote. At the end of the unit they could understand this new social situation and explain it to themselves, their parents, and peers. If and when they visit Germany, they will be more comfortable using their newly acquired skills.

We concluded the unit with another dialogue. Students wrote the conversation they would have with the German after finishing the dance unit. This time the students wrote in German.

*American:* Also, wir haben 2 Tage Tan-Unterricht gehabt. Es war wirklich interessant. Es war nicht leicht, aber es war Spass.

*German:* Ja, ich habe gedacht du wirs eine schone Zeit haben.

*American:* Ja, ich habe gelacht und alles hat Spass gemacht!

*German:* Siehst du! Tazen ist nicht schlecht. Wo hast du getanzt?

*American:* Oben mit meinen Klassenkameraden.

*German:* Ach, gut! Du kannst mit den deutschen Kindern jetzt tanzen.

*American:* Wir haben den Walzer, die Polka, den Ente Tanz, und den Swing Tanz gelernt.

*German:* Oje! Das hat mir DM75 gekostet.

## Translation

*American:* Well, we've had 2 days of dance lessons. It was really interesting. It wasn't easy, but it was fun!

*German:* Yes, I thought you'd have a good time.

*American:* Yes, I laughed, and everything was fun!

*German:* You see! Dancing isn't bad. Where did you dance?

*American:* Upstairs with my classmates.

*German:* Ahh, good. Now you can dance with the German kids.

*American:* We learned the waltz, the polka, the duck dance, and the wing dance.

*German:* Wow, that cost me 75 Marks.

The dialogues confirmed the dramatic change in student attitudes I had perceived during the dance unit. Step by step, student inhibitions dissolved as dialogue and dance lessons became more frequent throughout the year. A willingness and desire on the part of the students to learn about the culture being studied is clearly crucial to their success in mastering the language.

I attribute much of my success in fostering student interest in the German culture and language to using writing-to-learn techniques. In my large classes, writing-to-learn techniques have been invaluable in keeping all of the students actively engaged in the subject matter. In particular, the journal has provided a mechanism which organizes students' thoughts and work, displays student progress through the year, and gives me a means for evaluating student effort. Writing to learn facilitates a step-by-step increase in student confidence and competence, as students, through their writing, move smoothly from skill-acquiring to skill-applying. Used in such diverse areas as speaking, learning grammar, writing for real-life situations, and understanding cultural concepts, writing-to-learn techniques are an invaluable aid for helping students gain competence in foreign languages.

# Writing to Learn Social Studies

Bruce Beaman
Mountlake Terrace High School, Edmonds, Washington

I have been teaching for over fifteen years and have developed two guiding principles. First, good teaching requires variety and an infusion of new ideas and techniques. Second, do not get carried away with the latest trends or the current "in" methods of teaching. When the Writing-in-the-Humanities Program was suggested to me by Staff Development in the Edmonds School District, I was interested because I am always looking for new approaches to get course material across to the students. At the same time I was somewhat apprehensive, since the term "writing-to-learn" suggested creative writing or other aspects of English classes.

I teach several different high school courses including Psychology, Sociology, Contemporary Problems, and Psychology of Self-esteem. Psychology and Sociology are senior elective classes, both equivalent to introductory college courses. Contemporary problems is a consideration of the world and its complex problems. My goal is to have seniors graduate with a knowledge of the countries of the world and an understanding of historical reasons for the headlines we read about today. Psychology of Self-esteem, an elective, includes a mixture of grades nine through twelve. As the course title indicates, students are asked to give themselves a closer look and then are gently pushed towards a better self-image and given some strategies for self-improvement. With such a variety of courses, I did not see how writing could be used effectively in all my classes.

My work with writing to learn is still relatively new, and I change and adapt as I go along. Nonetheless, I have found that the strategies work in all my classes. Students gain not only because they are more involved in the learning process but also because they achieve a deeper insight into the material being studied.

However, I was hesitant to approach a non-English class with writing as one of the dominant teaching tools. I worried about how much time writing would take away from the lessons. What would my students learn from writing? My response at first was to add a few writing-to-learn techniques and see what happened. The students responded halfheartedly but not without some positive comments. I decided that if I were really to give writing-to-learn a chance I would have to be more assertive in using it in the classroom. Once I began using writing to learn seriously, I learned much.

First, I now insist that all students get the same kind of notebook. Otherwise, there was nothing special about the writing we would be doing. Students might be ready to write, but even if I had paper available, their compositions went into back pockets or disorganized folders. Now, I require a special, uniform notebook. This requirement not only makes the writing important, but I use the notebooks more frequently in my lessons. Second, I make writing in the journals a daily event. The students come to expect this and are, therefore, much more willing to produce. Third, I collect the notebooks at least once every two weeks because this reinforces their importance and reminds me once again that some sort of evaluation is due. Fourth, and perhaps most important, I found I had to get "into" the activity. I needed to make the students believe that this was something worthwhile and an enjoyable way to learn. A teacher must be assertive to give this teaching tool a chance at succeeding.

So what does one do in a subject area that is not English? How does one use writing to learn as an effective source of teaching? I was very concerned until I started using the journals on a regular basis. I found that having the students write is rewarding not only for the teacher but for the students who learn in the process. The first class in which I tried writing to learn was Psychology of Self-esteem. I felt that writing about both feelings and opinions would enable students to rethink some of their attitudes.

Psychology of Self-esteem offers the students a chance to look at their values and to develop some long-range goals. This class works on organizational skills as well as introspective techniques. Writing-to-learn techniques have proved invaluable in achieving these aims. Students gain insight while putting their thoughts on paper. Many assignments are of the completion variety, and students are amazed by their own responses.

The following are examples of the completions I use at the beginning of class.

> I get most angry when . . . .
> As a passenger in a car I . . . .

My best teacher was . . . .

To be most happy I . . . .

When someone tries to get me to do something I don't want to do
I . . . .

Some sample responses follow.

I get most angry when people brag.

As a passenger in a car I guess I can be pretty obnoxious as I am
constantly nagging the driver.

My best teacher was in seventh grade because he made learning
enjoyable and cared about us as individuals.

To be most happy I wish I was always as healthy as I am now.

When someone gets me to do something I don't want to do I usually give in because I hate the hassle of arguing my point of view.

Responses like these brought out some major points of the day's lesson. We were dealing with attitude and emotions, but the emphasis
was on peer pressure. The last example lent itself to a heated discussion
on being one's own person. One student finally commented, "Look, if
you don't learn to stick up for yourself now, you are going to have a
rocky road in life to follow." I didn't even need to comment because the
students had reached a valid conclusion.

This form of writing to learn also improves class discussions. When
I try discussion without the student writing, only the more vocal students respond. Writing to learn helps all the students to participate and
become a part of the daily assignment. They all have something to say
because they can read their writing when I ask for comments on the
day's assignment. In fact, when I ask questions in any class, I have all
students write their responses. Now, students have something to respond with, and I have a much better sense of how well the class is following me. It is much easier to keep the class on target.

The beauty of writing-to-learn Psychology of Self-esteem is that the
students often reach their own conclusions. In one assignment I asked
students to write a **dialogue** between themselves and a "friend" who
wanted them to do something they were opposed to but were unsure
of how to respond to because of peer pressure. This developed from the
students' admission that their friends had the greatest influence on
their lives. I asked if this was good or bad and was told it could be
either. Hence we did the following assignment. Students were told to
write possible responses to awkward teenage situations of peer pressure. The first two dialogues between Mary and Betty were put on the
board.

*Mary:* Let's skip class and go out on the parking lot. I have some awesome dope and a new tape by the Scorpions.

*Betty:* I can't. I've skipped second period one too many times, and I really want to graduate. Contemporary Problems is required, and I'm afraid I may fail.

*Mary:* Get serious, one class missed is not going to get you an F. You need the relaxation and besides the Scorpions . . . .

One response follows.

*Betty:* I wish I could say "yes" to you.

*Mary:* Say "yes" then, or are you turning into a real "school" girl?

*Betty:* You are pressuring me, Mary!

*Mary:* No pressure, just fun, come on . . . .

*Betty:* No, I'm going to class, I do want to graduate. You can go, but I'm going to class.

Writing a dialogue such as the example above is not necessarily going to prevent students from skipping, but at least it gives them an opportunity to think about the situation and to work through possible solutions. Writing helps students see their own views more clearly. The prime goal of this assignment was to teach that we can gain much from friends, but we don't have to be robots and do everything friends want us to do. We can say "no" and still be friends. One student told me that after she had written her response she compared it to a problem she was having with a friend who always wanted her to try marijuana. She said she wrote down a possible dialogue about her own situation and felt stronger afterward about responding to her friend and not feeling guilty about turning her friend down. Here again, students are involved and participating. No lecture I could devise would hold their attention as well. With writing to learn the class time goes by quickly, and often students are disappointed that the class period is over. "But I'm not finished" or "You haven't read mine!" are common comments. I can't think of a better compliment for writing to learn.

Likewise, I found in both psychology and sociology that students were able to develop understanding of the material through writing. A fine example of this growth through writing occurred when I asked, on the second day of a beginning psychology course, the definition of psychology. Several students responded that it is the study of how the brain affects our actions; others replied that they thought it was the study of mentally ill people; and some were not interested. I decided that this would be a good start for writing in their **journals.** My major objectives in this lesson were for students to know what they would be studying in psychology and to motivate them. To stimulate the class, I decided on a **dramatic scenario.** I had a rather officious-looking student come into class with a bulletin that I proceeded to read to the class.

> The Edmonds School Board met last night at the administration center and passed the following rule effective immediately. All seniors, in order to graduate, must take a new course entitled "consumer and community living." In case you cannot fit this into your current schedule before graduation, this class will also be offered at night.

Needless to say, since all in the room were seniors, the uproar that followed was lively and animated. After allowing the class ample time to register shock, I told them I was just kidding. They were asked to write their reactions to the announcement in their journals. One student wrote:

> I was shocked. I have just enough credit to graduate and my heart doubled in speed. I felt sweaty and nervous and horrified that this added pressure was put upon me. I couldn't believe what I was hearing but I believed it and felt panicked like I'll never graduate on time.

I then asked the class what they thought psychology was and the same student whose writing appears above responded with, "I guess it must be the study of how humans react to life." The book definition was that psychology is the study of human behavior. No student left that class period without understanding the definition.

During the first week of psychology, I asked students to write a dialogue discussing with a friend their reasons for taking the course. I wanted students to give some thought to why they take classes and to raise their expectations and demands on my role as a teacher. While this example did not contain the best reasons I could wish, at least this student found it easier to contribute to discussion.

> *Friend:* Why are we taking a stupid and boring thing like psychology?
>
> *Me:* Psychology is interesting.
>
> *Friend:* Psychology is for crazy people.
>
> *Me:* I think the mind is fascinating. It's a fun class.
>
> *Friend:* So what good will it do?
>
> *Me:* I might go into a field of psychology and even if I don't, it will probably be helpful in whatever field I do go into.

When we discussed states of consciousness in class, I wanted the students to comment on and think about states of consciousness, specifically daydreaming. I asked the students what they think about when they daydream. Most said, "I don't know." I wanted an exercise that would get students to write about some of their areas of daydreaming. Students were asked to do nothing for five minutes. They were told to refrain from speaking, writing, or reading. After five minutes I wrote on the board the following topics:

family

friends

school (outside class)

sports

religion

classroom (ours)

music

adventure

drugs

fighting or war

politics

money

clothes

sex

Students wrote these topics down and then indicated the approximate amount of time they spent thinking on each topic during the five minutes. Discussion centered on whether males and females daydreamed differently, and students expressed amazement over the variety of thoughts in one classroom during a five-minute period of time. The class did **focused writing** in their journal the last ten minutes of the period on one of the two statements I had placed on the board.

Daydreaming is wish fulfillment.

Daydreaming is healthy mental functioning.

The next day in class students read their notebook entries on their chosen statements. The colorful and varied comments showed me that the students were actually thinking about the subject matter and not just memorizing material to be repeated at test time. The following student comments speak for themselves.

I think daydreaming is healthy because it helps me to relax and makes me forget about my problems.

Daydreaming gives me a chance to be what I want to be and I think that is definitely wish fulfillment.

I had a hard time choosing between the two because for me my daydreams are full of wishes but they also are healthy because I sure wouldn't want to do some of the things I think about.

I heard a speaker on right-brain, left-brain functioning and she said someday daydreaming will be used in the schools to help develop our right side of the brain.

As time went on, writing became an increasingly important learning tool in my psychology classes. Because I taught sociology in much the same manner, it was not difficult to transfer many of the same processes to that area.

Sociology is a natural for many of the writing techniques that involved introspection and forced choices on the part of the student. I wanted the students to understand Durkheim's theory regarding suicide. Basically, Durkheim divides suicide into three distinct groups: "egoistic," in which individuals are not strongly supported by membership in a cohesive social group; "altruistic," in which individuals are deeply committed to group norms and goals to the extent that their own lives become insignificant; and last, "anomic," appearing chiefly during times of crisis or rapid change. Durkheim's theory is especially useful in sociology because it demonstrates not only the scientific method but the extensive use of statistics and their interpretation. In this assignment, students were asked to send a short **unsent letter** that would show their understanding of Durkheim's three categories and of the individuals who commit suicide. I put the following assignment on the board: Write a letter to a friend or relative that shows you understand Durkheim's theory. In your letter take the role of someone who will be or is contemplating suicide. Label your letter according to the particular kind of suicide you are representing.

Here is one student example.

November 3, 1978
Dear Aunt Marie,
All is well in Jonestown. We are one! I have never felt such togetherness in all my life but then I know the true meaning of our existence. We have now been in Guyana for two years and have established ourselves in the way to the true light and I do now comprehend so much more. We have been practicing committing suicide by drinking Kool Aid that may or may not be laced with poison. We do it gladly because Reverend Jones had told us that the political systems of the world are out to take Christ away from us, but we are ready to defend and die for Jonestown. We are in oneness. I know now that my life does have a purpose and I glow with an inner strength. My leader will guide me. If I must die I know that it will be for the greatest of all goals, a oneness with eternity.
Love,
Phil

(altruistic)

Everyone in class was able to recognize the symptoms of altruistic suicide, and the various unsent letters brought out discussion which was spontaneous and insightful.

In Sociology, as well as other courses, I have tried to make the students increasingly aware of the importance of the journals. Many, if not most, of these students will be going on to college, and I tell them they all will soon be using notebooks for most of their college classes. Students in sociology keep both their class notes and material copied off the blackboard in their notebooks. I use **dictation** for definitions and other major items I want learned. Dictation, which I once lumped with methods teachers last used during World War I, has been neglected as a worthwhile teaching tool. When I compare dictation to simply giving the students a handout, I find they do better at retaining the material after dictation. With handouts, students often glance over the page and file the sheet in notebooks, folders, or back pockets.

The use of these writing strategies can be as varied as the topic. I introduced a sociology lesson by asking whether social change is progress, referring the class to people who advocate a return to earlier, simpler times. Students were told they were going to be transported back in time, but they could not know the place or the period of time. They were to list five things they would like to take with them and to explain why each item made their list. The lists were many and varied as can be seen by the following example.

1. A computer with a large supply of batteries because this would give me an added advantage in so many different situations regardless of when and where I went in history.

2. A Bible so I could have a copy of the greatest literature of all time.

3. A trunk full of "how to do it" books so I could learn to do all the things that may be unfamiliar to the age that I am sent to.

4. A large supply of aspirin so at least I could fight off prehistoric headaches.

5. A gun with plenty of ammunition to protect myself against any and all circumstances.

Most of the items selected were modern. Perhaps one student said it best when he stated, "I never really gave it much thought before, but there really are a lot of things that would be hard to give up, especially those medical advancements we take for granted." When we discussed this issue, the class really began to question progress. It was an active discussion displaying real thinking by the students about the subject.

Contemporary problems is a broad overview of the political, social, and economic world. Much of what is taught is a repeat of the past twelve years, but for many students this is their last chance to learn about the world in an academic setting. I have always wondered how to get students past memorizing for tests and forgetting. My basic goals in this course are for students not only to know about where the various countries of the world are, but to understand each continent and its unique problems. Since much of the course is designed around geography and current happenings in various parts of the world, I wondered how I could effectively incorporate writing strategies in aspects other than dictation and notetaking. However, I soon realized that much of what we teach in contemporary problems class deals with feelings and emotions.

It is not enough for students to be able to blandly explain apartheid policies in South Africa or the conflict in El Salvador. They need to be able to sense, to appreciate, and to gain greater insight in the complexities of world problems. How would they handle apartheid? When we covered Africa I saw a remarkable change of images that can take place during the course of the unit. I asked students on the first day of the unit on Africa to **brainstorm** at least five images that come to mind when they think of Africa. We then **listed** on the board the majority of their images.

savages

deserts

bare-breasted women

snakes

hot

mud huts

animals

lions

blacks

natives

elephants

cannibals

jungles

spears

primitive

steamy

pygmies

poor

I was really not surprised by their responses, but I was not pleased either. I had lived in Africa for two years, and I wanted students to know Africa as I knew it. I had always assumed that by the 1980s the stereotypical view of Africa as a primitive jungle had been greatly changed or modified. This exercise proved me wrong. I wanted students to see not only the vastness of the African continent but its diversity as well. After teaching the unit on Africa, I asked the students once again to write down words that come to mind when they think of Africa. I was pleasantly surprised by the new words that were now included on the second list. I can look at the two lists and see whether positive learning has taken place during the course of the African unit. Below is a second list of words which were included at the end of the unit.

bush
animals
cities
gold
deserts
Arabs
natives
poverty
diamonds
oil
mountains
diversity
apartheid
tribes
coups d'état
jungles
colonialism
Nigeria
camels
surfing
diseases
lack of medicine

Writing to learn is fairly easy to adapt to contemporary problems especially when I want students to develop greater insight into a subject.

I have used unsent letters by a colonialist defending colonialism and by
Africans condemning colonialists. The class is divided and each side
takes the opposite position. I have used clustering at the end of the African unit to focus on the major problems facing Africa today. This
serves as an excellent review. In the following example students were
asked to list in their notebooks two or three major problems facing Africa. From these lists we as a class **clustered** the major problems on the
board:

                    Shiite-Sunni split                          high illiteracy rates
                  Christianity (many different)

                                                            **education**
**religions**
                                                            girls low
            Animism                                         priority

                                        lack of
                                        hospitals        poor
                                                         supplies
                            exotic
                            diseases
                                            **medicine**
                                        lack of medicine
            **problems of Africa today**

    diverse geography
                    encroaching deserts                  military dictatorships

    **physical**
            land-locked countries

    drought                                 **governments**

                        arbitrary boundaries

                                                lack of experience
    **family**

    arbitrary boundaries            family ties
    cross tribal lands              broken by industrialization

                                                    coups d'etat
                                    East-West power struggles
                                apartheid


   This chart by no means covers all the problems faced by Africa, but
it does give the students a broad outline of the continent. It is easy to
see how this clustering exercise could be utilized in many other areas

of contemporary problems. I have used this method with each continent we cover. It would be just as easy to use this with particular concepts like apartheid, nationalism, or even the arms race.

What, then, can be said about using writing to learn in areas other than traditional English classes? These techniques offer a variety of tools that enable students to participate in the learning process rather than just memorizing content temporarily.

# Teaching Special Education History Using Writing-to-Learn Strategies

Ray Marik
Seattle School District, Washington

It is easy to believe that special education students have many problems with writing. Many teachers have seen samples similar to the following and have regarded this as evidence that these students cannot and are not willing to learn even rudimentary writing skills, much less the more sophisticated aspects of expository composition. For example, Bobby has five-minute, **focused writing** assignments, but stubbornly writes these entries instead of responding to the history lesson.

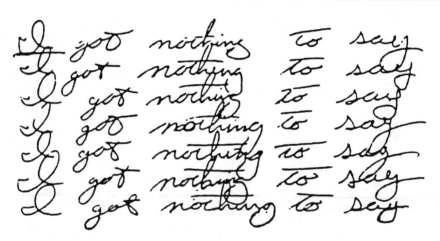

When occasionally he does have something else to say, it comes out like this:

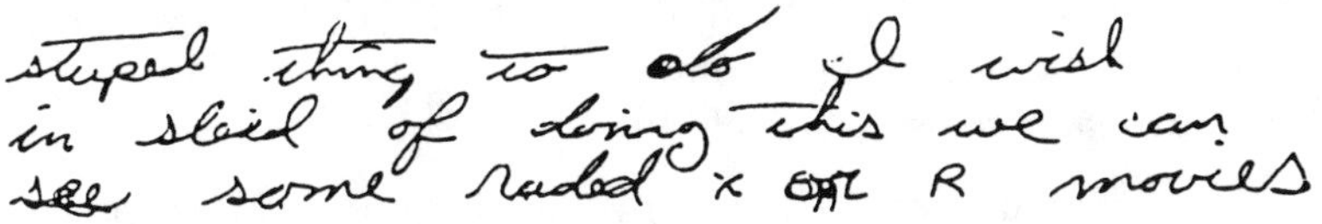
stuped thing to do I wish
in steed of doing this we can
see some raded X or R movies

> I wish we did not have to do this work, I think it is stuped thing to do I wish in steed of doing this we can see some raded X or R movies.

During this same time Paul writes about his main interest, sports.

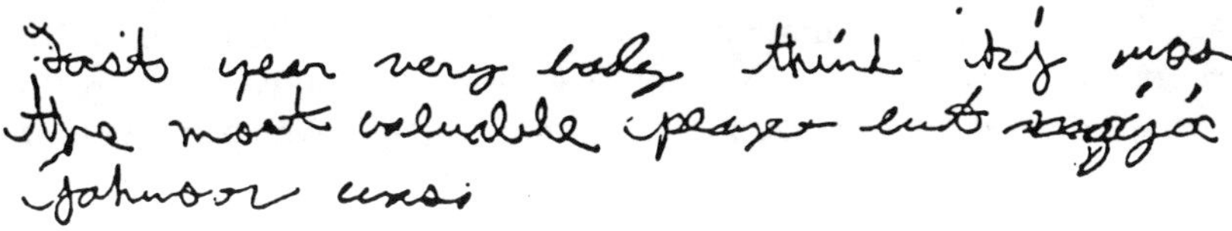

> Last year everybody think KJ was the most valuable player but majic johnson was.

From these and hundreds of other scraps of writing, I, too, concluded that special education students lacked the interest, academic background, and conceptual skills to benefit much from writing instruction. To some degree I still believe this, because the writing-to-learn approach described in this chapter will not work with all special education students. The more profoundly mentally handicapped and the severely disturbed benefit little from this approach.

There is, however, a "shadow" group in special education classes that goes almost unnoticed because of the enormous energy required to deal simultaneously with extremely disabled or disturbed students. This group represents a rough midpoint between the two extremes of disabled and disturbed which, when scheduled together for a period of instruction, can benefit from the writing-to-learn process. This chapter describes my work with such a group. In that group, the grade level averaged 4.5 and ranged in attitude from Bobby's initial antagonism at being required to say something to Scott's willingness to think and draw personal conclusions about selected events. These nine juniors in my U.S. history class still have substantial learning problems, but writing to learn helped them gain insights into history and themselves that would not have been possible in a "read the chapter," "answer the questions," or "do this ditto" routine.

I set four major goals for myself during this course:

1. To generate interest in history by having students make intense, personal connections with the material presented.
2. To teach some aspects of expository composition in the process of teaching about history.
3. To assist students to think on higher levels by giving writing-to-learn assignments.
4. To have the students produce a final essay as a complement to the writing-to-learn process.

Although my lessons are outwardly aimed at a final product or essay, I confess to a fascination with the excitement and mystery of the cognitive processes. These processes, more than any other, are the "guts" of what matters. As such, the final drafts, of which students are so proud, are anticlimactic in relation to processes they used to get there. For this reason, I do not feel a need to grade the essays, but I know I must grade nearly everything.

## The Journal

The U.S. history course starts in the fall with a **journal** or thinkbook writing assignment. Thinkbooks (a term used by Anne Wotring) consist of approximately fifteen pages of lined notebook paper, stapled together with a "fancy" cover.

The purpose is to provide a place where students can write five- to ten-minute personal reactions to a quotation, statement, or question from the teacher, from a reading assignment, or another student's comments.

Besides functioning as a method of keeping students "on task" (because they never can be certain when in the instructional hour a thinkbook activity may develop, or be assigned), it has a more important purpose. Primarily, I want to encourage students to make higher level connections among data, events, trends, and action. This is a sample assignment from the first day.

Write for five minutes on any of the following:

1. Tell how you feel about studying history. Write the first thoughts that come to mind.
2. List all the major events in U.S. history that you can remember.
3. Define what you believe is U.S. history. Begin: U.S. history is . . . .

4. Relate an important moment in history to your life.
5. Decide (evaluate) what might be the four most important events in U.S. history. Tell why.

The first word in each statement (tell, list, define, relate, decide) relates to a specific cognitive level in Bloom's *Taxonomy of Educational Objectives* (1956). Statements 1 and 2 relate to level 1, knowledge; statement 3 relates to level 2, comprehension; statement 4 relates to level 3, application; statement 5 relates to level 6, evaluation. Students are free to choose any statement to write about. Scott selected statement 3:

> United States history is the things that happened before we were a country, when we were in the wars, and all the stuff that happened afterward. It's the way people do things, how we got through crisis, and what happened after the crisis.

Students share these thinkbook entries by reading aloud what they have written, and when Scott finishes reading his entry, I ask the class for samples of "stuff" that happened in U.S. history. Their responses range from the 1980 Mount Saint Helens eruption to selected impressions from World War II seen on television. I ask many questions and try to move students into expressing higher-level connections. We may start with a lower-level written response but end up "seeing" higher-level applications.

Students became very much aware of cognitive levels when I drew a large triangle on a piece of cardboard and then printed Bloom's six cognitive levels on it.

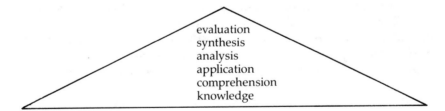

Whenever higher-level connections are written or discussed, I point to this card and ask what level of thinking is being expressed. At first this is a very slow process with many blank faces and little articulation. After a few months, those who are more academically able recognize, and strive to write comments on higher cognitive levels. When their entries touch, however minutely, on analysis, synthesis, or evaluation, I praise them for the quality of their thinking. For example, Scott later in the course wrote about the westward expansion from an Indian point of view:

> White men were coming in white covered wagons and everytime
> we investigate them, they'd shoot at us. I guess they basically ag-
> gressive. I wonder what's gonna happen to us in years to come.

He describes the clash between settler and Indian and evaluates (level
6) the settler as basically aggressive. (He then speculates on what impact this conflict will have on "us" in the future.) Discussion of his
comment involves questions of agression, both historical and personal.

> Can you think of any other examples where people other than set-
> tlers showed a fair degree of basic aggression?
>
> How would you feel if someone tried to drive you out of your
> home, neighborhood, or city?
>
> If you were an Indian, and saw the settler come into your home-
> land, would you view your reactions as aggressive, or defensive?

In answer to the first question, I want to stimulate recall of a major
war or armed conflict. Other questions evolve into considerations of
how defensive activities become labeled as aggressive reactions. Who
determines when this line has been crossed? How? Our discussions do
not always result in satisfactory answers. My intent, however, is not to
seek only "correct" answers, but to arrange a sequence of questions to
stimulate responses from mere recall to more abstract possibilities or
conditions.

This is an exciting and creative challenge because I never know exactly what students will write for their thinkbook entry and thus questions and possibilities evolve (or don't evolve) from the spontaneity of
the reactive moment. For students who are not able to make a significant observation at the time, success is possible because nearly all writing efforts can be praised by referring to the use of good descriptive
words, sensory details, powerful verbs, interesting or unusual observations. In this regard, Paul's focused writing evaluation of the most
valuable basketball player "majic johnson" presents an interesting
learner. This mildly mentally handicapped student that I took a chance
on and included in the writing-to-learn group, bears down and writes,
sorts out and evaluates data at the same time others in the class are
writing, and is trying to fulfill the assignment just as his classmates are.
Of course, he is not. We are writing about history, not basketball. In another sense, he is doing what everyone else is doing, except it is not on
the subject, but it is "on" the mental processes I wish to encourage and
develop. In sharing his writing, he gives evidence of interpreting facts
and drawing inferences in much the same way others are. And since
that is one of the expressed goals of the course, I must recognize and

praise the quality of his analysis. Ultimately, I place Paul in a history series more commensurate with his ability so he can pass the course. He is encouraged to continue to contribute to our discussions without doing the thinkbook entries. He lacks the mental flexibility to deal with all but a very narrow range of interests. Yet, if his P.E. teacher were using the writing-to-learn process instead of the traditional objective tests which Paul fails, his focused writing on sports, and excellent explanation of what he meant, could result in his not only passing the academic portion of that course, but excelling in it.

Consider another thinkbook use. When the class is asked to define "nationalism," John writes:

> I'm totally confused. I think that Nationalism is one heck of a word. I don't know too much about it but what you said I think it is one important word . . . some of the comments are all of the past like Goeage Washington in the boat going across and Paul Reavr . . . but America is one of the best I think, but I wonder if we all people could stop fighting.

John writes "Mixed up" in the margin at the end of his last sentence, but here is an expression of honesty with some deeper implications and insights. If he is confused, it is a safe bet that others who did not find much to write on about this topic are confused too. I now have an opportunity to clear up this confusion before going on. But there is more.

What came out of the discussion of John's statement was not his or the others' inability to define nationalism. It was that last sentence about fighting where he admitted he was "mixed up." The colonial revolutionary wars against the British are quite rightly portrayed as events of heroic importance. Yet, against the current background of highly publicized confrontations all over the world—Vietnam, Iran, Iraq, Afghanistan, Central America, Northern Ireland, and on and on—he finds it hard to view any armed conflict, however noble, in heroic terms. He has, at age seventeen, been burned out on the war issue, without having ever carried a gun, fired a shot, or spent one day in the military. I owe John much because his one small piece of honesty has helped me to understand something very significant about how some of our young people may react to the struggles and heroics of conventionally written history. Also, that acknowledgment increases my obligation to be more sensitive and aware of how young people view conflict in modern terms. All this from one thinkbook entry. Toby Fulwiler notes: "Journal writing works because every time students write, they individualize instruction. The act of silent writing, even for five minutes, generates ideas" (1980, 15). Yes, and some rather significant and unexpected insights too!

## The Multiple Question/Statement Approach

The multiple question/statement assignment previously listed usually contains from four to six statements placed on the front chalkboard (or overhead) and are used at an appropriate time in the instructional hour. Originally I reasoned that if I provided a hierarchical range of questions, those able to function on higher cognitive levels would be drawn to questions on levels four, five, and six. Interestingly, it was not the cognitive levels that always attracted them, but what seemed important at the moment. For example, Sarah, like Scott, took the same higher cognitive level question—writing about the westward expansion from an Indian viewpoint—and loudly concluded that the Indian-settler conflict was "Just like the blacks being pushed around by the whites." Students of both races expressed equally strong rebuttals. Were her comments an example of an inappropriate thinkbook activity? Not necessarily. Tristine Rainer, in describing basic diary or thinkbook entries, notes there are four natural modes of expression: catharsis, description, free-intuitive writing, and self-expression (1978, 72–114). Sarah's reaction thus becomes an appropriate catharsis/self-expression commentary of her perceptions on this historical event and demonstrates another opportunity for a unique insight into student thinking by using thinkbook journals. However, getting this system going at the beginning of the year, as Bobby's writing sample indicated, presented only one of many problems.

## Grading Thinkbook Entries

My initial inclination was not to grade these deceptively "simple" entries. However, after only the second thinkbook assignment, Mike said, "Hey Mr. Marik, what kinda grade we gonna get for this writing?" I had previously explained how many people such as Lewis and Clark, scientists, and prominent individuals throughout history had used journals for their own purposes and rewards. I also stressed how writing helps to clarify existing thoughts and generate new ideas, insights, and understandings of a topic. I marshaled all the arguments I could think of to convey my deep conviction about the worth of writing for its own sake, but in the end they nailed me to the wall with pointed statements to the effect that if they were not going to get a grade for this writing, then there was no reason to do it. I recognized the somewhat crass but eminently practical merit of the argument and reluctantly agreed to grade all entries so their writing time would not be "wasted." But how to grade every assignment?

I resolved not to get into the trap of assigning more writing and then losing energy and interest as the year wore on because of the paper load. The system I finally used permits students to get maximum credit for quality work, without increasing the paper load because these entries are not routinely collected. Here is how it works. I enter credit for work at the time of discussion by a zero (0), check (√) or plus (+) system. Students received zero for refusing to write anything, a check for writing an entry but refusing to share it, and a plus for writing an entry, reading it to the class (and discussing it, whenever questions arise). Later, when I'm pressed, the 0, √, or + can be converted to an *E*, *C*, or *A* grade. Very few students get many zeroes because most like to be asked their opinion. They write often, express their feelings and reactions, and get immediate comments and reinforcement at the instructional moment when it is most relevant.

In general, thinkbook entries take five to ten minutes to write, approximately the same time to share, and are used two or three times a week. They are used along with regular textbook work so that the interactive, perceptive nature of these entries are tightly bound in the student's mind to the expectations of the course. This bonding can be accomplished in half a semester. The thinkbook entry format is not used the second semester with these same students. By this time, the spontaneous response to reading and situations has become instead somewhat automatic, and we thus concentrate more on blending these unique impressions into stages of the composing process. The result is short pieces of writing or a longer expository essay.

## The Longer Essay

Unit one is a study of the structures that our first Americans built. I directed students' attention to a colorful page on which were displayed nine major sections of the country where Indian cultures developed distinct habitats. For example, the Eastern Woodland houses were made from wood, sticks, bark, and skins; the Northwest coast structures were primarily of cedar; the Southwest primarily of stone and mud. Students concentrated on these three concrete examples in preparation for their first essay assignment and started the prewriting stage by naming parts of the structure as I **listed** on the board the similarities and differences between parts of a modern house (their house), and what they can observe from the picture of Indian structures. Toward the end of the period, students made a copy of this list as part of their "research," because the board was to be erased. Here is a sample list.

| Modern House | Indian House |
|---|---|
| side | side |
| front | front |
| back | back |
| wall | wall |
| gutter | no gutter |
| air ducts | no |
| windows | no |
| locks | no |
| floor | floor |
| ceiling | ceiling |
| insulation | no |
| attic | no |
| basement | no |
| brick | stone |
| closet | no |
| bathroom | woods |
| wires | no |
| bathtub | no |
| plumbing | no |
| hot water | no |

The next day we focused on the two Eastern structures, noticing that one is a rectangular, wood and bark, Quonset-shaped hut, and the other is a circular, skin covered, igloo-shaped design. I brought in small pieces of tree bark, and as it was handled, weighed, inspected, and discussed, we **clustered** the relevant qualities opposite the word "bark" (see following). Once this visual, tactile, auditory, interactive process is experienced and learned, the class **brainstormed** the qualities of materials not brought in, such as sap, poles, skin, and materials common to the other two cultures (structures) we were studying.

| Naming word | Giving qualities to naming words | Giving actions to naming words |
|---|---|---|
| bark | covering, wood, chip, strip, light, brown, red, rough, from a tree, smell (stink), pine, thin, brittle, float, soft, waterproof, can be tied together | burning, grows, broken, bent, protect |

| skin | soft, furry, warm, brown, waterproof, tough, shrink, painted, stretched, sewed | make clothing, warmed, tied, sewed, cute |
| pole | wood, strong, thin, long, tied, straight | burn |
| sap | sticky, honey, thick, glue, syrup, brush on, smeared, smooth, shiny, pitch | dry |

We had now generated a wealth of detailed information on the three main Indian structures. However, care must be taken not to get the information mixed up in the process of transferring it into essay form. The data needs to be organized. To do this, students tree their information. Maimon notes that treeing helps students see different kinds of relationships and can be especially valuable for the visually orientated person (1981, 25). Treeing is thus more than a fancy or unusual way to outline because it taps the right-brain functions, from which associations can be more readily seen. Cynthia's sample shows her work in comparing the two eastern structures.

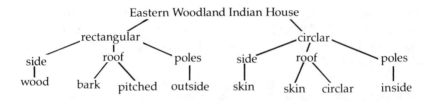

Once the treeing was finished, I modeled sentences orally using data from students' clusters and topic trees. After class discussion, students entered the drafting stage by writing their own sentences. Unfortunately, few students used many of the descriptive words we had collected. Most of the vocabulary was quite elementary. It did not seem very productive to expend energy generating words in the prewriting stage when students used only 20 or 30 percent of those words in the actual composition. However, John Freund notes in a *College English* article entitled "Entropy and Composition" that the brain may induce entropy or make energy (words) unavailable for use according to the second law of thermodynamics the same way that an internal combustion engine is only about 30 percent efficient. The prewriting or word-generating energy has to be necessarily wasteful in order to produce enough random word energy to move words onto paper where they are again selectively considered in the drafting and revising stage. Freund says:

> It should be clear at this point that communication and composition are no more exempt from the constraints of the second law of

thermodynamics than are countless other life processes. On the contrary, it would be unreasonable to assume that composition achieves the higher levels of organization it seeks without paying for them in some fashion. (1980, 499)

My alarm about special education students not using all their generated words or energy seems unfounded because their written efforts parallel processes essential and unavoidable in all writing. They are creating and producing as they should be, commensurate with nonspecial education students.

Revision in this assignment is limited to two main activities: (1) drafting introductions and conclusions and (2) checking paragraph accuracy and unity. The introductory paragraph is constructed using a "funnel" design which begins with a generalized statement and narrows down to one last sentence which is the essay's thesis. I help students draft this paragraph because they have not been taught this model. Further, at this point in the composition process we can proceed from prewriting to a drafting activity, using what has been discovered about the topic. The students are now in a better position to understand what it is we are to introduce, emphasize, and conclude. Revision for accuracy and unity means double checking the draft to determine that only the basic information clustered and treed in each category has been accurately entered in the correct paragraphs. Cynthia's essay demonstrates:

### Early Indian Dwellings

There are many types of Indian dwellings. The Eastern woodland was made of wood and skin. The wood dwelling was a rectangular shape. The skin was circular. The Northwest Coast was made of wood too and it is shape rectangular our houses today. The Southwest Pueblo was made of mud and staw. Its shape was square. They are all different in unusual ways. For example, Norrhwest Coast has nice totems with different shapes and colors. The of the most unusual are Eastern woodland, Northwest Coast, Northwest Pueblo.

The Eastern woodlands had rectangular house and circular. The rectangle used mostly wood. It has a door and two windows and bark is used for the roof and other things. The rectangular house is bigger then the circular house. The circular house has skin that is used and poles are used to help hold it up. There is a circular door and none windows. But it is painted with many shapes and colors. Sap is used to help the skin stick together.

The Northwest Coast have nice totem poles. The poles they got from cedar trees. They can be painted on with blue, green, brown eyes. Cedar is ued for other things like building a house. It is hard, it smells good it has rings on it to see how old it is. It lasts a longer time than other then other Indian more than anything else. The house of the Northwest Coast they usually have totem poles in front of the home. They have pitch roofs and use sap to help hold it together and the side together. They have circular doors.

The Southwest Indians home are very different than the Eastern and Northwest. To start with they use mud and stone, clay and starw, insaed of wood and skin. When it is windy and sunny they go inside because it cool. When the build they use laddlers and stairs to work there way up. Their house one square and tall. They have many window and doors with many rooms. After they get done with building, making sure they square and straight, they let it dry. After it drys, it is very strong and it last a long time. And when you look up it you can see that its many stories high.

Editing seems to thread its persistent way through all stages from the student's first thoughts to the final draft. This is true even for think-book entries. My reminders not to worry about spelling and punctuation early in the composing process are routinely ignored, a situation both frustrating and encouraging: frustrating because I believe the free flow of perceptions should continue unimpeded without starting and stopping midthought to spell "settlers" or "military," encouraging because of the students' desire to spell all words correctly. Interestingly, students new to my class (but old to our school system) never ask any questions about the relative quality of ideas, paragraph structure, topic sentences, introductory patterns, conclusions, or many other considerations relating to audience, tone, or style. Perhaps they saw their previous writing efforts floundering time and again in a morass of mechanical errors and thus perceived the absence of these errors as the sole measure of "good" writing.

Ultimately, I have to tell myself how much editing is enough. I do not want my students to feel their composing efforts will always end up hacked to pieces by this teacher. Hence, obvious mechanical imperfections are not relentlessly expunged. As long as the essays show evidence of learning, of reacting to, thinking about, and organizing data, they are acceptable.

To help students understand writing as a process or sequence of steps, I made a transparency (see figure 1) to convey the general ideas, but I explain that there is considerable overlapping and shifting back and forth between these categories. I display this transparency whenever necessary to help students see where we are in the composing process. We routinely start new assignments with prewriting activities which eventually touch all stages on the way to completion. "Eventually" is an important word because my students have a tendency to dash off a few sentences and turn it in as an "essay" without going through the process. I want my students to understand, as Randall Freisinger notes:

## Composing Developmental Process

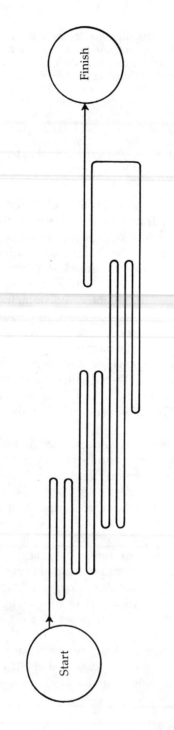

**Prewriting**
Free writing
Note taking
Scribbling
Dreaming
Talking
Listening
Research
Journals
Impressions

**Drafting**
Organizing
Introduction
Thesis
Paragraphs
Facts
Examples
Conclusion

**Revising**
Accuracy
Brevity
Clarity
Audience
Tone
Style
Sentence struct.
Paragraph struct.

**Editing**
Mechanics
Spelling
Punctuation
Grammar

**Publishing**
Send to
Teacher
Magazine
Journal
Newspaper
Customer

Figure 1. The Composing Developmental Process.

Almost all serious writing tasks, excepting mere copying, normally require a process, no matter how implicit and telescoped that process might be. For mature writers working on a single writing task, the process may be mostly unconscious and compressed. But if the writer's task is complex or if he or she lacks the confidence and fluency of a mature writer, the process becomes more explicit and protracted (1980, 161).

Essays similar to Cynthia's mark the conclusion of our first major unit. This effort takes about three weeks during the "September madness" of getting classes started. However, it is a productive time. Students learn some elements of expository writing and become accustomed to sharing thinkbook writings. Even students such as Bobby come around. He is still angry, noisy, and abusive, but as the trust level in the class rises, he is slowly coming to realize that we would really like to hear his comments and observations about the aspect of history we are studying.

## The Touchstone Concept

However, not all of our written work can take as much time as the First American unit if we are to deal with over two hundred years of U.S. history in one school year. I resolved this problem with the "touchstone" concept. This approach provides a sequence that allows time for students to interact with selected events without losing a sense of historical momentum.

Using writing to learn means making rather arbitrary decisions to skip sections of American history because the writing process is more time-consuming than a more conventional approach of moving through an entire text, page by page, in one year. The basic idea is to select key events relating to times of major historical importance.

Historians are compelled to be selective, partly because details on all aspects of life hundreds or thousands of years ago may not be available. They are also selective because not all events are factors in the thesis a historian is pursuing. As a result, most textbook versions of history are arranged to follow a chosen format, with contributing causes and events neatly bundled into sequential chapters. Further, as new evidence surfaces, analysis changes, and history is rewritten to clarify our elusive heritage. Thus, at best we read and teach selective history, and the touchstone concept is an extension of this selective gathering of events. The purpose is to enable the special education student to react to and identify with an event directly and personally. Students briefly pause here, touch an event, then proceed to the next touchstone on their way to a major topic or theme which can be explored in greater detail.

In order to maintain a sense of continuity between selected historical events, my curriculum contains major and minor historical events. The touchstone concept provides a more intensive look at certain events to permit the special education student time to absorb, write, and react to the material. The following are two examples of touchstone assignments.

*Narrative Writing*

> Write a story recalling the most memorable smells, sights, and sounds in the "Battle of the Wilderness" between the combined forces of the French and Indians, against the British. The PENTAD may be helpful. You may start *anywhere* on the PENTAD for your story. Refer to the picture on p. 48.
>
> 1. *SCENE*—What was it like that morning in the woods before the battle began? Describe a beautiful fall day in the early morning woods. What do you see, smell and hear? Be specific i.e. A squirrel (not animal) scampered across our path.
>
> 2. *ACTORS-AGENTS*—What do the French smell like? What do the Indians smell like? What did they eat for breakfast? What do you think the British smelled like?
>
> 3. *PURPOSE*—Why are you all in the woods this morning?
>
> 4. *MEANS*—(The way) What means have you chosen to solve the problem? What is the problem?
>
> 5. *ACTION*—How does the battle begin? What smells, sights, and sounds were noticed as the British forces approached? What noises did they make? What smells can you describe during the battle? What sounds did people make? What did they say?
>
> END—Anything else? Who won? What significance (So what?) Did you notice any ironies or contrasts in your story?
> Further suggestions for getting started.
> Brainstorm a list of impressions about the woods in the fall. Do the same with the pentad categories. You may wish to use this guide.

| Naming word | Giving qualities to naming words | Giving actions to naming words |
|---|---|---|
| *Trees* (Better) | | |
| *Leaves* (The more specific the better) | | |

This lesson is on the French and Indian war. The link with previous composition skills learned is near the end of the assignment. It is a reminder to utilize previously learned skills such as when we wrote descriptions of bark, skin, poles, and sap in unit one. Here a similar process leads to clustering and brainstorming descriptions from a picture in the textbook, and using categories like Kenneth Burke's pentad as the primary essay form. Craig's sample shows how it is done:

| | |
|---|---|
| Indians | mohawks, feathers, racoon hats, barefeet, canten, haff reed, metal arm bark, leather boots, gin, dark skin, maccians, blackhair, buffalo, head bands, pauches, knives, pistols, deerskin clothes |
| Scene | mss, rocks, grass, tree, shrubs, branches, ambush, leaves, smoke, haze from guns, Indians, British, French, covered wagons, horse, blood, red, people bleeding, Ohio Valley, time of year (fall), bark |
| Action | fighting-shooting guns, horse back riding, yelling, running, hiding behind tree, bushes, dieing, wounded, booming, falling people and cussing, horses sweating, smell gunpowder smoke |
| Purpose | French and Indian war started because the British wanted to be the power of the New World but the French and Indians were there also. The British wanted land, and the French had and the French didn't want to give it up. |
| Means | To solve this problem the British were going to fight the French and Indians for the Ohio Valley the problem to who is going to have power of the land. |

Note that the left-hand margins list the five pentad categories. Opposite each category he has clustered his descriptions. From these words he will arrange sentences in much the same manner as in unit one, work these into paragraphs, and then into essay form. His essay was one of the best in the class. The pentad permits students to start with any question and then develop any other categories they choose.

Craig begins with explaining why the war was started and its purpose.

> The French and Indian War started because the British wanted to be the main power of the New World, but the French and Indians were there also. The British wanted land the French had and they didn't want to give it up.
> To solve this problem the British were going to fight the French for the Ohio valley and a lot of other land.
> In 1754, it was a fall morning in the Ohio valley and he French were planning their attack on the British . . . .

Cynthia begins with setting or scene.

The morning was a little on the cold side. It was wet from the dew. The leaves were full of color like reds, yellow, browns. The trees were almost naked . . . . The smell was of trees and smoke from our campfire. The fire was crackly from the wet wood that was drying too fast.

The French and Indians smelled of sweat. They all needed a bath. The campfire was just hot enough to fix eggs and good old oatmeal . . . . A rider cam by and told them that the British were coming. Plates, cups, forks, spoons, went flying up in the air.

Then the French and the Indians surrounded the British. There were horses going around, there were guns shooting, there were stabbing of knives . . . .

Bobby has by now found much to say and begins with action.

The Indians and the French came down into the valley for fight the British in the year 1755. Then all hell broke loose when all of a sudden there was a lot of killing and suffering from both sides . . . . all guns were going off there was a lot of loud racket and smoke coming out from the end of growing from the people just before they died.

## Role-playing

In another example of a touchstone assignment the students **role-play** by assuming the identity of a reporter for the fictitious *Boston Times* newspaper during the Boston Massacre. Marie's graphic, descriptive involvement with the topic leads one to believe she will not easily forget this historical event.

Five Innocent People Get Killed!
It was March 24, 1770 the early evening about 6:15 p.m. When a special British Military force from Canada was sent to the Boston area. Soldier's and colonists soon were invole in quarrels. A force of soldier fired on crowded of people. There was five people killed out the crowded. Five people killed was badly wound. Some got shot in the head, neck and chest. One man got shot in the head. Five innocent people that killed among the crowd there was one who was a runaway slave Crispus Attucks, who had been in anti-British working along the water front. Sam Gray was shot on the left side of the head. Pat Carl was shot three time, once in the chest in the right leg and in the eye. It was two more people who killed. James Caldwell who owned A little store in Boston. When he heard the gun went off he ran out of the store with his gun started shooting shead and they shot him down and his best friend Gay Maverick.

What started this big quarrel was over the Sugar act 1764. . . .

Marie summarizes some of the less graphic frustrations of the colonists, such as the Townshend and other precedent acts. From this brief sample, it is not easy to appreciate the relatively enormous amount of energy she expended in research, creativity, organizing data, and the tremendous satisfaction she received when her classmates complimented her on the story. Her success is worthy of note if only because her initial thinkbook entry indicated an ambivalence toward this subject:

> I think history is important to learn and I think everybody should now something about history. I don't like history to much But I wont to now something about the united states of america.

One advantage of the touchstone concept is that the progression of events and causes leading up to major events may be more clearly understood by focusing intensively on specific representative happenings rather than trying to deal with the multiple causes and contradictions traditionally surrounding historical analysis and synthesis. Assignments in regular classes at this level are very complex and "overload" students with learning, cognitive, and conceptual disabilities. Thus, a curriculum that touches on smaller selected issues recognizes these students' learning difficulties and helps them understand some of the causes of the Revolutionary War.

## Conclusions

The main advantage of writing as a way of learning is the active participation it generates from all students, and the opportunity it provides for them to embrace assignments in intensely personal ways. It encourages a stretching of intellectual and conceptual thinking and insights on an emotional involvement in learning. Students cannot sit through entire semesters with minimal engagement in the academic processes as some have routinely done for years. Indeed, they do not want to, because the excitement of ideas expressed through their writing keeps them interested.

From my experience, there are a few cautions to consider when using the writing-to-learn approach with special education students. First, decide well in advance on limiting the kinds of writing assignments. There are so many different ways to come into a piece of writing that confusion can easily result. My students did not show an easy flexibility in adapting to new genres and techniques, and for this reason the frustration level was at times unusually high. Ian Pringle, in an article entitled "Why Teach Style: A Review Essay," notes: "One of the marked correlates of intellectual development in student writers is growth in ability to move up and down the ladder of abstractions, and particularly the ability to move further up and down it within one pa-per" (*College Composition and Communication*, 1983, 96). To increase the chances for success, repeat a few selected approaches many times rather than introduce many new ones throughout the course.

Second, repeat selected methods of putting a piece together. For ex-ample, I used the listing, clustering, and sentencing of the "First Amer-icans" expository writing activity in the French and Indian War narrative assignment, and again much later in the Civil War writing as-signment. Stick with one method until it becomes as well learned and automatic as possible.

L.N. Landa, in the book *Instructional Regulation and Control, Cybernet-ics, Algorithmization and Heuristics in Education,* states: "In order to reach some major instructional objectives more effectively and efficiently, it is advisable to teach cognitive operations and processes (algorithmetic or heuristic) purposefully and explicitly" (Englewood Cliffs, N.J.: Educa-tional Technology Publications, 1976, 134). He suggests processes be learned so well that they become part of an automatic system of re-sponse to be used whenever solving problems of a repetitive nature.

Finally, we ask the inevitable question: What has been learned by us-ing the writing-to-learn approach that could not have been learned with a more traditional presentation of history? Of course, students learned to write sentences, paragraphs, funnel introductions, theses, revisions, and conclusions, and they learned techniques of naming, listing, clustering, brainstorming, along with the pentad, role-playing and many other genres not described in this chapter. These techniques and forms, however, are not the truly important learning. They are just the framing that bordered the display of personal discoveries. The truly important learning came when students began to understand how the writing-to-learn process helped their thinking processes. They did not know how to generate first thoughts, how to lead these initial impres-sions to higher levels of abstraction, or how to work them into a piece that expressed what they really wanted to say and feel about a topic. Perhaps most important, this method opened a way for them to come into a subject and make it live through unique, personal reactions to flat pages of old facts and faded pictures.

In a larger sense, there is something strikingly appropriate about us-ing the writing-to-learn method in history. It has to do with the activity of gathering, interpreting, mulling over, and making personal sense out of those democratic processes we wish for our students as respon-sible adult citizens. The tangible evidences of this activity, their written descriptions, are not flawless. But these students discovered the es-sence of many historical moments and were left with deep impressions that are likely to remain long after detailed facts are forgotten. In the end, even Bobby became drawn into this process and could not go on maintaining, "I got nothing to say." He had found much to say. And, much to my relief, it was about history, not about his desire to see X-rated movies in my classroom.

# Writing to Learn Science

Patricia Johnston
Shorecrest High School, Shoreline, Washington

English and social studies teachers expect writing to play a major role in their classes. They regularly assign and evaluate essays and research papers. Most science teachers I know do not think of writing as an important part of their classes. To be sure, they assign lab reports and occasionally ask students to answer questions at the end of a chapter, but writing is not really important in their class work. Moving and caring for delicate and expensive equipment takes a great deal of time. Then there is the demanding problem of preparing for laboratory sessions and the subsequent clean-up, repair, and replacement of equipment. "With all these other concerns," they say, "who has time for writing?"

I used to share this view with my colleagues, but in recent years I have come to value writing in my classes, not just writing to show that a lab task has been accomplished, but writing to learn. What I have discovered is that writing helps my students understand science more fully than any other teaching strategy can. The learning fostered by written reports more than compensates for the time they require. Written reports that must be scientifically accurate, interpretive, creative, analytical, and evaluative demonstrate those highly prized goals of abstract thinking which all teachers hope to foster.

Arnold Arons and Robert Karplus, science professors who have studied levels of intellectual development, state:

> If it is indeed true that one-third of the school population is formal operational by the age about 14 while one-third is still concrete and that these proportions do not change substantially from then on in spite of schooling, then we face the implication that our educational system is not contributing significantly to intellectual development (abstract, logical thinking) (*American Journal of Physics* 1976, 44).

These researchers also state that helping students to make progress in becoming formally operational should be a major objective of education.

One of the first ways I use writing in my classes is to help students learn the vocabulary of the discipline. I do this by having students write poems which they call *biocrostics,* an adaptation of the **biopoem.** Some serve as unit summary; some are just a welcome break from lectures, labs, and tests.

Students are asked to produce a poem by using the letters in the name of one of the plants or animals we are studying. Biology students believe that the "bio" stems from biology and no one tells them differently. The only other rule for these poems is that each line must include some fact about the organism which is being immortalized and, if questioned, the student must provide supporting evidence for a given line. The following examples are from a life science class which students take as a last resort for fulfilling science graduation requirements.

Points are given for correctly using vocabulary words from the study unit. Each statement (line) must begin with the first letter of sequence in the spelled animal name. These exercises require conceptual understandings of the basic "lifestyle" of the animal as well as creativity within the constraints of the letters in the name. Notice that the life science class uses the common name.

Pedra Santos
Mollusks (CLAM)
C alcium PROTECTS the average BIVALVE
L ike a HATCHET a foot gives the movement they have
A ll people think the SIPHON'S the neck
M uscles close the shell quick to save them by heck!

Todd Bennett

Phylum Mollusca
SQUIDS
S hells are VESTICLE and we call them a "pen"
Q uick is the movement that caves them again
U nder their suckers is a toothed horny nail
I nk sacs protect them by making "smoke screen"
D eep sea kinds are LUMINOUSLY seen
S trong vicious jaws make them not like a snail.

The next examples are from a vertebrate zoology class for which biology and chemistry are prerequisites. The class requires much reading and writing as well as laboratory projects. Only binomial nomenclature is allowed in these biocrostics. The other rules are the same, but the complexity and application of higher cognitive levels are immediately apparent.

Shannon Joplin and Carolyn Gross
STRONGYLOCENTROTUS FRANCISCANUS
S ea
T ube feet

R  adiating spines
O  rganisms
N  ot human
G  onads good with French bread
Y  ummy
L  ow tide line
O  ceanic
C  rawling
E  ggs fertilized outside body
N  ot a land animal
T  able delicacy
R  ich in taste
O  mnivorous non est
T  hree jaws in pedicellariae
U  rchin
S  even inches across

F  rench bread good with gonads
R  ed or purple
A  ppendages
N  ot a dinosaur
C  oiled intestine
I  talians like to eat 'em
S  tarfish relation
C  ommensal and parasitic worms
A  ristotle's Lantern
N  ot caviar—but close
U  nplentiful
S  low locomotion

Because I feel that biological terms are as difficult for students to master as any foreign language, I use other forms of writing to help students learn them. Crossword puzzles provide a challenging way to test mastery of vocabulary. I have a computer which will generate a crossword puzzle when I type in definitions or "fill-in-the-blank" answers with a list of vocabulary words. Crossword puzzles only match words. After using a couple of examples of computer-generated puzzles, I ask students to generate their own (without computers). The crossword puzzles are a good warm-up for learning to write biology.

The next step is a one-period exercise which has proved stimulating for the students and enlightening to teachers. It has been dubbed: "Use as Many as You Can Correctly," and it begins with a list of words dealing in a relatively broad field recently studied. The amount of material covered is roughly equivalent to a chapter on which students would be tested.

Students are encouraged to be imaginative, which will reveal whether or not they are comfortable enough with the vocabulary to express themselves freely and intelligently. The exercises build a sense of awareness and mastery of the principles of biology as well as a knowledge of acceptable usage and mechanics. No matter how well a student grasps a scientific concept or how beautifully an experiment has succeeded, unless the student can explain that concept or experiment clearly to someone else, he or she does not, in fact, understand the concept or the research project very well. As E. Fred Carlisle says, "A young scientist must be able to represent and communicate well" ("Teaching Scientific Writing Humanistically: From Theory to Action." *English Journal* 67 [April 1978]: 35–39.).

Fifty to sixty words seem to fit a fifty- to fifty-five–minute period. I tell my students that they may write fact or fiction, but what they say must be biologically correct. A good score for the average student is correct use of about thirty words. The example shows imagination as well as an innovative approach to include more words.

Grading is based not only on correct usage of biological terminology, but also on cohesiveness and organization. This exercise could be used in almost any unit in secondary science.

Here is the list used by the student whose example is included:

arthropods

chiton

exoskeleton

jointed appendages

analogous

thorax

abdomen

head

compound eye

simple eye

fused

crustacean

antenna

legs

coelom

air tubes

pupa

chrysalis

metamorphosis

transformation

differentiation

nymph

molt

social colony

cephalothorax

carapace

telson

wings

internal segmentation

beeswax

green gland

barnacle

arachnids

mites

scabies

centipede

millipede

cheliceras

mandibles

nectar

adaptive radiation

gills

air tubes

tactile hairs

pollen

proboscis

caste

naiad

wing

Bellacia, Juan

### Arthropods

We went to the beach during spring vacation. My mom said that it looked like everything at the beach was some kind of clam, snail, or worm. I said that couldn't be right because I learned in biology that there were more ARTHROPODS in the world than anything else. I started looking around and sure enough there were little crabs running all around. They don't look much like the grasshopper or crayfish in our biology book because they walk sidewise and their ABDOMENS are tucked under. But they have EXOSKELETONS made of CHITON. Their HEADS and THORAXES are FUSED. They sure have JOINTED APPENDAGES and they can really move fast on their LEGS. I think that the crabs are CRUSTACEANS and breathe by GILLS (into CEPHALOTHORAX). At the dock they were selling big crabs for one dollar each alive! My mom didn't want to, so my dad cooked two! Then I knew what a CARAPACE was. Some people pulled it off while the crab was still alive. Ugh!! After the crabs were cooked I looked at the way they eat. They had big pinchers and I think pinchers should be on your list! They sure didn't have WINGS but those mosquitoes that came to our camp that night had WINGS and long PROBOSCIS. I think that what the crabs ate with were MANDIBLES!

The next morning my mom yelled because a spider had built a web across the flap of our tent. I told her that it was just an ARACHNID that ate bugs and that it might have at least six SIMPLE EYES. She didn't care.

When we went down to the beach to go swimming I cut my feet on all the BARNACLES. No one believed that barnacles were any relation to the crabs. So why take biology if nobody believes you? Huh! I suppose I could get more points if I talked about bees and NECTAR and POLLEN and BEESWAX but I really don't fool around with them. But I know they live in SOCIAL COLONIES.

I think I get 25.

Once students are comfortable with the vocabulary of what we are studying, I move them toward more extended writing tasks. One of these is a form of **role-playing.** My assignment follows:

Become an animal and write authentically about that animal's existence for a day, an hour or whatever length of his lifetime is appropriate depending on how much detail about your animal is available in our library. Do not anthropomorphize your entity. If you choose to be a reptile, use a *reptilian* brain. Some of you will choose mammals to be on the "safe side." Your grade depends on accuracy regarding the animal's habitat, diet, movement, (in other words, all the ways it satisfies necessary life processes). You will have one period in the library for research . . . An extinct animal is acceptable. Try to choose a creature about which you can find sufficient data.

We write a paper because we have a story to tell: an introduction, a narrative, and a conclusion. If the message that the paper is to present cannot be precisely or concisely defined, how can the paper be written? A review of brain evolution is appropriate as a reminder that the reptilian brain can have limited responses which relate only to survival, that all three brain layers may exist in a mammal, but that the surface area of a cerebral cortex determines thought processes. In this paper all levels of learning—facts, concepts, values—must be woven into the paper. Grading is based on focus, coherence, clarity, emphasis, and organization.

This role-playing prepares students for the written reports I require later in the term. For example, a vertebrate zoology class was given a semester project which included the articulation of a vertebrate skeleton (which each student obtained from a local veterinarian, the zoo, or a road kill). A report included with the completed skeleton required a detailed life history of the species as well as a comparison of the analogous and homologous parts with that of some other vertebrate class. A detailed bibliography was also required. I ask students to use the same form as that required by the English and social studies departments in our school district.

Occasionally these projects go awry. One meticulous student overtreated her cat skeleton in a sodium hydroxide solution and completely dissolved it. With no time to prepare another, she collected bones from several specimens, and produced an extremely unusual project. The articulation of the bones of these unrelated species provided impetus for her paper.

> HOMO DERANGEO: A New Theory in Human Development
> Many evolutionists believe that the stages of man's recent development include the Ancestral hominid, Australopithecine, HOMO ERECTUS, primitive HOMO SAPIENS, and finally, modern man; in short, human beings have descended from the ape. We, however, cannot accept this absurd, erroneous idea. Based on our own archaeological discoveries, we are proposing a new theory of evolution: man evolved from the HOMO SEPULAR CAROLIFIC GROMIFULUS RUTHENOSIS AMMONEOZOIC DERANGEO, a degenerate bird form. We believe the HOMO DERANGEO first appeared on October 9, 1732 B.C., and evolved to modern human form in less than twelve days. Additional evidence has shown that the HOMO SAPIENS' evolution was completed in the seventeenth hour of this twelfth day.
> We can begin to support our assumptions with this original skeleton of the HOMO DERANGEO, discovered on December 30, 1981. As we were making our annual ascent of Mount Bonaparte, Washington, we uncovered a small, indistinct animal skeleton encased in glacial ice. Being unable to arouse the 951 residents of Tonasket, a nearby town, we transported the fragile specimen to our laboratory in Seattle. After carefully melting the ice and revealing the skeleton, we discovered many interesting details. The decomposed, putrified remains of a small flag, of unknown nationality, were found tightly clutched in the specimen's right palm. Naturally, we must assume that this primitive creature, the HOMO DERANGEO, was engaging in an obviously human activity while climbing Mount Bonaparte's 7,280 feet: it was simply claiming this

territory for its own native homeland. Logical evidence such as this is only a minute portion of the overwhelming factors which point to the HOMO DERANGEO as man's predecessor.

The theory of man's descent from the ape is flawed by the inability to draw accurate family trees and several "missing links." There are many aspects of the HOMO DERANGEO's development which we believe connect this degenerate bird to human evolution. Modern men, like modern birds, inhabit nearly the entire earth; however, apes are limited to more specific living regions. Also, apes have a continuous brow ridge, the torus supraorbitalis, which both modern men and birds lack, as did the HOMO DERANGEO. These dissimilarities between man and ape, coupled with the likeness of man and bird, can only exemplify man's obvious descent from the HOMO DERANGEO.

Another evident factor which links man with the HOMO DERANGEO is the placement of the teeth. Human beings are distinguished not only by their basically identical molar patterns, but also by the shape of the shape of their canines. The beginnings of these canines can be observed in our HOMO DERANGEO as enlarged, flesh-tearing devices. After the fossilized teeth had been exposed, we found distinctive remains of tissue fragmentation; we believe that this represents a primitive gum disease, providing a clear link with man's modern periodontal disease.

The derivation of the HOMO SAPIEN's ear can also be detected in the HOMO DERANGEO. Rudimentary ear canals appear in our specimen as two horn-like protuberances emerging laterally from the top of the cranium. It is apparent to us that during the twelve day evolution period, these horns collapsed down the sides of the head, imbedding themselves in tender flesh to become the first human ears.

The inverted rib cage of our degenerate bird obviously provides an evolutionary link with modern man's ominous abdominous: the pot belly. Through the amazing development of the HOMO DERANGEO, the flabby tissue surrounding the abdominal cavity remained intact while the upper ribcage expanded. Another intriguing element of the human evolutionary process involves the transformation of the HOMO DERANGEO's wing. On the seventh day of the HOMO DERANGEO's evolution, the muscles collapsed, lowering the wings into another position. They became adapted to this new location, and served as primitive scapulae. This development of the bird wing into the pristine human scapulae, along with the customary abdominous, provides yet another convincing indication of man's evolution from the bird.

The progression of the HOMO DERANGEO was also marked by changes in its arms, legs, claws, tail length, and posture. The placement of these items on our HOMO DERANGEO show that our specimen must have expired within the first or second days of this evolution period. The size of the HOMO DERANGEO increased eightfold during the twelve day interval, therefore accounting for the disproportionate limb growth. As the evolution process

continued, the HOMO DERANGEO began to develop clawlike fingernails, and we have deduced that our specimen was unquestion-
ably of the female gender; indeed, fingernails of any great length
are truly distinct feminine characteristics. The tail, unlike the fingernails, was swiftly degenerating, and we have estimated that the
caudal vertebrae were completely detached by the sixth day of evolution. Finally, we can see the rapid development of upright body
position as a clear link with modern human posture.

Thus, we have introduced our new theory of human evolution,
and have supported our contentions with legitimate scientific data.
Now, we can only hope that our enlightening discovery will become the accepted theory of evolution, and that our intensive research and analyses will help convince future generations of their
true ancestor, the HOMO DERANGEO.

BIBLIOGRAPHY

Falwell, Jerry. *Homo Derangeo: Man or Myth?* Lynchburg, Virginia: Creationist
Express Publications, 1981.

Frye, Eustachia. "Evolution of Man: Ape or Bird?" *Scientific American* 245 (December 1981): 112–18.

Goosby, Dr. Zuretti. *A Scientific Approach to Inventing False Data.* San Infesto,
New Mexico: Al's Quickie Publishing Company—"Publishing while you
wait."

Joad, Horace. *Gimme Some Grits—I Ain't No Bird.* Paducah, Texas: Podunk University Press, 1980.

Leaky, Louis Z. *The New Guesswork Method of Preparing Fossilized Skeletons.* Tulsa,
Oklahoma: "No Questions Asked" Publishing Company, 1978.

Nimoy, Leonard. *In Search of Man's Evolutionary Origins: Development of the
Horned Ear.* Crow Agency, Montana: The "Copyright—What Copyright?"
Publishing Company, 1981.

Sagan, Carl. *Homo Derangeo: Billiyuns and Billiyuns of Years Ago.* Poughkeepsie,
New York: Birds-Eye Printing Corporation, 1981.

Snodgrass, Helga. *Tarzan—The Bird Man?* Humptulips, Washington: Stu's Slap-
and-Stick Print Company, 1981.

Stowe, Harriet Beecher. *Uncle Tom's Cabin.* Boston, Massachusetts: John P.
Hewett and Company, 1852.

Thudpucker, Lucretia. *Do It Yourself Carbon-14 Fossil Dating.* Piney Buttes, Montana: Piney Buttes Publications, 1981.

Although the student shows some lack of knowledge regarding binomial nomenclature and putrefaction, the paper could be considered
a success. Even the bibliography of this paper is creative. This student
would not have been able to turn her lab disaster into such a successful
comedy if she had not had plenty of experience with writing to learn.
Specifically, I think the role-playing we did in writing made it possible
for her to write a fine satire on the abstracts all students were required
to read for this assignment.

Students in natural science courses are not the only ones to profit from written techniques. Chemistry and physics students quickly learn what they understand and what they do not when they are asked to "explain" their laboratory findings.

Chemistry laboratory reports usually follow a standard format: title, purpose, procedure, data table, computations, and answers to questions or problems. The individual preparing the report has little opportunity to demonstrate conceptual understanding or abstract reasoning. A different approach can be used in most laboratory reports. Students may be asked to write an interpretation of the laboratory exercise and include the data table as an addendum. To eliminate verbosity and to expedite evaluation, the interpretation should be limited to one page. In traditional reports, there are few clues as to whether or not the students understand the real purpose of the lab. This student, however, goes beyond the recipe stage to draw conclusions, raise questions, and propose new theories.

John Okimoto
Int. Chemistry
11/1/83
Labtime!

### Stoichiometry Stuff

It's that time again, when chemicals react and balances balance, yes, it's lab time! In this most recent lab, we reacted Potassium Chromate and Lead (II) nitrate and got Potassium nitrate and lead (II) chromate. And here is that equation, in living black, white, and incidental blue:

$$K_2CrO_4 + Pb(NO_3)_2 \longrightarrow 2 KNO_3 + PbCrO_4$$

Each of the reagents was measured semi-carefully so that there was .005 moles of each, .97 g of $K_2CrO_4$ and 1.66 g of $Pb(NO_3)_2$. After reacting this stuff in water and separating the products, we were left with Lead Chromate ($PbCrO_4$) and Potassium nitrate ($KNO_3$). We had .0052 moles and .0084 moles each, respectively, and the mass difference between reagents and products was $-0.09g$ (2.63g before and 2.54g after). Apparently something got lost somewhere.

As for our results versus theoretical results, we came sort-of close. Since mole relationships are given by the coefficients in a chemical equation, we should have gotten .005 moles of $Pb(CrO_4)$ (1:1 ratio) and .010 moles of $KBNO_3$ (1:2 ratio). Checking the results on the data table shows we came pretty close on the $Pb(CrO_4)$, off by $+.0002$ moles, but we were off by $-.0016$ moles for the $KNO_3$. Since we had too much $PbCrO_4$ and too little $KNO_3$, I guess we didn't decant right.

Since moles are derived from mass, our mass measurements worked the same way. We should have ended up with 1.615g of $PbCrO_4$, but got 1.69g $-$ .075g too much. We also got .85g of $KNO_3$ instead of 1.01g, a difference of .16g. Oh, well.

Finally, we will address that all important question, "Why are some filtrates yellow and some not?" An informed source has told me that chromate is yellow, so it seems to follow that any substance containing chromate will be at least a little bit yellow. Or so it seems.

DATA TABLE
Mass of beaker A                                                       101.12g
Mass of $K_2CrO_4$                                                        .97g
.............................................................................
Mass of $PbCrO_4$                                                          ?
Lab analysis.

We added 20 ml of distilled water into 0.97g of yellow $K_2CrO_4$ = .005 mole. It turned out as a yellow solution. We also added 30 ml. of distilled water into 1.65g of $Pb(NO_3)_2$ = .005 mole. Then we added the clear $Pb(NO_3)_2$ solution to the $K_2CrO_4$ solution, a few milliliters at a time. At first white precipitate was formed, but then later the whole mixture was turned into yellow. The mixture was heated to the boiling point, then we let the precipitate settle. We decanted the liquid into the funnel again. When the filtering was complete, we removed the filter paper from the funnel and placed it in the beaker with the precipitate. We then let the beaker #1 and beaker #2 dry overnight in the oven. When both beakers were dry, we measured the masses carefully.

The precipitate that was formed was PbCr so the equation for the reaction is . . . .

$$K_2CrO_4 \text{ (aq)} + Pb(NO_3)_2 \text{ (aq)} \longrightarrow 2KNO_3 + PbCrO_4 \text{ (o)}$$

From our data, the determined mass of the product is 2.82g. There are two moles for $KNO_3$ and 1 mole for $PbCrO_4$. The calculated theoretical masses of reactants and products from our experimental results are 2.625g for reactants and 2.82g for products. Their difference might be caused by our mistake in measuring and in filtering. Some filtrates were yellow and others were not, because some people used a little too much of $K_2CrO_4$.

Questions for Problems:
1. $2HCl + Mg \longrightarrow H_2 + MgCl_2$
2. 25.41
3. 4.51

Not only do students demonstrate greater understanding of concepts in their interpretative lab reports, they show greater mastery of material as a result of their writing to learn. In the classes which have used writing to learn, students have higher test scores than students in other classes. Putting the material down on paper seems to improve retention. In addition to higher unit tests, I find that students do better on semester or year-end multiple choice tests when they have written to learn science. Students understand more and remember it longer because of writing.

Many college-bound students take advanced placement examinations. A score of three through five on these tests earns them college credit in the subject. The examinations given in biology and chemistry consist of a battery of multiple choice questions and a list of four or five subcategories from which two areas must be chosen as subjects for essays. The evaluation of these essays constitutes 50 percent of the total score. Since students have been writing to learn science, they have gained self-confidence in taking these AP tests, and their scores in the essay section have improved steadily since 1981, the first year we began the writing-to-learn program. An added bonus is the measurable improvement of scores in the multiple choice portion of the test. It appears that writing helps students with all types of learning.

# Writing in Math Class

Don Schmidt
Woodbrook Junior High, Tacoma, Washington

Writing is not a sure-fire way to help students understand or like math, but it does open lines of communication and helps to build a sense of community and trust so that students can take risks. It also gives students another way to look at math problems. Mathematics is, after all, communication, but communication in math involves a compact, unambiguous symbolism that to many students is cold and rigid. Writing, on the other hand, is a less structured way of expressing ideas. Since learning in math class depends on communication, I use writing mainly as a way of opening lines of communication.

## Admit Slips

The first method I introduce is the **admit slip**. Admit slips give each student a channel to write something and to get an immediate audience. There is no wait for each student to see how his or her writing is accepted. There is also modeling because the students get to hear what their classmates have written. Everyone gets quick, class-wide responses.

Because I work with junior high students, I feel that I must put some constraints on them. The constraints are

nothing nasty,

nothing personal,

the slips are to be anonymous, and

everyone must write something.

Nasty can mean the scatological words and phrases so dear to junior high students, or anything that I feel may hurt someone's feelings, mine included. Personal messages are rejected so as to encourage messages of universal import. Slips that violate these rules are not read aloud. Students write their own thoughts then fold the slips once. It takes two passes to pick up the slips. The first pass gets all but the most reticent started. The last couple are usually finished when I remind them that they're not writing the great American novel.

I then tell students to practice their listening skills. I shuffle the admit slips and have them cut before reading them to help to preserve anonymity.

Admit slips can give new students a chance to tell how they like it at this school.

> When I first came to Woodbrook, I didn't think I would make any friends. I had a whole bunch of friends at Lockburn who I like being with, but the people at Woodbrook seem to be a whole lot nicer.

Or the students tell me how they feel about admit slips.

> I have to admit that I really have nothing to admit. I have been a good girl. Very shocking . . . Last period was boring, and I hate having algebra last period because then I almost miss my bus.

Many of my students suffer from math anxiety. They have not been successful with math, and a page of numbers fills them with panic. Admit slips provide a comfortable arena to write about some of these fears.

> I am having problems in algebra. One of which is I don't know how to do it. Although I am trying I'm not getting anywhere. I'm worried about my report card for this quarter.

> Friday's algebra homework was hard.

> Page 227 was hard.

> Mr. Schmidt,
> Can you explain 227 to me today?
> Thanks.

> I wish I understood my algebra.

> Hi class,
> Friday's algebra homework was too difficult for the average dumb student.
> [Signed]
> Dumb student.

It is difficult to give an objective measure of the effect that admit slips can have on math anxiety, but if students can share anonymously their successes and failures in the math exercises, they'll be able to deal with them better themselves. Admit slips let the students know that they are not alone in their fears and that they can celebrate successes.

Some students use their admit slips to share their successes with the class.

> The test was pretty easy today. Thanks. Why are you so grouchy today? Hi.

> Hurrah!
> I GOT AN A ON THE TEST!

> Yah, I got a
> B-plus on the
>     test

>         HIP
>             HIP
>                 HURRAH!

> Algebra is getting a _____of a lot easier, and I'm so happy and proud. And it's all because of my fantastic algebra teacher. Maybe not fantastic but I gotta give him some credit.

> Life can be totally awesome! I have a pretty good grasp on algebra, because Mr. Schmidt is a very good teacher, even though he gets sarcastic, he's usually rather sharp!

> Mr. Schmidt,
> Pre-algebra is so easy. You should make it more difficult for some of us smart ones.

> I've gotten used to this class so it is not as bad as it used to be!

Problems that can be verbalized can be discussed; they become something that can be attacked and handled. Sometimes a problem that comes on an admit slip will prompt a student with a related problem to see me before or after school.

Students also use admit slips to express their feelings about issues outside math class: their concerns about growing up, their difficult days.

> Sometimes I wish I was little so I wouldn't have to worry about things like school, money, friends, and just plain old people.

> Responsibility is a heavy burden and even though I'm still very young I dread growing up.

> There is a guy in the class that I like, but he doesn't even notice me. But sometimes he acts like a nerd.

> There will always be a Monday. This morning I woke up 10 minutes before the bus is supposed to come. The jeans I wanted to wear were wet. My dog got loose and ran all over the neighborhood and got picked up by the M.P.'s. My cat knocked over the aquarium, and I accidentally threw away my geometry.

The first admit slips are often tentative standard junior high buzz phrases, but once the trust and sense of community builds they become more venturesome: mentioning math or computer successes. Often, they ask math questions or share puzzles:

> Two algebra jokes.
> 1. When does 2 + 1 = 2?
> 2. When does 12 + 1 = 1?
> answers: 1. 2 teaspoons of water and 1 teaspoon of sugar.
> 2. 12:00 + 1 hour is 1:00.
>
> If you have five lines but have to make six spaces how would you do it?
> answer: draw a star.

When computers were introduced in class and began to be used as problem-solving tools, students shared what computers mean in their lives:

> Computers are fun to work with. I wish we were still using them in class.
>
> I want to play the computers eat and sleep and hit my sister eat and sleep.
>
> How about that, we got are selfs a TRS-80 home computer, it is neat.
>
> I will be very happy when I get my Apple II computer with 2 Disk drives and an A.M. Desk Color T.V.
>
> You know what makes me mad is when you have a computer and you can't use it until you you mom sees you brought up your English grade and report cards don't get sent home until June 23rd.

When the class rings with "That's not fair!" as it did when I gave a cumulative algebra test to a prealgebra class, it is not easy to tell if the vocal ones are really expressing the feelings of the class. If I had listened to my accusers, I would have learned a different lesson than the one I learned when I asked students to write admit slips to tell me if they felt I was being unfair. Taking the time to write gives students a chance to reflect and maybe change their point of view.

In reading the paragraphs from the entire class, I could tell that many students did see the connection between the test problems in algebra and the things they had been trying to learn in prealgebra.

> The math test I thought was a good idea. It helped me to see what I had to review before going into algebra next year. I don't think I did too well on the second and third pages, but now I know what to expect in algebra. How I can review all of it before going to high school.
>
> The math test I took wasn't really hard. Some of the problems were sort of hard, but I still tried to work them out. It was a challenge. Most of the things in the test we've already learned from our prealgebra math book.

I thought the test was okay. It is only testing what you know. I knew how to do 50% of the problems. Others I guessed how to do, hoping to get them right. I hope to be able to get a good grade on this test so I can bring my grade up.

The first few problems of the test were easy. As I got further and further into the test it began to get harder. The test was fair. I wish every test was like that one. It was fair because if you didn't like your grade it wouldn't count but if you liked it you could keep it.

The algebra test was okay. If you think a student can do it let them. The first couple problems were okay. Like I said let them do it if they want to.

I thought that the test you were giving to us was going to be easy when I saw the first page, but when I got to number 22 the problems just started getting harder and harder. I did not understand how to figure out the rest of the test. So I had to make some educated guesses. I did not enjoy taking this test.

These admit slips gave students a chance to stop and consider what they had learned and how much there was for them to learn still. Because they use admit slips in so many ways, students begin to see math class as a place where feelings can be shared, and they can approach me for help without fear. Admit slips also make students more reflective about their own feelings.

## Unsent Letter

Towards the end of the year I build on students' ability to reflect on their own language by assigning an **unsent letter**. I ask them to write to an imaginary cousin who is coming to Woodbrook Junior High and who will be in my class. The letter should tell the incoming student what she or he needs to know to get along in my class.

These letters are from an eighth grade math class in which students average two years behind their grade level on a standardized math achievement test.

Dear Nanci,

I got your letter and will tell you what you need to know to be a good student in Mr. Schmidt's class. He likes it when you bring pencils, your book and whatever else you might need. Be sure to bring everything you need before the bell rings. (Also be in your seat when the bell rings.) Mr. Schmidt does like to pick on people but he does it only to make people pay attention and do good in his class. I am really glad to have him as a math teacher. He will explain assignments, but sometimes he doesn't like to repeat him-

self. I can understand that. Well there's a lot more to say but I gotta go.
See ya soon,
Gladys

Dear Al,
    I heard you are going to have Mr. Schmidt for math. He is sometimes nice and sometimes mean. He will yell at you if you do not bring your math book, pencil, and paper. If you are going to pass his class you have to do all the homework. You better listen when he talks to you. Sometimes when he is nice he lets you work on a computer.
    Love,
    Herman

The lesson that is repeated in almost every letter is that students need to bring books, paper, and pencil and that to learn in class, it is necessary to do the homework. That is a different attitude than they start the class with. It is a step toward accepting the responsibility for their own learning.

Admit slips have made the students realize that their feelings and concerns about school do have an audience and value. One unsent letter assignment gave them an opportunity to share their feelings about school with a student who has been taught at home by a computer teacher and who has no chance of peer contact.

The students wrote to a girl in a Ray Bradbury short story. Here is a short synopsis of the story: In the twenty-second century Margie is upset with her computer. She finds an ancient twentieth-century book, and she longs to be in a school with real kids and human teachers instead of at home alone with her computer teacher. These unsent letters give students an opportunity to analyze their feelings about school.

Margie,
    I think you would enjoy the twentieth century school system. The teachers are real human beings and know and understand feelings, and they sometimes get to be real nice friends.
    I personally enjoy school the way it is, and I don't think I could live with having a computer for a teacher. I wish you could experience a twentieth century school day, even it it is just one day.
    Friends forever,
    Jim

Margie,
    Hi! My name is Rorie Alfaro and I was wondering if I could be your new friend.
    I am in my math class called algebra. I have a man teacher and his name is Mr. Schmidt. I think you would like going to a school

because you get to meet a lot of people and when you're in a regular
school, if you don't understand a problem a teacher could probably
help you better than a computer.

We have six classes a day and then they are called periods. In the
morning when I wake up I eat, etc. When I come to school I go to
my locker and get my books. My books are for me to learn from, its
something like your teacher.

Got to go now. I'll write more after.

Friends,
Rorie

Margie,

Howdy! You asked me earlier, "What is my school like?" Well, I
think its kind of hard to explain my type of school.

Unlike yours, we go to different classes for different subjects (assuming you're in 7-12 grade.) The teachers are human, and they all
have different personalities.

It really is fun. You have time between classes to visit with your
friends and a certain amount of time to eat lunch.

In each class you hand in your homework, the teacher explains
the next lesson, he asks you some questions on that particular lesson or subject. And towards the end of the period, you're usually
assigned some homework.

It sounds as if your school is only 2 or 3 hours long. Well, you're
really lucky ours lasts about 6 hours.

I have to admit the school of the future sounds boring. I
wouldn't want to be taught in my own home and by a computer.

Well I gotta go. See you around.

Friends,
Shaunna

Dear Margie,

I am in the 20th century, the year 1983 and I am in school right
now not your school of course. I am in a public school in the Clover
Park School District. That means all the kids that live in a certain
area near here come to this school.

The schools here are probably funner than the ones there. Here
all the kids come and gather at school at 8:55 a.m. At school we
have different teachers to teach different things and it's great! I
know you have computers now we do too. Probably not as advanced and as good but we have them. I'm sitting at one right now
in my math class.

Well I have to go now it is time to go home for the day.

Signed,
Dan

Dear Margie,

School in this time is mostly like it is in your time, we have computers, homework, and teachers except our teachers are human
unlike yours which is a computer. But it's mostly the same. I would

trade yours at times if that were possible, because I think I would like being able to stay home and pick the times I wanted to go to school.
Your friend,
Dale

Teaching is not a good way to get rich. The rewards come from human contact. Once communication has been opened between my students and me by admit slips, I sometimes get unsolicited letters from students. Some are little notes attached to homework and some are lengthy explanations.

> Mr. Schmidt, I understand this pretty well, I just made careless mistakes.
>
> I will turn in p. 306–9 late on Monday.
>
> Mr. Schmidt—I think I understand better now.
>
> I figured out what I did wrong.
>
> Mr. Schmidt—This assignment was pretty easy. See ya.
>
> Mr. Schmidt—I only worked for 30 minutes on this because I had a lot of homework. I understand it a lot better now.
>
> Some answers I didn't reduce until I saw the answers in the back of the book.
>
> I know what I did wrong.
>
> Mr. Schmidt, I think I understand this pretty well, but I need more practice on it.
>
> Mr. Schmidt, I understand this okay, but I don't know how to change the equations to the right form.

I think the following three letters, even though very different in tone, are a result of the lines of communication that admit slips have opened up and that the unsent letters have strengthened. The students sometimes write me about the concerns they have and we can discuss them as a class if they are concerns that may affect everyone (like the letter from "anonymous"). An atmosphere where concerns can be discussed seems to mean there are fewer students who sit there not knowing what to do except stop trying when things aren't going smoothly.

> Mr. Schmidt,
> I spent a lot of time on this assignment. My mistakes were all on the 4th step. I didn't change or I had an equal number in the beginning. I understand this very well though.
>
> Mr. Schmidt,
> I'm a concerned student. I feel you are not doing your duty in explaining our tests and assignments. For instance, it is very hard to

take a computer test when you haven't even corrected your assignments before that. I feel that one of the reasons I got a lower grade on the test was because I was not informed of the correct answers on the assignments. After we got the test back, we never even went over it. Instead of keeping the wrong answers from the test in mind, I would like to learn something by knowing the right answers.

Another example is that you give us the assignments at the end of the period so that when we do a problem and need help, it's too late.

This is not to be a rude note, but I am honestly concerned with the welfare of my fellow students and I.

Sincerely,
Anonymous

To: Mr. Schmidt,

I am very proud of myself. I did what you said: If you don't understand something try and figure it out yourself. So that's what I did. I've been lost since p. 166 and haven't tried to figure it out so yesterday I did just that.

I figured out how to do pages 166–191 so I'm not lost anymore.

Here are all those assignment. I've finished all of them except 176. I didn't understand that page no matter how hard I tried. I would like to take the tests for these pages Thursday after school if you're not busy.

Now I am caught up and can do the next chapter.

Thank you for offering your help. But now I think I understand what I didn't earlier.

Sincerely,
Beth

P.S. From now on I will try harder and will also try to get my assignments in on time.

## Dialectic

Not only do students use writing to deal with their feelings about math, they also use writing to explain problems to themselves. When Beth says that she was able to figure things out for herself, she is referring to a process of writing about the math problems which stumped her. Like many students, she is not a good number cruncher and finds $2x + 7 = 9$ strange and frightening. It is easier for her to put such problems into words such as "seven more than twice a number is nine." I encourage students to use writing to explain math to themselves and remind them that they learned words before they learned numbers as children. This process of writing about math problems resembles the **dialectic** described in other chapters of this book, but instead of recorded notes on the left side, students put numbers on the left and then write their explanations on the right.

## Book Reports

Even when they write to express feelings and to learn math, some students still cannot succeed in my course. With another form of writing I offer my students an opportunity for success: I allow them to write book reports.

"Book reports in math?" "Read a book about math?" These are the usual responses writing book reports in a math class bring. When I took math, I never considered it a human discovery, but through my reading I've learned about the people who invented math: humans with foibles like the rest of us. Reading about these people and their inventions has heightened my interest in math, and it seems to do the same for my students.

I've gleaned all of these delightful esoteric facts from reading junior high math books:

> Rene Descartes who invented, along with Fermat, graphing on the Cartesian plane had to move secretly from place to place because he was so popular that was the only way he would escape the society that sprang up around him.

> Pascal gave up math to devote all his energy to worship God, but when he got relief from toothache pain while working on a math problem, he took that as a sign from God that working that problem was okay. When the pain left, his asceticism again stretched to math, and he again gave it up as others give up smoking for Lent.

> A googol, 1 followed by 100 zeroes, was invented by the son of a physicist to name his concept of a BIG number. A googolplex, 1 followed by a googol zeroes (ten to the googolpower) makes a bigger number.

> Decimal fractions were invented in 1585. While fractions were used in ancient Egypt.

> There are infinitely many counting numbers, an equal number of fractions or even numbers but somehow there are infinitely many more nonrepeating decimals (irrational numbers).

> Hypatia, an accomplished mathematician, philosopher, beautiful woman, and pagan was stripped naked, dragged through the streets and had her flesh stripped from her bones by those professing to be Christians.

There is also a delightful mathematical analysis of why an elephant can't jump as high as a flea.

Men and women invented calculus, zero, multiplying logarithms, even methods of determining "pi" to as many decimal places as you like.

Eratosthenes, again of Alexandria, measured the diameter of the earth quite accurately using trigonometric ratios before Christ's birth.

It's good for students to realize that mathematics is part of their human heritage.

The report must be on a book with Dewey decimal classification numbers 510, 793, or 001.64. It is further to be on a book the students enjoy reading. The specific directions follow.

1. Write it in ink at least one page long but no longer than two pages.
2. Give the title of the book, the author, and the number of pages.
3. Tell what the book is about.
4. Tell what you learned by reading the book.
5. Tell what you like about the book.
6. Tell what you didn't like about the book.

The book report format asks the students to exercise their judgment about the book, thereby telling them that their judgment is important. Rarely do they fail to find something that they like about a book, especially since the students have the responsibility of searching through the books to find one they'll enjoy reading.

Here are some examples of student reports.

> Ricky
> Period 4
> Mr. Schmidt
>     The name of my book is Computers:Machines with a memory, by Doris and Stephen Kinsler and it is 54 pages long. A computer has 5 main parts: the control unit, the arithmetic unit, memory devices, and input and output devices. The control unit interprets and carries out the instructions of the program, and it also controls the input and output devices. The arithmetic unit does arithmetic problems such as addition, subtraction, multiplication and division, also logical problems such as comparison of 2 letters, numbers, or symbols. All the information the computer will work with must be put in its memory, the storing place for information. What someone puts in the computer is input, and what the computer gives back is output. I learned what a computer is made of and how it works. I liked how clearly it explained everything in this book. You know as well as I do I don't like math, but I did think this book was interesting.

Not all students like math, yet Ricky did read a book and learned from it about computers. Ricky says he doesn't like math, but he found the book interesting and presenting a clear idea about how computers work. Students often look for someone to blame when they don't learn, but now Ricky knows that he can learn about math by reading and that the responsibility for what he learns lies with him as well as the teacher.

> Duane Linker
> Geometry
> Period 4
>
> The Age of Mathematics—Volume I
> (The Origins)
> Author—Michael Moffett
> 133 pages
>
> *The Origins* is the first book of a four book collection which covers the history of mathematics. This book explains how mathematics was developed in many different regions of the earth. After reading this book I realize how complicated the number system could be if we didn't have our system of counting. I used to think also that our system of numbers was the best anyone would ever think of but now it seems there are ways our system can be improved too.
>
> What I liked about this book is that it made me realize how important math was long ago and even now. If we didn't have math and a number system almost everything in our society would be impossible such as space travel, cars, computers, designing things, etc.

Duane is beginning to see how mathematics fits in with human history and to understand the role math plays in a liberal education. Duane has begun to see that mathematics has evolved and changed and that these changes have made a difference in his life in that it is easier to use math now because of the changes made long ago.

> Teresa Zimmers
> Geometry p. 4
> June 3, 1983
>
> THE HUMAN SIDE OF COMPUTERS
> by Daniel Cohen
> 82 pages
>
> *The Human Side of Computers* is an "attempt at a balanced view of computers, how they affect our lives, and our attitudes toward them." Since many people become very emotional about computers, because they fear their impact, this book tackles some of the questions the American society has about computers: do computers constitute a threat to our society? What steps can be taken to ease the threat? Is increasing computerization of society good? Is it inevitable? These problems bother most everybody, and they are discussed in this book.

The book also discussed reasons people resent computers, computers and crimes, polling and politics, computers at war, fun and games, privacy, artificial intelligence, and all humanizing computers. Those incidentally are the names of the chapters.

I liked this book because these questions are ones I have been wondering about. So much of our society is based on computers, from businesses to the CIA.

I would recommend this book to junior high students because it is written in our technical terms about the concerns of today's society.

Teresa is learning about the consequences of computers for society. She shows a more reflective view than the admit slip students who want to "play" on the computer in class or at home.

## Summary

I'm amazed sometimes how far written communication can go and how rewarding it can be. The following are examples of the kind of notes I have received on assignments.

To Mr. Schmidt,

I know I'm not a very good student as far as grades are concerned and I'm sorry. I will miss you a lot. You're one of the best teachers I know. I really enjoyed having you as a teacher.

Love,
Sue

P.S. Have a very happy life and I hope everything you do turns out for the best.

Mr. Schmidt,

No, I'm not mad at you, my parents are getting a divorce, and I don't feel good. Thank you for caring.

Buffy

Writing in math class is not a panacea. Students still fail—there hasn't been a test yet where every student got a perfect score. Much of the writing isn't even about math. Still, by learning and writing about related topics, by writing about problems which puzzle them, by writing about their fears and feelings, students begin to see math in more human terms. For me it is a way to get to know more about those varied and wonderful people who are my students. Thinking about how I use writing to learn in math classes I've become aware that what I do would work equally well in a shop, home economics, or English class.

I feel that writing gives students more of a chance to communicate feelings about a subject or to tell a teacher they need more feedback. The teacher–student connection is one of communication, and writing can help to make that communication two-way.

# Writing to Learn Philosophy

Jessie Yoshida
Inglemoor High School, Bothell, Washington

Both philosophy and writing to learn are process oriented and intended to help students connect images of self and the universe. As Randall Freisinger notes of writing to learn, "The goal of this method . . . is to allow the students to enlarge their image of the world . . . by connecting the existing picture to the new experiences. As they encounter new materials, they must either assimilate the materials into their new image or they must accommodate . . . And the key point is this: These connections must be personal" (*Language Connection* Urbana: National Council of Teachers of English, 1982).

Four goals were developed to help students "enlarge their image of the world" and connect meaningfully with philosophic issues. They are:

> to understand with Socrates that the "unexamined life is not worth living,"
>
> to "know thyself,"
>
> to confront the problems of existence as revealed in literature and in life, and
>
> to clarify personal values and develop a philosophy of life.

In this chapter, I will describe how writing-to-learn strategies helped students achieve these four goals. While there is a sequence to the strategies (writing interview questions follows **dialectics,** and **admit slips** with **metaphorical questions** follow **community building** metaphors and questions on poetry), these strategies are layered more than sequenced to help students think substantially and imaginatively about philosophical issues.

To begin this quest into the nature of wisdom (philo: love; sophia: wisdom), individual students list in five minutes their reasons for electing philosophy and the questions they hope to clarify during our twelve weeks together. Then then form groups of five to six, combine their lists on newsprint, and add any reasons or questions that the group interaction generates. Then one member of each group reads its list to the entire class, others note similarities and differences, and clarify meaning. Following are some of the goals and questions students listed.

Why are we in this class?

> to become wise
>
> to explore inner self
>
> to learn how to make our own decisions
>
> to compare philosophies
>
> to communicate with and understand other class members
>
> to learn to support our own beliefs
>
> to keep an open mind

What questions do we have?

> What use do religions serve?
>
> What will happen after death?
>
> What is happiness? Why do people continuously look for true happiness?
>
> Is there truth? What is it? How can we find it? Can there be more than one truth for different people?
>
> What is and how important is success?
>
> How can we make our lives fulfilling?
>
> What and who is God?
>
> How do people develop certain "trains" of thought?
>
> How can people believe in evolution?

As students performed this task, they called upon **brainstorming** and comparing and contrasting skills. In addition, they clarified goals which would later be written up in individual contracts. In these contracts students list questions they hope to answer, goals to accomplish, and course requirements to fulfill. A third function of this listing is that it is a community-building exercise.

A sense of community is essential for the success of a philosophy class. Revealing deeply held beliefs and values requires courage on the student's part, and sensitivity on the teacher's to plan activities that lead to trust and a sense of belonging. Students can take risks when they trust that others respect their positions and share their concerns and feelings. This initial listing exercise is a safe first step in getting acquainted and discovering mutual interests, first individually, then in small groups, and finally with the entire class.

Another activity that aids community building as well as "knowing thyself" is forced-choice response to **metaphorical questions.** Students gather at room center and step to one side or the other in response to questions such as "Are you more like a daisy or a rose?" "More like winter or summer?" "More like no trespassing or public fishing?" Again, students first share in pairs, then volunteer to share with the entire class. They enjoy the novelty of metaphorical questions, and this imaginative, indirect route to self-knowledge and revelation seems less threatening. They weigh and sort who they are, "re-cognize" themselves in new images, and distinguish the variety of characteristics others assign to a "rose" or "summer," none of them right or wrong. This paves the way to being open-minded and willing to explore and experiment, important for achieving the four class goals. Through these initial activities, students begin to dance to Neruda's truth:

> There is no insurmountable solitude. All paths lead to the same goal: to convey to others what we are. And we must pass through solitude and difficulty, isolation and silence in order to reach forth to that enchanted place where we can dance our clumsy dance and sing our sorrowful song. But in this dance and in this song there are fulfilled the most ancient rites of our conscience in the awareness of being human and believing in a common destiny. (Pablo Neruda, "Toward a Splendid City," Nobel Address).

This community building segment ends with the Neruda **dictation** which students write in their journals. However, building community is only the first step toward the difficult work that lies ahead.

Not snap reading for adults, Plato, Sartre, and Niebuhr present a genuine challenge for juniors and seniors. Students need to understand syntax, vocabulary, and concepts, and to connect meaningfully to works such as Hesse's *Siddhartha* and Dostoevski's "The Grand Inquisitor" (from *The Brothers Karamozov*). **Dialectics** offer one useful approach. Unlike traditional notetaking or answering study questions at the end of a chapter, dialectics ask the student to identify main points in a reading, and then to respond personally: what does the passage stir in his or her thinking, memory, imagination, associations, or feelings? Does the student agree or disagree? Is the student unclear about or confused by a passage? In addition, students are encouraged to keep an eye out for "jellybeans," lines from a reading that strike them as well turned, not only true but also beautifully phrased. They often incorporate these "jellybeans" in writing more formal papers. For example, on a series of poems on truth, students make two columns: on the left they summarize the author's ideas, and on the right, they comment.

| Poetic Truth | Comment |
|---|---|
| "Truth Is As Old As God" by Emily Dickinson | |
| Truth is God's twin. It will disappear the day God perishes. | I don't understand what is meant by the last three lines. |
| Truth and God are dependent on each other—one can't exist without the other. | Is she saying that truth is like her God? Why assume that truth would be gone if God didn't exist? |
| "The Wayfarer" by Stephen Crane | |
| The paths of truth can be deceiving—but more importantly, painful and difficult. | Without a willingness to sacrifice, the path of truth will not be chosen. |
| "Preludes" by T.S. Eliot | |
| First part of the poem shows a regimented life where everything goes as planned. Second part shows hope for individuality. Third part shows that it's futile and people are slaves to society. | This reminds me of a thing by Steve Martin where he conceded that things are terrible. Then he says maybe we can change them. Maybe . . . maybe. Na a a ah. |

As students comment, they begin to question, compare, interpret, and modify. They move from simple requests for clarification and information to higher-level analysis and evaluation. They begin to distinguish between the poet's ideas and their own ideas stimulated by the poem. In the writing-to-learn approach, as Freisinger noted, "the expressive function of language assumes a crucial role" (1982). Through expressive writing, students initiate a dialectic with the self as first audience, attempting to get ideas straight in their own minds before transacting with others. Dialectics develop the expressive mode of writing, legitimizing the uncertainty and tentativeness natural to the discovery process. This focus on formative writing in the expressive mode contrasts with more typical transactional assignments which focus on summative writing to the teacher as expert or examiner. Utilizing strategies that help students give words to vague images and shadowy ideas enables them to experience writing as a learning tool. All too often teachers have overlooked this important function of language by assigning writing as a test or show of fully formed ideas. Through exploratory dialectics with the self, the unknown becomes familiar. This kind of initial writing leads not only to more fruitful class discussions as students have ready responses, but also to more effective summative papers and essays.

A series of metaphorical questions further facilitates the journey into difficult territory. To the toughest poem, T.S. Eliot's "Preludes," one student answers:

1. What color is this poem?
   A glossy pumpkin orange with a grimy black film covering.
2. What kind of weather?
   The kind of day that as soon as you put your umbrella up, the sun breaks through the clouds and as soon as you take it down, it pours again.
3. What means of transportation?
   This poem would be a subway, crowded and dirty.
4. If T.S. Eliot were a guest on the Phil Donahue Show, how would Phil introduce him?
   Our next guest on the show today is an intelligent writer whose poetry has raised many questions about the future, and hopelessness of mankind.

Responding to metaphorical questions helps students grasp the tone and texture of a poem, and generate images that reflect their judgments and inferences.

After students read their metaphors aloud, they choose one they've written, and engage in a **dialogue** with Eliot to discover his truth more fully. In the following dialogue, a student elaborates on her transportation metaphor.

> *Me:* Mr. Eliot, your poem reminds me of a subway that is crowded, grimy, and always moving, with lots of graffitti on the walls. But on this subway there would be a small child that smiles and giggles in the chaos—only to be silenced by the authoritative smack of her mother.
>
> *TS:* That is ridiculous, why?
>
> *Me:* Your poem revealed the essence of everyday grit and grime, but in the fourth stanza, the words chosen reminded me of a child and a child's dreams (fancies, curled, images, cling, gentle). But it is ended on a very bitter, sarcastic note. Does this conclusion reflect a viewpoint that there is no concrete hope for mankind?

*TS:* I only suggest that the world becomes a vicious cycle—it is for you to decide whether this is positive or not. Judging from past history, I would say that man can't get out of his rut—his nature is basically evil. Especially since the industrial revolution, we have seen how quickly technology and success brings out the greedy selfishness in man. It's almost laughable.

*Me:* Why do you choose to laugh at these problems rather than doing something about them? Isn't laughing an acknowledgment that you can't deal with the problems?

*TS:* Laughing is also a way of preserving one's sanity. I wrote the poems to express my own ideas; perhaps they have opened some eyes and minds, but I doubt it. You can't fight society and human nature.

*Me:* I disagree. I think we can do something about our problems or at least help others find satisfaction with their own lives. I prefer to "cling to your notions of an infinitely gentle, suffering thing."

*TS:* Perhaps you will be "moved by fancies," but you will soon look back on these immature idealistic ideas with scorn. The more things change, the more they remain the same. History will repeat itself for eternity—if we make it that long (which I doubt).

By engaging in dialogue, this student enlarges her world by "becoming" the author, and seeing two viewpoints. She wrestles with her own picture of the universe as well as the author's. Unsure if she wanted to "grow up" and see what adults called reality, this student liked to "think positive," clinging to childhood assurances which risked wounding in jousts with Dostoevski's Grand Inquisitor, Stace's agnosticism, and Niebuhr's Christian existentialism. As she wrote eleven weeks later in her final paper, she considered dropping class at the time of this dialogue; class raised so many uncomfortable questions, and feelings. Instead, she chose to remain and expand her "image of the world." Writing to learn helps students connect the heart as well as the head to course material.

The dialogue technique is wonderfully fitting for a philosophy course, not only because of its Socratic history, but because it helps students understand an author's view in depth. I use it often, and with each assignment, give a clear purpose, a question to be explored and a possible opening line. I also hand out sample dialogues and share with the students parts of dialogues I write. In the following dialogue with Dostoevski's Grand Inquisitor, the aim was to understand the inquisitor's (GI's) beliefs about human nature, and his motivations for burning the heretics and ultimately setting Christ free. Christ had returned to the world, and while holding him prisoner, the GI carries on a monologue defending the church as the highest authority, and chastising Christ for granting people the freedom to choose.

> *PS:* You obviously are sincere in your wish to make everyone happy, but will losing freedom make them happy?
>
> *GI:* Of course it will! People will no longer have to face agonizing questions or choose between right and wrong.
>
> *PS:* But what about the freedom they have lost?
>
> *GI:* First of all, they didn't lose it; they gave it away, and second, the only thing they lost was the agony of their choices.
>
> *PS:* Let me ask you this then, would you make the trade: your freedom for your "agony of choice?"
>
> *GI:* No, not now, the people need someone to lead them. It is because I am strong enough that I keep my freedom. Mankind is weak and cannot handle freedom. I know this but I love people and will help them to be happy.
>
> *PS:* What about those who are strong enough?
>
> *GI:* They must be sacrificed for the good of the whole just as I have sacrificed my life for the good of the whole.
>
> *PS:* This is what you perceive to be true?
>
> *GI:* Yes, I searched and found the truth. It wasn't nice but it was and still is the truth.

Following this dialogue, the student concluded:

> The Grand Inquisitor was a man who had searched for and found what he thought was truth. He accepted it and lived by it even though it wasn't very pleasant for him. He was unselfish and gave his devotion to the job he felt had to be done. His love of mankind and the truth exceeded the value he placed on his own life. I think the GI was a very moral person in that he was true to what he believed.

While I could wish for a great deal more discussion and clarification, the student grasped the GI's view of humankind. Also, as the GI, he came up with firm statements about what the issues were, and why he behaved as he did. Without agreeing, the student came to appreciate another perspective and to see the humanity in an apparently "evil" person, much like the silent Christ who kissed the Grand Inquisitor and left the memory of that kiss glowing in the old man's heart. A dramatic technique, the dialogue engages students in what James Britton calls the "language of being and becoming," through which students clarify who and how they are in the world. It differs from language for informing and explaining in its concern with personal connections and values. In the preceding example, both analytical thinking and personal meaning-making are evident.

Later, students wrote **biopoems.** Then in small groups, they read their poems aloud, and selected one to read to the class. The following biopoem differed from most in the student's use of metaphorical language and imagery. Typically, students analyze character in literal terms; the poet in them remains silent. Paul's Grand Inquisitor, however, "radiates cold shafts of broken glass," and "fits all mankind with a collar and chain." Paul paints an unflinchingly cold portrait of the GI. So clearly does he see the GI, that he takes the thinking process a step higher and fuses it with imagination.

> Inquisitor,
> Cynical, bold, all knowing, and fearless.
> Friend of no one, peer of few.
> Lover of self, wisdom, and unconquerable knowledge.
> Who feels neither pity nor compassion nor the love of God.
> Who needs no man, save for himself.
> Who fears the kiss that warms his heart.
> And the coming tide which will not retreat.
> Who radiates cold shafts of broken glass
> And who fits all mankind with collar and chain.
> Who would like to see the deceivers burned
> And Christ to be humbled before him.
> Resident of ages past,
> The Grand Inquirer.

Paul has moved from the expressive mode where one gets ideas straight first with the self, into the poetic mode where connections are reflected in imaginative word play. Where the transactional mode is functional, aimed to inform or persuade, the poetic mode is imaginative, creating a poem, play, short story, or other art form. In the biopoem, language for its own sake, language toward artistic expression dominates. Also, unlike previous journal entries which were only read aloud in class, this biopoem was revised, edited, and submitted for a grade.

Consensus statements and **exit slips** are two additional strategies which help clarify key ideas in a literary piece. Consensus statements force a more thorough discussion of word meanings, reasons for agreement or disagreement, and consideration of alternative views. In the exercise, students first mark under the *self* column, A if they agree and D if they disagree with the statement. Then in groups of 4 or 5, they must "as a group" agree or disagree under the *group* column. They may not vote, but must use persuasion. Later, each group is polled for further discussion. The following example shows how one junior changed two opinions after group discussion.

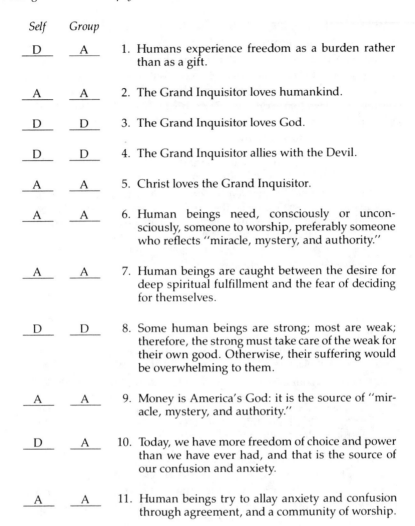

| Self | Group | |
|---|---|---|
| D | A | 1. Humans experience freedom as a burden rather than as a gift. |
| A | A | 2. The Grand Inquisitor loves humankind. |
| D | D | 3. The Grand Inquisitor loves God. |
| D | D | 4. The Grand Inquisitor allies with the Devil. |
| A | A | 5. Christ loves the Grand Inquisitor. |
| A | A | 6. Human beings need, consciously or unconsciously, someone to worship, preferably someone who reflects "miracle, mystery, and authority." |
| A | A | 7. Human beings are caught between the desire for deep spiritual fulfillment and the fear of deciding for themselves. |
| D | D | 8. Some human beings are strong; most are weak; therefore, the strong must take care of the weak for their own good. Otherwise, their suffering would be overwhelming to them. |
| A | A | 9. Money is America's God: it is the source of "miracle, mystery, and authority." |
| D | A | 10. Today, we have more freedom of choice and power than we have ever had, and that is the source of our confusion and anxiety. |
| A | A | 11. Human beings try to allay anxiety and confusion through agreement, and a community of worship. |

Students then write exit slips in the remaining five to ten minutes of class. The topic is anything relevant to the discussion: a personal connection, a dangling question, a summation. One junior identifies a conflict of values:

> I have thought a lot about money as America's God and the desire for spiritual fulfillment. I don't see how people can ever find fulfillment through money. Yet at my church, they always want to know how much money we are giving, for the new church.

Whereas the exit slip synthesizes the student's thoughts after a period's activity, the **admit slip** starts the day's activities. Usually anonymous, admit and exit slips are collected by the teacher and read aloud. What students write on the back of scratch half sheets clues the class to everyone's thoughts on the subject. The admit slip is a good warm up, helping the class focus on task. Two thirds through Hesse's *Siddhartha*, students were asked in an admit slip to describe a passage, idea, or event that was personally meaningful:

> The only way I can relate to Siddhartha is that I am confused too, as to what I want to do in the future. I am a little lost.

> In the book Siddhartha felt he was merely playing a game in life abiding by the rules, while the real life was slipping past him. Recently I came to that realization myself. Though I do still "play the game," I believe that I am getting more out of life than I used to. Hopefully someday soon, I will completely stop playing the game.

> I believe the event which hit close to home was when he went to the other village to pick up merchandise and they had none. Instead of looking at it like a loss, he gained something. He wasn't angry. I'm never patient and when I lose something it's lost and I lose my control. I fall to pieces. Instead, I realized something can be gained. It's already helping me.

> It seems significant to me that Siddhartha could get "lost" in the "garden of pleasures" but he eventually finds his way out.

> I thought about a relationship that I had, what I had thought was real but wasn't, about playing games, and losing parts of me, changing my values for another person. I don't want that to happen again, but I also think that you have to take a risk, and be in control. It's hard to find the point between risk and control.

Another time, a metaphorical question was combined with an admit slip, to help students focus on a difficult Niebuhr essay on Christian commitment: (1) What is a key idea that Niebuhr expresses? (2) What season of the year would represent his impact on your thinking?

> That the Bible is not true historically but is true spiritually. Niebuhr impacted me like the end of winter, and the beginning of spring. His ideas sounded dark and cold, but I also see warmth and brightness in his ideas.

> Reinhold Niebuhr's main point is that a Christian must have the faith to change his or her perceptions with time and discovery, because Christian doctrine can be interpreted in so many ways, like art. This had impact on me because it was a refreshing look at the Christian faith, almost a springlike approach to the old dead winter ideas.

> That you need to teach the truth by deception—in order to make the truth clear. What season? I would say fall because everything

seems to fall down around you when you see the truth. The leaves come off the trees, and everything seems to open up. There's a mess for a while, while the leaves are still falling, but once they stop falling and are cleaned up, you can live again.

The Bible's truth lies within deception. Winter—what appears useless is actually quite essential. What is barren on the outside today may contain the seeds of truth for tomorrow.

Thoroughly enjoying what students had written, I remarked, "Isn't it amazing what we can come up with when we're not even sure what we think?" A number grinned and nodded agreement. Each student had summarized a key Niebuhr idea slightly differently so that by the end of the reading, we had a rich collection of understandings. Beyond that, we had an appreciation for the personal responses Niebuhr's Christian existentialism had evoked. Students completed this activity with warm regard for their imaginative and intellectual skills, and heightened respect for the feelings each experienced while wrestling with new "images of the world."

Writing interview questions is another way for students to comprehend a philosopher's ideas. Each philosopher or literary character is interviewed about his beliefs and experiences. Over each section of reading, students write comments or questions to classmates who **role-play** Plato, Sartre, Siddhartha, or Ivan. The two or three role-players confer for ten minutes and begin the interview with a brief autobiography and position statement. Following are questions on three works: On Dostoevski's "The Grand Inquisitor"

> It said, "They have vanquished freedom and have done that to make man happy." How is that going to make man happy?
>
> You say freedom does not support man in a society. What does support society?
>
> What do you mean when you say, "We shall deceive them again, for we will not let thee come to us again. That deception will be our suffering for we shall be forced to lie"?
>
> Christ, why did you stay so silent when the Grand Inquisitor was talking?
>
> Why is Ivan writing this story if he is an atheist?

On Hesse's *Siddhartha*

> How does Siddhartha's searching relate to the "Allegory of the Den"? Could the wisdom of the "true light" be incommunicable to the prisoners according to Siddhartha's philosophy? Must the prisoners discover the truth for themselves?
>
> Why does wisdom sound foolish to ordinary people? You did not think Gotama's words were foolish.

On Stace's essay "Man Against Darkness"

> You say nature means nothing, has no use, no purpose. What do
> we do then if we are to disregard dreams, ideals? What do we do if
> we're not supposed to believe in these things? Are we then to give
> up our hopes? Do we then have nothing in our lives that means
> anything, and are to look for nothing to help us either?
>
> If you don't know if God exists, then why do you condemn
> religion?

Through their questions, students request information and clarification. They compare with concepts studied earlier, criticize logical fal-
lacies and infer meaning. Preparing for role-playing supports the
students' journey into unknown territory by legitimatizing uncertainty
and tentativeness. Zen teaches that while the questions are profound,
the answers are often shallow. Questions students write generate more
questions and connections so that while role-players' answers clarify, it
is the process of questioning and seeking that empowers. The process
of discovery in writing to learn parallels philosophy as discovery, life as
discovery. The educational, intellectual, and personal realms richly
reinforce each other.

Following the interview and before a major paper is due, I assign a
**focused write.** Students ignore spelling and mechanics and simply
write all the thoughts that come to mind for at least one page. The focused write proved to be a solid technique for developing student
fluency and appreciation for inner resources. From feeling they have little to say, students move to the truth that they'll write something
worthwhile. Also, instead of the minimum one page, many, caught up
in the momentum of their thinking, write past ten minutes. Perhaps
because they know this formative paper will help them make a summative statement and because they are freed from worrying about correctness, they give themselves more fully to the task. In her focused
write describing the process of enlightenment which Siddhartha experienced, one student wrote:

> Siddhartha had to go through a lot of experiences before he was
> enlightened. By enlightenment I mean he had a sense of unity in
> the world. He had inner harmony and harmony with the world. He
> lived for the present and had no need for material possessions. To
> reach this enlightenment, Siddhartha's first step was to break away
> from his father and the beliefs he had held as a child. He went out
> alone and tried out many different teachers. He deprived himself,
> learned the art of love, surrounded himself with material posses-
> sions. He had to go through all this before he realized he did not
> want that. He didn't want to follow others' beliefs or play a game
> instead of really living. He then went into a great depression, came

> close to suicide then thought, "Wait a minute! All this time I've been playing a dumb game, when what I really wanted was right under my nose!" He was able to see the unity of all things, good and bad. Yet it was like he had to go through all these other things before he could see past them to something more. He realized that people share desires and needs and this all makes up the world. After experiencing these desires, he could then understand why people do what they do and that life is a continuous cycle. I think that this is true wisdom.

At the end of ten minutes, this student was able to define wisdom. Engaged in "explaining the matter to herself," she discerned the pattern underlying Siddhartha's life experiences, generalizing this as a process common to all. She identified turning points in his life and drew her own conclusions.

Sometimes students exchange focused writing with two others. Besides continuing to build community, the exchange helps students discover alternative interpretations and strengthen appreciation for their own and classmates' skills and insights. Other times they underline their best, most effective, or "right on" sentence and read to us. Or they read aloud in groups of four to five and select their best to share with the class. This last option asks them to be critics as well, and to define the criteria by which the paper is chosen.

After all of these activities we arrive at the marriage of formative and summative writing. We shift from writing to learn to writing to inform in three summative assignments. One is the *Siddhartha* paper which discusses wisdom and the process of enlightenment. Students include where on this path they see themselves since personal and intellectual connections are important. A second summative activity discusses key ideas garnered from their supplementary reading. In selecting the supplementary book, students considered how it would meet their personal contract goals, since they are asked not to summarize, but to discuss ideas that shaped their understanding of self and the universe. For their final summative activity, students write their philosophy of life.

Summative writings are evaluated for content and form. This is unlike formative journal entries that are exploratory responses to content which students read aloud, or refer to in class discussions. Each student is expected to read aloud ten times during the twelve weeks, and is simply checked off in the grade book after each reading. In this way the sense of community is continually nurtured, I have constant feedback on the degree of student understanding and confusion, and the paperload is manageable. Any writing-to-learn strategy may remain purely at the formative level; however, many can be taken to the summative stage, by students revising and editing their initial drafts to meet particular requirements.

There are four parts to this philosophy final. First is a map drawn in oil pastels indicating personal turning points during the course, with a brief description of what was learned at each turn. Second is a set of metaphorical comparisons, third is a biopoem, and fourth is an essay on their philosophy. This sequence assists students to synthesize their ideas, and focus their essays. They appear not only to enjoy the process more, they also write more authentically and effectively. To that end, they are asked and assisted to be artists, poets, and imaginative essayists.

While the class had a map—four course goals—to follow, the journey was unique for each individual. As Mike describes the turning points on his map, he reveals how each new idea shaped his image of himself and the world, and how he accommodated. His needs, interests, and concerns gave a unique inflection to his learning.

1. "The unexamined life is not worth living"—the clarity of this statement more fully impacted me when I was offered the opportunity to view man as insecure, and for the most part in need of an illusion. Then I began to see that we choose.

2. "To know all is to forgive all"—at first glance I was not able to accept this idea. After some thought, however, I came to the conclusion that everyone has reasons for everything they do. I was in a way shocked by the power of this statement. Somehow I felt as though I, at this point, opened my eyes.

3. Siddhartha's first enlightenment—at this point I started to participate more in the ideas of enlightenment. This was largely true because I could equate myself with Siddhartha since I was experiencing similar feelings.

4. Siddhartha listened to the river, hearing himself—the idea of finding oneself helped me understand enlightenment. I also feel that American society has become too hung up on external stimuli to listen to what the body or mind needs. This may have to change for society to continue.

5. Indulgences are modern illusions—society is not looking out of itself. We all (almost) are engaging in indulgences that actually keep us from facing uncomfortable situations. Because of avoidance, we will not have the chance to grow.

6. Examination of Sartre and Stace—through these two I have become more aware of the need for questioning the old ways. Everything else changes; why not beliefs? Rebellion against society has been repressed, but now I have a better understanding of the need for rebellion and I have relocated my challenging mind before my accepting mind.

7. Attitude—recently I have been exposed to readings which express the importance of attitude. The idea of using positive attitude has been a key to my getting back together.

8. "The fall upward"—this idea unlike others explored in class is totally new to me, and I feel more reassured that man as a force may be able to grow up and mature into a rational civilization. There is still hope!

In part two of the final paper students answered a set of metaphorical questions about themselves which tied in to our second goal, "know thyself." Students were free to use any of the metaphorical questions asked in earlier exercises or to create their own. They asked class members how they were seen as a dance, color, means of transportation, body part, dessert; then they wrote how they saw themselves. Students "re-cognized" themselves in the following metaphors:

Ellen

If I were a means of transportation, I would be a bicycle, because I think that getting there is not only reaching a destination, but also how you get there, and because a bicycle is powered solely by man . . . self-reliant.

If I were a type of dance, I would be ballet, because it is traditional and somewhat reserved, but is very expressive to those who realize the depth and discipline ballet portrays.

Rhonda

A foggy day with the sun trying to show through. I have a hard time showing others my feelings and thoughts. Some think I try to hide my feelings and put on fronts. I really don't. I just don't know how to show my thoughts.

I'd say an elbow or knee because I am bendable in the way I can see others' sides or views, but you can only bend me so far.

Mike

Perrier. Not really a dessert, but I think it fits—you don't get it often, and when you do, you savor it. I don't see the self in me that is truly me very often. But when I do, I savor it. Perrier is also simple, basic, and natural—but with a touch of "class."

Alley cat. A loner—I know what I want—I don't need anything new—I can live off leftovers.

In their metaphorical comparisons, students described themselves in authentic and touching ways. By this point in the trimester, sharing one's "true self" was received as a welcome, rewarding activity. Their honest and imaginative self-reflection demonstrated how trust had grown so that students could sing their songs and dance their dances in a world made larger and more comprehensible.

Metaphorical comparisons led students to the biopoem, a much more direct statement of self. In these later biopoems, students exhibit more imaginative, metaphorical language than in their first characterization on the Grand Inquisitor.

Paul.
meticulous, headstrong, grey matter, naive.
Relative of the burdensome.
Lover of untouchables, intellect, biting satire.
Who feels the weight of the stone, spiteful, the wrench of cold reality,
Who needs love, something beyond the formula, the ever-elusive lady luck,
Who gives disillusionment, lies to veil the clockworks, and who plays the tragedy to par,
Who would like to see his day arrive, the future which awaits him, the silver lining before the cloud appears
Resident of the big blue marble,
Rowe

Jan
Energetic, serious, opinionated.
Friend of Jodi
lover of Tim, life, good friends
Who feels free, content, hopeful
Who needs to learn, to love, to experience
Who fears failure, loss of choice, not being loved
Who gives criticism like acid and support like a rock
Who would like to see less pettiness, more communication, more caring
Resident of the world I choose to see.
Smith

Mike
Curious, cloudy, sensitive, longing
Brother of two who need to care
Lover of hair, art, the Grateful Dead
Who feels frustrated, misunderstood, free
Who needs forests, music, love
Who fears leaders, obligations, dark houses
Who gives love in hopes of receiving love
Who would like to see the world and its people at peace
Resident of The Earth.
Dove.

Finally, students write the essay, presenting those beliefs and values they have clarified, changed, and confirmed in encounters with various philosophers. In discussing their philosophies, students illustrate how writing to learn expanded their world pictures. Excerpts are grouped according to the four course goals, though they overlap in many ways.

## On Examining Life

One of the key tasks of education is nurturing curiosity and a questioning attitude. These first two excerpts demonstrate growth toward analysis and reflection.

> One of the most important things that came clear to me this trimester was the fact that "the unexamined life" is the height of immorality. If a person doesn't analyze what he's doing and just goes along with everyone, then he is voluntarily giving up his freedom.

> By reading and discussing different philosophers and their significance, I have learned the importance of thinking and questioning. There is a lot of truth in the quote. "The unexamined life is not worth living." At the beginning of the course I did not fully realize the importance of that statement, but now I do.

## On Knowing Oneself

In the following, three students have taken to heart Socrates' enjoiner to "know thyself." The first writer describes the fear that accompanies encountering oneself and others and the fear, especially for adolescents, of "what will others think of me?" It is through entering a dialogue with self and others that students forge a clearer identity. By encouraging dialogue, writing-to-learn strategies nurture mastery and self-confidence.

> This is the part I liked most about this class. I learned a lot about myself. When I got into this class, I thought I was just going to learn about other philosophies, but I learned more about myself than anything else. I learned I don't have to agree with people just to make them happy. If I do all this agreeing, I'll never know what I feel, and other people will never know what I feel, but if I let people know how I really feel; they will like me for what I am, and hate me for what I am.

> My idea of happiness lies beneath the music of wisdom within myself. When I lose my love for wisdom, happiness seems like a million miles away. Wisdom, for me, creates a passion for knowing myself and how to live.

> When I started philosophy, I thought that all my religious questions would be answered, but it's not a matter of learning all the answers, it's a knowing where the answers are going to come from. Not from someone else, and not from knowledge of facts and figures, it comes from inside, from what you find through knowing yourself and experiencing life.

## On Confronting the Problems of Existence

Again, the first writer echoes the fear of revealing himself to others and struggling, not with not caring or not having enough to say but with

how to appropriately express intense feelings and beliefs. How could
he develop tolerance, if not appreciation, for different views, to respect
others? Through participating in dialogues, role-plays, and metaphorical questions that actively engaged him, he learned to put himself in
others' shoes. The other three students describe wrestling with issues
of purpose, commitment, and independence. They show how involvement with literary ideas and characters helped them resolve personal
issues.

> After the first two weeks of the class, I knew I was in for it, because
> I could see that I was going to have to deal with one of the things I
> fear most, which is revealing my true, most inner feelings to people
> I hardly know. So this class rapidly became my most feared class.
> Getting into groups with people I don't know gives me the feeling
> that I wish I could be beamed up or just fly away, until the group
> had broken up . . . .

> One thing I learned from this class was to respect other people's
> opinions. I used to want to come right out and attack people that
> didn't agree with me. And if I didn't attack them, I would always
> think about attacking them. Through this class I've learned to put
> myself in other people's shoes and try to see some positive aspects
> points to their opinion. Even if I still can't see some positive aspects
> or where they're coming from, by doing this I can at least carry on
> a somewhat calm conversation.

> One great understanding I now have concerns the meaning of my
> life. Confusion had overpowered my thoughts to the point where I
> asked myself, "What am I doing here? Would I be better off dead?"
> But after reading *Man's Search for Meaning* by Vicktor E. Frankl, I re-
> alize life's meaning changes from man to man, from day to day,
> from hour to hour. As the existentialist philosophers say, "You,
> yourself, make your own life."

> Though I approached this class with the attitude that I was simply
> taking it to fill a junior English elective, I quickly decided after the
> first day that I had two choices. I could drop the class, or commit
> myself to an open, honest reevaluation of my beliefs. Uncon-
> sciously, I had my first experience with philosophical commitment
> at this point. Though I had made a Christian commitment before,
> this was a new kind of commitment. It was a commitment to
> growth, and a willingness to change. It was a commitment to ac-
> cept ideas and really look at other beliefs. Whether I retain all of my
> Christian beliefs at this point is questionable, but my commitment
> to growth is one that I can make and uphold no matter what beliefs
> I might support. Spiritual death results from a closed mind and a
> closed heart.

> After making this commitment, the class became an experience
> with inner turmoil. As a result of examining poetry and "The
> Grand Inquisitor," I concluded that truth, beauty, and goodness

would serve as an adequate definition for God as I perceived Him. This certainly did not threaten my Christian beliefs, and it also integrated what we learned. But something was gnawing at me. I soon found out why after analyzing "The Allegory of the Den." I began to recognize my own resistance to new ideas. As a Christian that is what I had been taught to do, but I knew it wouldn't work for philosophy. I began to experience the pain of trying to let go of some old ideas.

When I first came into philosophy, I was in a state of confusion. I had just begun to question my values and to wonder about life. I was unhappy, yet hiding behind a mask of indifference. At the time I had discarded my friends that I associated with in junior high, not being able to accept their values any longer. I could no longer live thinking that clothes, who I was friends with, and my current date were the most important things in life. I didn't know what my values were, and I was unhappy. Joyfully, I now see a clearer picture of myself, others, and the world.

First of all, the readings of philosophers helped open my eyes. The main eye-opener was *Siddhartha*, by Herman Hesse . . . . Young Siddhartha was frustrated with the teachings of parents and other authority figures . . . . He did not want to live by someone else's version of truth; he wanted to discover it for himself. This is exactly how I feel . . . . Siddhartha taught me that naturally I want to break away from my parents, and go on with my own quest, and it is totally natural, and I do not need to feel guilty about doing it.

## On Clarifying One's Beliefs

On this last course goal, one student came to define himself as an existentialist while a second was able to define wisdom and to recognize the unceasing nature of the journey.

I am fundamentally an existentialist. Like Sartre, Stace, and Niebuhr, I believe that "existence precedes essence" and not vice versa. In other words, what I become I am solely responsible for. I must take the credit or the blame for what I make out of my life. Man must learn to accept the world as it is, looking at it neither through "rose colored glasses" nor the darkened glasses of negativism.

Epictetus is reputed to have said, "A life entangled with Fortune is like a torrent. It is turbulent and muddy; hard to pass and masterful of mood: noisy and of brief continuance." This class has helped me to understand how to deal with this torrent of life. Through reading and thinking about the existentialists, and after assuming the character of Stace in class discussion; I understand that I must be responsible to myself and to others. If I am to make sense out of the torrent, I cannot lapse into "quietism," but instead must try to change the world to what I want it to be.

My definition of wisdom, taken from *Siddhartha* and my own limited experience is: a state in which one has knowledge and conception of oneself and one's relationship to the universe. In *Siddhartha,* "this stone is a stone, it is also animal, God and Buddha . . . it has already long been everything and is everything." (*Siddhartha,* p. 117) Everything is itself and all other-things, and it is this realization that becomes and is wisdom.

I ask myself: who am I, what exactly do I believe (which has been clarified by this paper), and do I believe it because of myself, or my parents, or the society I live in? Do I really want enlightenment, and how much will I work or give up to get there? I have, indeed, not gone very far toward experience and wisdom, but I am learning and experiencing more every day.

In every case, students commented on the process of discovery they embarked on. They view life now as a process, with themselves as involved actors. They express greater confidence in their ability to grapple with the challenges life offers. They are less concerned with the product or destination and more absorbed in the myriad patterns of the journey itself. As one student concluded, "Life is a trip. Saddle up!"

Writing as a means for learning played a key role in facilitating this journey, helping students formulate a philosophy and shape an image of the universe and their relationship to it that had lain unformed and inarticulate until they began to write.

Teaching philosophy in this way is enormously pleasurable and satisfying. To see students grow in trust, self-understanding, critical thinking skills, and imaginative sensitivity is a joy. Since I believe strongly in the inquiry approach and the student as an active learner, the techniques I've described have greatly enriched my teaching repertoire and increased my effectiveness in the classroom.

# Writing to Learn History

Tom Watson
Shorecrest High School, Seattle, Washington

Effective thinking skills are an important part of the social studies curriculum. It is not enough for students to be able to see, hear, or read material; they must understand and interpret it. Under the influence of writing-to-learn techniques, students improve their ability to understand and interpret, thereby gaining greater mastery of the material in my courses.

I use the **journal** for most of the student writing during the semester. Journals, if used conscientiously, can help students to develop their thinking skills. By writing, students move toward more complete understanding of what the class is studying. Journals also help me to be a better teacher because if students are confused about something, scanning the journals usually makes it easy for me to locate their confusion.

I have students write **lists, clusters,** and **focused writing** in their journals so they and I can see how well they have absorbed material covered in class. I also use **dialogues** to help students develop an understanding of different points of view. Other techniques that help students take a new perspective are **biopoems** and **unsent letters.** Although this chapter concentrates on Washington State History, I have used the techniques discussed here in my other social studies classes as well.

## Introducing the Techniques

The ninth graders in my state history class are new to the high school and many are strangers to one another. Although a few are accomplished writers, most of them "know" they don't write well; at least so they've been told. All of them have to be eased into the idea that they are going to do a lot of daily writing in a history class.

My first goal for these students is that they loosen up their writing. It is hard for students to accept the notion that writing, like other skills, can be improved with practice and conditioning. I want them to write freely and openly, without concentrating on each thought, to realize that not all the writing in their journals needs to be good writing.

The first writing assignment I use is ten minutes of focused writing in their journals. Students are to select a favorite vacation spot in Washington and describe it. This gives them a topic they'll be familiar with and enjoy writing on. The key is to write for ten minutes without stopping.

After writing, students are asked to share what they've written. My purpose here is to have the students describe the natural geography of a part of the state they're familiar with. They will have to think of the specifics that make its geography appealing. These writing exercises will help them better understand the environment they live in. For the next day's assignment each student selects one place name from the state and researches its origin.

On the following day we discuss legends briefly just to make sure they all understand this genre. Then I give students a ten-minute journal assignment of creating a legend about the origin of the place name they've chosen. This gives them an opportunity to write imaginatively about the information they gathered the previous night, and it is also a stepping stone to the next assignment.

On the third day the ten-minute focused writing asks students to assume the role of one individual from their legend and write about it in the first person. This **role-playing** helps students think about a situation critically and makes the learning experiences more personal.

Up to this point, the students have had fun writing, the topics have not been threatening, and we've established several things in the class: journal writing, creative thinking, nonstop writing, and writing about history in the first person. All of these will make it easy to slip into more academic subject matter later. The important thing is that students have already started developing their skill for writing to learn, so the time is not "lost."

## A Natural History Unit

The first unit in my course presents the geography and geological history of the Pacific Northwest incorporating several types of writing activities. After viewing the film *Cascade Winter,* students list all the words or phrases that they can recall from the film. As the student example illustrates, this is an alternative to traditional note taking.

## Cascade Winter

fog    snowy days    white    Alpental    trees without leaves

silent snow fall

wet snow    icicles

sculptural ice    frozen waterfalls

thick underbrush covered with snow

Beakoning Summits

long ice ridges    summit ridges and slopes

wind    isolation

Mt. Rainier    cold that doesn't end

blowing snow    jagged ridges

rock    crusty snow    wind sculpture

black rock    contrast white snow    Sea of Mountains

snow covered trees    patterns in the snow

clouds    majestic    cloud cap    lazy ridges

isolated peakes    many peaks

rock & snow & ice    cold    clear and cold

clifts    knife edge ridges    quiet

beautiful sun on a new snow    ice crusted trees

Mt. Baker    covered & rounded with snow

trees in the open

sparkling snow    sun reflecting off snow

surrounded with snow

jagged peaks on skyline    Glacier Peak

Listing requires students to concentrate on what they've seen and forces them to work on recall. In addition, it provides them with a cache of ideas to draw on for later writing assignments. I ask several students to read their lists so that everyone can benefit from what others remembered from the film. Then I help them to organize their recollections by assigning them a clustering exercise. As the following student example illustrates, clustering helps students see relationships among the various items in their lists.

glaciers        wind

Mt. Rainier

cloud cap

isolated groups
in snow fields

snow
covered
                    jagged          sharp
ice                 peaks           ridges
encrusted

green        deep
            forested
                                    snow
trees                   mountains

**Cascades**        sea of peaks

7th heaven          deep valleys

new snow                                boulders

skiing          water           long hikes

moguls      Stevens Pass    rivers       streams

bums

cruising    teaching equipment      dams

chief                                   electricity

PUD

Seattle Light

The following day I assign a ten-minute focused writing on *Cascade Winter.* The ten-minute focused writing makes students write quickly. Like many entries from the class, Julie's entry catches the feeling and meaning of winter in the Cascades. Her use of metaphors adds to her understanding of the theme of the film.

Julie Potter
Cascades in Winter

The snowflakes fall gently through the air and trees then land silently on the snow that has fallen before. The trees are caked with white powder and they droop with its weight. All the trees that in the spring will turn green are now empty, barren of leaves.

Through this stark whiteness a stream flows, cutting its path through the fallen snow, dipping and turning in waterfalls and over rocks. Icicles hang everywhere, clear points ready to drop and pierce any living thing passing below. Looking closer you can imagine yourself in a magically haunting world where these wet stalagtites are fortresses that are ruled by powerful ice-lords. The sun reflected from the ice and snow gives everything a crystaline aspect. Now the snow has stopped, the whole world stands still except for the sound and movement of the running brook.

Something is moving farther up, among the high peaks of the mountains. The winter wind sweeps over the slopes, slowing moving the snow. The wind creates and destroys clouds and mists as it goes. The wind-swept mountains stand and take the beating majestically, as if they will stand forever.

This sequence of listing, clustering, and focused writing helps students move from scattered recollections to coherent thinking on what they are learning. If I choose to assign an essay about the film, students are well prepared to write it, but in any event, they have used writing to learn about the Cascades.

Following the general introduction to a study of the geography and geology of the Pacific Northwest, I use the film *Volcanic Landscapes* as the springboard for a look at the role volcanic activity has played in creating the environment of the Pacific Northwest. Before I show the film, I tell students to select one item from the film to write about in the first person.

That item can be a form of volcanic rock, a volcanic land form, or a kind of volcano. The film is in two parts, and I use only one part a day. After seeing each segment, the students list thoughts as they had done earlier. Next, they individually choose one item and cluster it. They use the remaining five to eight minutes to write in their journals on the topic they had selected. These writing exercises helped the students assimilate and organize a lot of new information.

After viewing the film, listing, clustering, and completing journal writing, the students had a day in the library to do additional reading on the topic they had chosen. They were to write about their chosen item in the first person, describing how a specific volcano landform was created, what it looks like, its texture, and so on. This became the first of what students dubbed "I am . . ." papers. They joked about it at first but ended up having fun writing them. Almost anyone could go to the library and select information on a topic, organize it into a standard essay to be turned in and graded, without really understanding the topic. Students who write "I am . . ." papers, however, seem to understand their material.

Writing from the first person personalizes the assignment. It requires students to understand what they are writing about so that they can be creative with it. This level of student involvement has sold me on writing to learn. Students were excited about turning in what they had created.

I remember trying to talk one young student, Crystal McCormick, out of selecting the topic she had chosen: lava stalactites formed in lava tubes. I anticipated she would have difficulty finding enough information to complete the assigned one to two pages. When she turned in the following piece, it was evident she had caught the essence of the assignment completely.

> I am lava all around,
>> Gases emerging and burning into steam,
>>> Taking everything that stands before me
>>>> I move sluggishly across the land.
> Slowly,
>> My outer layer cools,
>>> But my inside still turns
>>>> Forming a tunnel.
> I feel movement beneath,
>> Rushing air,
>>> The still liquid part
>>>> Tries to fill the tunnel
>>>>> cooling as it descends.
> Forming
>> A column of basalt
>>> dangling from the roof of the cavern.
> I am
>> A pillar formed from fire,
>>> now frozen as ice.
> I am
>> A stalactite.
> I am.

My goal was to make sure each student's writing demonstrated understanding of one volcanic landform in depth. Although she chose to use a different format than essay, Crystal creates with very few words the correct image of a lava tube forming, the hot gases melting its insides, causing remelted lava to drip down forming stalactites. Her words are well chosen, especially when she compares them to icicles, pillars formed from fire now frozen.

Another example is written by Jessica Chinn, who assumes the role of obsidian. She is accurate in describing it and very creative in putting the material together. Both of these students had time to learn and understand the material in order to be creative with it. Writing caused them to make a personal connection with the learning. I believe that will make the learning and thinking they went through more meaningful.

> My friends and I are anxiously waiting for the time when we shall have the chance to see a brief glimpse of the outside world. For

days I have been waiting ever so patiently underground, my inside boiling and raging with anticipation as I hear my friends and relatives asking the much repeated question, "Is it time? Is it not yet time . . . ?"

I can not believe it. Today is THE day! Somewhere deep within me I can feel it . . . for suddenly I feel myself being pushed upward. Higher and faster are we going; melting and completely destroying every obstruction that blocks our path.

For some unknown reason I am feeling a great pride for being part of this particular lava flow. Just think, I am destroying at least 50 square miles and enjoying myself at the same time; very unusual for lava like me . . .

. . . but wait! What is the matter with me? Why do I feel this terrible hardness slowly creeping through my body . . . ?

. . . "Hold on!" I shout, "Please wait for me. Don't leave without me!" Alas, there is nothing my friends can do, they have no choice but to keep on moving forward, occasionally turning around to cast me one last sorrowful glance . . .

I am just now celebrating my ten thousandth birthday. And during those 10,000 years I have gone under considerable change.

Instead of merely being a lava flow. I am now a shiny, black piece of obsidian fashioned into a jagged arrowhead made by some desperate Indian hundreds of years ago. I lie in the dirt now, waiting for fate to do its job . . .

At the end of the semester students seemed to remember far more about Washington state geology than they had in previous years. I think this is because they had spent more time thinking about the material and using it on a higher level of thinking rather than just memorizing for tests.

From geology we go to a unit on geography and a study of the internal regions of the Pacific Northwest. **Guided imagery** is one of the best tools for this unit. It was a way of asking students to think about and describe what had been studied in class. We start with the Coastal Region, and I show the film *Hoh Rain Forest* without sound and then ask students to list and cluster information about the forest. Next they write about a hike through the Hoh Rain Forest. This exercise takes the better part of an entire period. Using guided imagery I gave them situations, and they filled in the details using what they had learned of the region. My guided imagery is in the first person, and it begins as they get up early the morning of the hike to catch the first ferry from Edmonds and drive around the peninsula to the trail head. After they have been hiking (in their minds) for about an hour, I recite aloud to help them with their writing.

Describe what you are thinking about, what the river looks like, what the trail is like, and make other general observations about what you see.

The sun has come out, yet it is still cool . . . Why?

Something brushes your face. . . . What is it?

Time for a rest stop. You look around and find an ideal spot. Describe it. Then you begin to speculate how it got there and why it was there.

Hiking along later, you observe some animals off in a clearing. Describe them.

Later, along the trail, you crouch low to look at something. What is it?

Midafternoon, you set up camp. What are you going to do with the rest of the day?

After dinner, as the sun is setting you listen quietly to the sounds of the rain forest. Describe them.

Describe the weather the next morning.

Here is one student's response to the guided imagery:

### A Hike through the Rain Forest

We're starting on the bark-covered trail into the wild wonder of the Rain Forest. There's moss growing over the trail so you can barely tell there's bark underneath it. I can tell they haven't covered it with bark in a long while. The river is moving rather rapidly, dodging the rocks and fallen trees and branches. The sun is coming out and shining rather bright. The forest is still cold though. It's like there's a giant reflector over the forest reflecting the heat so it will stay cold. We're taking a break to rest up a bit. There's an old nursing log with some trees and rocks by and on it. We like this place because there's a good place to sit and rest. There's a lot of action going on here. Some birds are in the trees above us. We're back on the trail now some moss hanging from a tree brushed my face. It's fascinating how it just hangs from this tree. . . .

This assignment has the student doing several things at the same time. As it moves along, they have to recall information; interpret what they have seen, heard, and read; and apply that information appropriately. Not only do they recall information, they demonstrate understanding by recalling appropriate information at the right time. Also, it allows them to be creative in how they use or describe the information. My students take pride in the writing they do in response to guided imagery.

You can adapt this technique to any region. Use a car trip, vacation trip, bike trip, or anything that causes the student to move through an area and think about it. I don't teach world geography or world history, but I believe guided imagery would be fun and productive in these courses.

Later, while studying the Columbia Plateau region and after show-ing the film *Fresh Country Apples*, I asked each student to select a loca-tion for their apple ranch and role-play about being an apple rancher. I felt this was a way of helping them understand more fully what it would be like to live in the Columbia Plateau area. They were to start with the winter season and describe what chores they had to do and then cover spring, summer, and fall. The following example was writ-ten by Shelley Grasmick, a student who has learning difficulties and previously had trouble writing. She had not read a single journal entry until her reading group chose this to represent them. I felt she had come a long way.

In the beginning of the semester she had difficulty completing es-says. Here she had no trouble describing the seasons of an apple ranch. It was exciting to hear her read it without hesitation.

Agriculture-History
Apples

Well, its about 9:00 and there's a foot of snow on the ground. We're going to start trimming the trees today and get them ready for spring. It's about 22 degree above 0 degree right now and the sun is shining bright. It's a perfect day for work.

The glaciers have been melting now for about a month and the trees are starting to get leaves and blossoms on the branches. It's still real cold at night. The frost detector has gone off four times this week. It's a good thing we have technology or the crops could be totally ruined. The weather has been mostly sunny the last couple weeks, and the bees have been buzzing around pollinating the trees.

The apples are small right now and I'm not worried about them yet, in about a week I'm going to have to start thinning them out so most of the apples can get lots of sun.

It seems to be a real good crop this year. The apples have been progressing wonderfully in the last few months and are ready for harvest. Everyone is going to start harvesting the apples in about 3 days.

Writing to learn helped Shelley understand course material more com-pletely and gave her the confidence to share her learning with the class.

## A Unit on Native Americans

Unit II focuses on the Native American Indian culture of the Pacific Northwest. As we progress through different aspects of each culture's food, clothing, shelter, religion, and customs, students often write in the first person. Usually I assign them a specific role such as young adult (male or female) or elder. Topics include building your long house, fishing for and preserving salmon, winter ceremonies, and food gathering among the Coastal Indians. Among the Plateau's culture area they could describe their housing (there are several types to choose from), fishing for salmon along the Columbia River on a tributary, hunting in the fall, or pressing food for the winter. The important thing is that I take time every day to have them write something in their journals that summarizes or reflects on what was covered that period, or allows them to ask questions about it.

Students are motivated and often ready to talk a lot after seeing *I Will Fight No More . . . Forever.* This excellent movie was created for television in 1977 to depict the historic struggle between the Nez Percé Indians and the U.S. Army in 1877. I start by asking students to list words in their journals describing General Howard, Captain Woods, and Chief Joseph. They then write two unsent letters from Captain Wood to Chief Joseph. The first is to have been written shortly after the Nez Percé surrender along the Canadian border in Montana. The second was to have been about two years later and to reflect the change in events, broken promises, and unanswered pleas. Captain Wood was the conscience of General Howard and the U.S. Army. His role was an interesting one, and by writing from his point of view students had to look at both sides of the issue. The Captain Wood assignment allows them to choose either the position of the U.S. or the position of the Indians, but they do have to make a choice.

After looking at the various treaties, Walla Walla and Medicine Creek in particular, students write a dialogue between General Stevens and the Indians for each site. As a follow-up activity, students take turns role-playing the drama. After writing the dialogues, they have definite ideas about the roles and are anxious to play them out. It is fun to see the shyness barriers come down as everyone gets involved in reenacting history. Dialogues not only involve students directly in history, they demonstrate whether students really understand what they study. Here, for example, is a dialogue a student wrote for a later unit when we studied the Pig War in the San Juan Islands. This was a controversy caused by an American farmer shooting a British farmer's pig on San Juan Island. Writing a dialogue allowed students to "step into" the moment of history we were studying, and it helped students develop an understanding of how the participants fit into the situation and how the controversy arose.

### The Pig War

"Here's your pig Griffin! And if you don't keep you sheep off my land there'll be lots of mutton, besides pork. I've asked you before to keep your pig out of my potatoes, I just got tired of asking."

"You Americans are all 'alike.' You come barging around, acting like you own the place, build your shacks, plant your weeds, and then you don't even fence them properly! You should have kept your potatoes out of my pig! Now what do I do with my best breeder dead?!! How will I replace him?!!"

"Hold on now! I'll pay for your pig. Here's 10 dollars Griffin and be glad I'm paying you that much with all the damage he's done to my potatoes."

"Ten dollars!" choked Griffin. "Ten dollars; that pig was worth upwards of 100."

"Fine then, we're going to court."

"Fine, when do we go to England?"

"England! we're going to an American court. There's no way I'm going all the way to England."

## Other Units

As this class moved into contemporary topics related to industry, foreign trade, and government, the journal writing continued. I had students write letters of application to industries to demonstrate their understanding of the nature of that business. Controversial issues like energy, and especially the Washington Public Power Supply System were natural topics for students to write letters of complaint or letters to the editor.

This discussion has focused on my Washington State History classes, but I use writing to learn in my U. S. History classes as well, and I believe these strategies can be adapted to any social studies class. No matter what the subject matter, writing improves students' ability to learn. Not only do students perform better on tests and write better final essays when we use writing to learn, they also contribute more to class discussions. I have noticed that students who are willing to read from their journals are not always the same ones who regularly participate in class discussions. Writing helps students develop ideas and deepen their understanding of history at the same time that it makes them more able and willing to communicate their learning to others.

# Better Writers, Better Thinkers

Stephen Arkle
Lake Washington School District, Kirkland, Washington

Many chapters in this book provide a good sense of what writing to learn is and how it works. I will explain in this chapter how I use writing-to-learn techniques to help students to think through an idea more clearly. Two aspects of writing to learn are very important: it helps students to understand content better, and it shows them that writing is a process with various stages. When students have a full grasp of material and can use the stages of writing to develop their ideas, they become better thinkers.

One of the biggest hurdles for most students is finding meaning in what they read. Lectures do not always help them to understand the piece of literature being studied. The lecture isn't their experience: their personal connection with the material. Louise Rosenblatt has explained the importance of getting students to think on their own about material.

> Although all students should not be required to give the same sort of expression to their reaction, in most cases a personal experience will elicit a definite response; it will lead to some kind of reflection. It may also lead to the desire to communicate this to others whom the boy or girl trusts. An atmosphere of informal, friendly exchange could be created. The student should feel free to reveal emotions and to make judgments. The primary criterion should not be whether his [or her] reactions or his [or her] judgments measure up to critical traditions, but rather the genuineness of the ideas and reactions he expresses. The variety and unpredictability of life need not be alien to the classroom. Teachers and pupils should be relaxed enough to face what indeed happened as they interpreted the printed page. Frank expression of boredom or even vigorous rejection is a more valid starting point for learning than are docile attempts to feel "what the teacher wants." When the young reader considers why [she or] he has responded in a certain way, [she or] he is learning both to read more adequately and to seek personal meaning in literature (1975, 70).

Rosenblatt emphasizes three points here and throughout the rest of *Literature as Exploration*. First, students need to be engaged with what they read. Second, students need to learn to trust their reactions to what they have read so that they might reconstruct their ideas. And third, thinking should be done by students. The teacher should not interpret material, that is should not provide meaning or ideas about the text. Interpretation will carry more weight with students if the ideas are their own. It is their "exploration of experience" (Edward DeBono, *Teaching Thinking*, (London: Penguin, 1976), p. 33).

The writing-to-learn process offers the kind of engagement with material that Rosenblatt recommends. Students have a basis from which to respond, even if the response is boredom or rejection. The students are no longer passive receivers of information. What is gained by allowing students to draw on their own resources and experiences is ownership of ideas. This ownership of ideas provides the foundation for quality in writing and thinking because of the students' investment in ideas.

With the teacher directing and intervening in the writing and thinking processes, the students develop ideas in writing which will help them to understand and to communicate material more thoroughly. As the students evolve their own ideas, they also realize that writing is a process: a process that is not completed in one sitting. My writing-to-learn program consists of eight stages, each gradually increasing the complexity of thought required. These are dialectics, first thoughts, metaphorical questions, metaphorical characteristics, comparative lists of comparable concrete textual evidence, controlling idea, instant version, and draft. I will explain how students use these stages to develop the framework for a critical essay on Mary Shelley's *Frankenstein*. Following the explanation of these stages, I will describe how I evaluate the final written product. I include this evaluation "process" because it helps reinforce the concern for student-centered learning and the growth of ideas through writing.

### Dialectics

From the beginning I wanted the students to begin developing and dealing with their ideas about the novel, so I turned to **dialectics** because they help students develop ideas by responding to and reflecting on what they have read. Dialectics give students a place to record ideas, to think, to discover, and to begin the long process of refining ideas. In the broadest sense, the dialectic gives the students a chance to begin translating or grasping the meaning of the material in a way only they can understand. At first, I like to have my students focus on particular aspects of a piece to let them get used to the dialectics. For example, one time they may only focus on the interaction between characters or another time only on what a character thinks. This focus usually depends on the type of paper they will be writing. After they have done a dialectic response, students usually have some new ideas as well as a sense of personal engagement with the topic. Here, for example, is what one student wrote after doing a dialectic response to *Frankenstein*. (The numbers in parentheses refer to text pages from which the responses are drawn.)

I. Nothing contributes so much to tranquilize the mind as a steady purpose—a point on which the soul may fix its intellectual eye.

Walton is enthralled with the stranger. Almost infatuated. His description of the stranger narrating is so complimentary that it borders on the naive (16).

II. With this deep consciousness of what they owed towards the being which they had given life . . . (Frankenstein's childhood) (33).

Frankenstein's motive "I will pioneer a new way, explore unknown powers, and unfold to the world the deepest mysteries of creation" (47).

"Learn from me how dangerous is the acquirement of knowledge and how much happier that man is who believes his native town to be the world" (52).

"No father could claim the gratitude of his child so completely as I should deserve theirs" (52).

"A human being in perfection ought always to preserve a calm and peaceful mind and never allow passion or a transitory mind to disturb his tranquility."

He will not end up creating the perfect human being (54).

The description of the monster's "birth" (56).

This sounds like Raskolnikov (58).

I can't believe it. He brings life to this monster, and then makes no attempt to destroy it—instead, abandoning it totally to run free as it will. His behavior is similar to Raskolnikov's during his illness, and while he recovers from it.

Victor discovers the monster. Becomes convinced his monster is the murderer. Spends the night in a rainstorm (68).

III. A being whom I myself had formed, and endued with life, had met me at midnight among the precipices of an inaccessible mountain (74).

Frankie's first words with the monster high in the mountains—what drew him there (95–96).

The beginning of the monster's tale (98).

Like Adam, the monster eats the fruit of the tree of knowledge. "Was man, indeed, at once so powerful, so virtuous and magnificent, yet so vicious and base?" (114).

"What was I?" (116).

IV. Compares himself to Adam.

Compares himself more to Satan—does this fit into his image of an alter ego?

Frankenstein's guilt at creating the monster and consequently leaving it immediately after creation is like a young girl who has committed adultery. She no longer wants to see the face of her lover and the very thought and fear of the act she has committed makes her sick (124).

The monster demands Frankenstein create another monster. This would destroy him though. He would surely fall prey to another bout of sickness. If Frankenstein became the monster's friend he would have him completely under his thumb (137).

"The prospect of such an occupation (creating a female monster) made every other circumstance of existence pass before me like a dream, and that thought no longer had to me the reality of life" (142).

Frankenstein imprisoned in the dungeon of his own mind, of his own grief (189).

It is obvious to me that the monster meant he would kill Elisabeth on Frank's wedding night, because he had avowed to revenge himself by killing F.'s family. Evidently, F. thought it was he the monster was to be after because he couldn't emotionally accept the possibility of Elisabeth's death. It was too horrible to be true.

If the monster was F.'s alter ego, F. has now become his own alter ego since he is so intent upon his revenge (197).

"I was the slave—not the master, of an impulse which I detested yet could not disobey" (the monster at F.'s deathbed) (209).

Walter to Fred—"You throw a torch into a pile of buildings, and they are consumed, you sit among the ruins and lament the fall" (289).

Both the monster & Frankenstein feel that their crimes have degraded them "beneath the meanest entrance (?)." They both compare themselves to the "fallen angel" in the end (209).

The monster. "I am an abortion. Your abhorrence cannot equal that with which I regard myself. Where can I find rest but death?" (210).

Types of thinking presented here range from comprehension to paraphrasing information about plot to analysis (breaking down selection of material) such as the comparative statement about Raskolnikov of *Crime and Punishment* and Victor of *Frankenstein*. This student has begun thinking independently and making broad personal connections to the text. Ownership of ideas has begun.

## First Thoughts

In the next stage of the process I ask students to narrow their observations. They review their dialectic writing and then summarize pre-
dominate ideas or impressions they have about Victor or the novel.
Although primarily concerned with comprehension, this part of the
process also focuses on application because they are selecting and con-
verging on a particular idea or ideas. These **first thoughts** often focus on
very specific responses to characteristics, images, and colors. Here is
an example of one student's first thoughts.

> My first impression dealt with Walter. His fascination and admi-
> ration of Victor is so strong that it borders on infatuation. Victor
> seems to be immersed in his own occupations and self during boy-
> hood—a kind of introvert I would think that the morals he learned
> from his parents would have prevented him from "playing God"
> and creating the fiend. Victor seems to have no sexual attachments
> to Elisabeth which I think is odd. He doesn't seem to care for
> women much at all. As a matter of fact Walter is kind of the same
> way writing home to his sister, instead of a lover or wife.

Although short, this first thought focuses on the quality of Victor's
relationships. When viewed in relation to the previous writing on
which it is based, this selection demonstrates a narrowing and refining
process because the focus is more particular and less general than the
dialectic. First-thoughts focus attention on the whole of a character or
novel and pull disconnected thoughts together. These responses, like
all the responses in the prewriting stage, are shared orally with the
class while I act as a director of discussion. This peer feedback benefits
both the writer and the listener.

## Metaphorical Questions

With a more specific focus in mind, I next invite students to consider
the metaphorical aspects of *Frankenstein*. Some students need an explanation of these aspects. I provide them with an example. If the metaphor of a gathering storm has been chosen, one could focus on certain
qualities of the storm (gray clouds, giant thunderheads, and thunder itself). After I have demonstrated the qualities of a particular metaphor,
the students are usually able to generate their metaphorical lists. Drawing on the list of previously answered questions, one student listed
these characteristics.

Metaphor: Dark Forest

Characteristics: hiding good
　　　　　　　animals
　　　　　　　multi-faceted
　　　　　　　depressing to humans
　　　　　　　yet hiding things we consider good

Metaphor: Volcano

Characteristics: unpredictable
　　　　　　　full of inward turmoil
　　　　　　　steam released
　　　　　　　heaving
　　　　　　　under unnameable pressure

After students have selected metaphors, I have them begin analysis. They are to pick one metaphor they are drawn to and think of characteristics typifying that metaphor—the more the better. I ask students to broaden and refine their thinking about the character or novel with metaphorical questions, reminding them that they should use their "first thoughts" as only a guide, and that they may revise the response later, if they wish, but that first responses are often more perceptive than carefully considered ones. One student's responses are given after each question.

If this novel were:

a machine, what would it be? can opener.

a color? gray, peppery and black.

an animal? wolverine.

a weather condition, what would it be? turbulent.

a poison, what would it be? cyanide.

a weapon, what would it be? a dull knife.

history, what important moments would it be? civil war or medieval.

a mood, what would it be? angry, depressed, edgy, miserable.

nature, what aspects would it be? avalanche, dark forest or volcano.

a person (specific character, or relative, or man, woman, or child), what would it be? God, or small impulsive child.

After students respond to these questions the class discusses what they did. Metaphorical questions allow students to judge, infer, and see things that they hadn't previously noticed. The switch to associative thinking at this stage keeps students flexible in approaching their essays.

## Metaphorical Characteristics and Textual Evidence

The analytical step is further refined when I have the students compile a list of the metaphor's characteristics on one side of a journal page. Opposite this list, they provide another list of concrete examples from the text, examples that best "fit" the metaphor's characteristics. Working through these comparative lists, the students are forced to recognize, first, workable metaphors and second, clearly demonstrated relationships between the metaphor's characteristics and the textual evidence. Susanne K. Langer refers to this metaphorical relationship as "the recognition of a common form (pattern) in a different thing" (*An Introduction to Symbolic Logic*, 2nd ed. New York: Dover, 1953. p. 31). Once this linking is completed, students are asked to explain the relationship between the example cited and that metaphor's characteristics. This task forces students to think, to synthesize—not to approach relationships mechanically.

## Controlling Idea

Specifying a controlling idea for an essay is a difficult task for some students because writing this statement forces them to evaluate their ideas. I decided to have the students write their thesis statement (controlling idea) after the metaphor, complete with characteristics and textual support, had been developed. Writing a thesis at this point allows students time to explore the feasibility of relationships between their metaphors and text. They were to use the analogy to help reveal and reinforce their essay's controlling idea.

## Instant Version

After they have developed a controlling idea, students use their comparative list with metaphor and textual examples to write an **instant version** of their essay. I remind them to deal with only one part of their metaphor and to limit themselves to an example or piece of evidence for each point they make. I ask to provide an order for characteristics which they feel best typify it and then to provide some overt reasoning pattern for the chosen order. They are also to explain how these examples support their controlling idea. The points then become less isolated because they are discussed in relation to each other and to the controlling idea. The metaphor or analogy allows for personal connections and perceptions, an important aspect when the teacher doesn't want to force a totally artificial organization on the writer. Although analytical in nature, this stage also requires students to judge the effectiveness of their idea in an explanatory format. The following excerpt is from one student's instant version:

> Just as the characteristics in the fiend can be understood more clearly through the analogy of the forest, the characteristics of his creator can likewise be examined in relation to nature and better understood. It is easy to compare Victor Frankenstein's fate to an avalanche. The only way to keep an avalanche from sliding out of control is to not start it in the first place. An avalanche can never be controlled once it has started, and exploring the possibilities of creating a person, there was no going back. The snowfields that contain so much potential for destruction are seemingly pure and innocent, yet underneath they are shifting layers of treacherous ice. Frankenstein claims that he could never escape the fate of creating his disaster, the fiend.
>
> The results of playing creator seemed to him so innocent, all the world would love him; yet the consequences of his deed were deadly and ruinous.
>
> Once Victor starts playing with the dead, the chain of events leading to the creation of the ruinous fiend seems inevitable. Like the avalanche, he slides out of control.
>
> My application was at first fluctuating and uncertain; it gained strength as I proceeded and soon became so ardent and eager that the stars often disappeared in the light of morning whilst I was yet engaged in my laboratory. "None but those who have experienced them can conceive of the experiments of science" (49).
>
> Victor starts out in the scientific realm, slowly and full of uncertainty, but as he gains knowledge, he gains momentum. His thirst for knowledge becomes so great that he sacrifices normal human comforts to satiate it. The avalanche too, begins slowly and nothing deters it as it gains momentum. But in the end, we see that the avalanche results in a crashing destruction. Victor's situation also ends in wanton destruction. The creature is horrible from the first, and moves on to destroy family and friends, as well as others the creature meets along the way.
>
> The avalanche, which inevitably and ultimately ends in destruction, is hardly even preventable. The warming and cooling shifting layers of ice beneath the snowfields are so delicate that even the slightest events will touch off an avalanche. So it is with the events of our lives or a book read, that may change our outlook on life, so delicate is the thread that weaves it. Such is the case with Victor Frankenstein.

Although this instant version is in the early stages of the writing process, it shows the writer's attempt to deal with both metaphor and meaning found in the text.

The instant version step of the process allows students to write whatever comes to mind about their controlling idea—to play with relationships more fully. Second, students need not be concerned about mechanics, as the excerpt about shows. And third, students are able to see if the ideas work as well on paper (in essay form) as they do in lists and in their minds.

Once the instant versions are finished (usually two to three days, plus class time), students share them with their **writing groups.** I have the writing group members focus on the whole instant version of their essay with questions like: Does the piece make sense as a whole unit? If it doesn't, which parts specifically distract from the whole and why? Students find writing groups valuable at this stage because they can try various ideas or approaches without the fear of being overly committed to an idea. They also know that they will have time to revise the material which does not work well. The writing group stage further reinforces the process and the concern for student-centered learning.

## Draft

After the students have shared these instant versions I have them move to the final stages of writing the completed essay. They write a much tighter essay, fill in gaps of thought and finally edit. They then have a draft which can be revised again and finally edited for clarity. Once this "draft" is done they go back to the writing group where questions are asked again. Has the writer been specific? Is it clear where the writer is headed and has he or she developed a train of thought which is easily followed? Has the writer been specific in explaining points in relation to the controlling idea? Again the goal is to elaborate and clarify. The following openings from two students' essays show how the metaphor was used to help shape their essays on Frankenstein:

Example One

> When I was a child, I was interested in the culture of the North American Indians. It fascinated me. I read everything about them that I could lay my hands on and carefully handcrafted copies of their artwork. Indian art was my pet, my infatuation. As I grew and began to understand the people around me, I realized everyone has a pet, whether it be their hobby, religion, or career, and that sometimes the infatuation becomes obsession. In the novel *Frankenstein* by Mary Shelley, the main character, Victor, is extremely interested in natural science. He discovers how to create life and decides to try it. Creating the human becomes an obsession with him; he cannot give up the power that he has. And the possibilities of becoming famous if he is successful in creating life entices him. Once his goal is set in his mind, Victor cannot ignore it; the mo-

mentum of his previous successful experiments carry him until he completes his creation.

The characteristics of Victor Frankenstein's personality can be understood more clearly if they are compared to an avalanche. A delicate thread keeps the snowfields from becoming an avalanche, and once that thread snaps, the resulting avalanche is impossible to control. Similarly, there is a delicate thread of fate running through Victor's life that seems to snap when he becomes fascinated with science. This leads to obsession with the idea of creating a human, and Victor falls out of control. The snowfields that contain so much potential for destruction are seemingly pure and innocent enough—if it were just a dream—but his inspiration and the ability to make good the dream renders it deathly and ruinous.

Like the terrible dream-turned-reality, an avalanche is deadly and destructive. However, the realizing of the dream is more easily prevented than an avalanche. The warming and cooling shifting layers of ice beneath the snowfields are so delicate that even the slightest events, such as changes in temperature, and sound vibrations will touch off an avalanche. So it is with the events of our lives. A book read, or an hour spent in a new situation may rotate our outlook on life, lending new goals to strive for. Such becomes the case of Victor Frankenstein. Two events which would seem minor to any other, touch off the force that leads Victor to his demise. The first is his introduction to the ancient alchemists, who stirred his spark of scientific curiosity during youth. It was at a party that he chanced to come on the works of Agrippa. When he enthusiastically showed them to his father, his father told him it was "sad trash." This aroused his curiosity to the point where he "continued to read with the greatest avidity." Frankenstein relates that, if his father would have explained to him that the works were simply outdated, "It is possible that the train of my ideas would never have received the fatal impulse that led to my ruin." If Victor had not, on that day, picked up the works of Agrippa, he would have "thrown Agrippa aside and have contented (his) imagination, warmed as it was, by retuning with greater ardour to (his) former studies." But once his scientific curiosity is put into play, he becomes obsessed, full of "a student's thirst for knowledge."

## Example Two

"Adam had come forth from the hands of God a perfect creature, happy and prosperous, guarded by the special care of his Creator; he was allowed to converse with and acquire knowledge from beings of a superior nature." This quote explains the manner in which God has created man. It shows the care and wisdom he needed to assume the role of Creator. As Creator, God, out of love, gave man the provisions needed to survive and live a happy and prosperous life. In the novel *Frankenstein*, Victor Frankenstein attempts to play the role of God by bringing forth life. Victor, though, does not possess the qualities needed to successfully nurture his creation. Lacking in these qualities, Victor only brings about destruction for himself and others because of his creation.

This destruction comes about in different stages of the novel. These stages can be thought of as the life of a child. When the child is first born it has no understanding of the world, its ways of communicating, or its customs. As time goes on the child's parents use their "love" and "knowledge" to teach the child the essentials needed to survive and live a happy life. If the parents do not give the child the right amount of caring and teaching the child can turn out to be what our society calls a "backward child." When Victor creates his creature, he is stepping into the role of a parent, the creature being his "child." As Frankenstein grows in knowledge and understanding, Victor is unable to love and accept him as he should, this leading to destruction for both. It is because Victor lacks the qualities of love and acceptance that he cannot successfully raise Frankenstein into a prosperous and happy being.

Granted, these opening sections have some drawbacks, particularly in mechanics and sentence flow, but because of the pass/rewrite system of evaluation I use (which I will discuss in the next section) they are more than acceptable. Spelling errors and construction problems aside, these essays are interesting to read because of the student's personal involvement with the metaphor. In Example One the student moves from a childhood goal to Victor's obsession to the avalanche metaphor to obsession. In Example Two the chain of God—creator, Victor— monster and eventually parent—child is established. The writers have established a framework from which the reader can understand—to agree or to disagree with the writer's viewpoint.

The *Frankenstein* sequence reveals important aspects of the writing-to-learn concept. First, the assignment is broken into steps that facilitate the narrowing of material from general to specific. Second, as the sequence narrows, ideas need to be further and further qualified, forcing students to think, make choices and decisions. And third, the process itself fosters intellectual independence because the ideas which are narrowed and refined are the student's and not the teacher's. With this independence also comes ownership and with ownership comes the desire to do high quality work.

## Evaluation

So far I have barely mentioned evaluation, that time-consuming task all English teachers face. In evaluating a final written essay, I believe that one cannot base everything on some subjective criteria or become so objective that we are impersonal. The evaluation "processes" I use help to reinforce the process and the concern for students' own ideas.

To begin with, it is important to draw a distinction between two types of evaluation, formative and summative. Formative checks the student's work as it progresses. I like to think of it as a monitoring of the thinking process that the student goes through in the process of writing. I might check the steps used in the sequence of an essay or even monitor dialectics so that I can adjust learning if necessary. I can record in my grade book a plus ( + ) for students who have done an exceptional job for a series of dialectic entries while those who did only an average job receive a check (√). Summative evaluation, on the other hand, is evaluation that takes place when the essay is turned in—it evaluates the finished product, the student's "performance."

The process I use to evaluate finished essays draws on the two types of evaluation. I call it the pass/rewrite system. Every essay assigned has criteria for evaluation. For example, in one essay I might emphasize construction of an argument, and in another I might emphasize the use of a metaphor for clarity of argument. I refer to these criteria as my "Specific Evaluation" criteria for the assignment itself. I also use what I refer to as my "Primary Evaluation Considerations" which are adapted from William Irmscher's (*Teaching Expository Writing*. New York: Holt, 1979) criteria for letter grades on essays.

> Primary Evaluation Considerations for Essays (P/R, Graded Revisions & Final)
> When evaluating your essays, I will use: first, the primary criteria listed below; second, the specific criteria for the particular essay being written or rewritten (this is linked very closely to the first); and third, (for the Graded Revisions only) how well you follow those items listed in "Notes On Graded Revisions."

The A essay:

1. An ability to avoid the obvious and thus gain insights that are personal and often illuminating.

2. A capacity to develop ideas flexibly and fluently, yet with control and purpose.

3. A special concern for expressiveness, as well as clear communication, even if it entails coining a word that the language does not provide.

4. An ability to use punctuation rhetorically, using it for effect as well as for clarity.

5. A willingness to be inventive with words and structures in order to produce a clearly identifiable style, even though at times the effort may be too deliberate or fall short of the writer's intentions.

The B essay:

1. An ability to absorb ideas and experience and to interpret them meaningfully in a context of the writer's own conception.

2. A capacity to develop an idea with a clear sense of order.

3. A capacity to draw upon words adequate to express the writer's own thoughts and feelings.

4. An ability to use mechanics as an integral part of the meaning and effect of prose.

5. A capacity to consider alternate ways of expression as a means of making stylistic choices possible.

The C essay:

1. A tendency to depend on the self-evident and the cliché and thus to write uninformative discourse.

2. A tendency to make the organization obvious or to write aimlessly without a plan.

3. A tendency to limit the range of words and thus a dependence on the clichés and colloquialisms most available.

4. An ability to use mechanics correctly or incorrectly in proportion to the plainness or complexity of the style.

5. A general unawareness of choices that affect style and thus an inability to control the effects a writer may seek.

The D and E essays:

1. A tendency to exploit the obvious either because of lack of understanding, inability to read, failure to grapple with a topic, or, in many instances, lack of interest. The substance of essays therefore ranges from superficial to barren.

2. A tendency to wander aimlessly because of a lack of overall concept.

3. A tendency to play safe with words, using those the writer can speak or spell.

4. The incidence of mechanical error is high in anything more than a simple sentence.

5. A tendency to write either convoluted sentences or very simple sentences.

One final consideration is the student's growth in writing skills (growth in one or all of the primary evaluation criteria), which I monitor from assignment to assignment.

Using the pass/rewrite system, I keep the "Primary Evaluation Considerations" and "Specific Evaluation Criteria" in mind as I respond to student writing. The five areas of content, form, diction, mechanics, and style are all reflected in some way. If the student does not meet the criteria for "The C essay," either on the primary criteria or on the specific criteria, the essay is given a "rewrite." The student is not given a summative grade, but a formative one indicating that the essay is not yet acceptable. The student then rewrites the "rewrite" (within one week) and turns it in again.

To receive a grade for the course students pick two of four pass/rewrite essays they have written and revise them for a grade. I use the same evaluation criteria (primary and specific), and I consider how much improvement students have shown on the revision. The pass/rewrite system relieves much of students' anxiety because the thinking process and clarity are emphasized, not the grade.

Since I began using writing-to-learn techniques and the pass/rewrite system, the papers are much better. This evaluation system encourages growth in student writing. Formative evaluation encourages the process of writing and the development of thinking, much more than does summative evaluation alone.

Students need to learn and respond to the world around them, to develop their thinking and writing abilities to the fullest, and writing to learn fosters all of this. Through sequences like the one described here, my students learn that there is more than one way to write an essay. Students are given the opportunity to think on their own and to present their own ideas. They don't have to write an essay based on foreign ideas presented by an outside source. The writing-to-learn strategies themselves create the framework from which to work, and the writing process (data, prewriting, writing, sharing, revising, editing, evaluation) complement or carry the thinking process (data, comprehension, application, analysis, synthesis, evaluation) to such an extent that the two became inseparable. Because the students own their ideas, because they spend time moving through the process, they not only become better writers but better thinkers capable of dealing with almost any material.

# Writing to Learn Means Learning to Think

Syrene Forsman
Roosevelt High School, Seattle, Washington

As teachers we can choose between (a) sentencing students to thought-less mechanical operations and (b) facilitating their ability to think. If students' readiness for more involved thought processes is bypassed in favor of jamming more facts and figures into their heads, they will stag-nate at the lower levels of thinking. But if students are encouraged to try a variety of thought processes in classes, they can, regardless of their ages, develop considerable mental power. Writing is one of the most effective ways to develop thinking.

I assume that my students are all capable of thinking, but that they don't all recognize how the process feels, nor do they know how to di-rect their brains toward a product which I can evaluate. By using writ-ing-to-learn strategies, I can get students thinking, show them how to record the ideas that crop up, how to organize the wealth, how to sort out and select the one gem they want to polish, and I can give them a critical, yet supportive audience to help them to clarify their ideas in writing.

Writing to learn is learning to think, on paper, about what the stu-dents already know and how that fits with new informtion being stud-ied in our curriculum. When I look over the material to be covered in a semester, I have to remember that "learning" is allowing, not forbid-ding, a newly discovered rock to be fitted into the wall, the construct, of a student's reality. Learning may require moving some older rocks around, or even out of the wall. Teachers can't forcibly pile a semester's worth of new rocks into their students' minds. Each mind picks through the rocks, quickly or slowly, to rebuild or enlarge the structure that is that person's image of the world.

To begin incorporating new material into existing world views, I cap-italize on the students' innate drive to discuss their lives by inviting their opinions, fears, emotions, values, questions, and analyses into the **journal** "storehouse" for later application to composition assignments derived from required reading. Tying such newly "learned" information to the student's experience makes the new information stick far beyond the next scheduled quiz.

I use journals in my classes throughout the year. Students savor and save their journals because they provide a map of where their minds have been during a period of intense growth and change. Its stored material, when utilized in what Linda Flower calls reader-based prose, can give students confidence in the diversity as well as the importance of their own ideas. "I have nothing to write about" is no longer a valid excuse to avoid writing an essay, because the student has written pages and pages in response to the carefully structured sequence of daily writing topics.

During the daily journal writing, I insist that students write continuously for a specified number of minutes (five, to begin with); that they write whatever is in their heads about the topics, with almost no regard for someone reading over their shoulders (they can always remove material they don't want to share before turning in the journal for credit); and that they keep a record of the number of words they get down on paper during each timed write. This word counting is mechanistic, but it allows students to scrutinize their own growth as writers. When presented with this concrete evidence that they can write more than they ever thought possible, students develop the confidence and comfort that characterize fluent writers.

Students become accustomed to a few minutes of dictated topics, a prewriting discussion or exercise, and then the words, "Please begin writing. I will set the timer." When the time is up, I ask students to calculate their word total as follows: "Count the number of words in any three lines. Find the average number of words per line. Multiply the average by the total number of lines you wrote during the timed exercise. Record the number at the end of the entry." My first goal for all students is that they increase the number of words they generate in a timed write, and counting words provides concrete evidence of their progress toward that goal.

The class can choose from three questions in this **focused writing**, so that if they run out of ideas on one, they have something else to write about. They can transfer this approach to more academic composition assignments, recognizing that "if I can't attack this essay from Angle A, let me try B, or even C." I construct the questions with several goals in mind: (1) to direct their minds to the subject matter of the day, (2) to encourage ever more complex levels of thinking, and (3) to increase the flow of ideas onto paper.

During the first weeks, I pose questions that invite students to dip into their own backlogs of experience. Events that have sparked interest—a new school rule, the band at last Friday's dance, and the kitten found on the front steps—all offer students chances to write as well as to examine their lives more closely. My experience has been that when students have had little experience writing in the school setting or when their writing has been inhibited by fill-in-the-blank exercises, they need to develop self-respect for their own generating power. Before I can ask them to write to learn, they have to know they can write at all.

Since fluency is my goal, I grade by awarding points for filling a set number of pages every two weeks. The number is negotiated after the first two weeks of recording word counts so that the students can see that they are capable of generating more and more words in one ten-minute write, and they are reasonably confident that they can continue the curve. The requirement of four pages a week (in some classes six or seven depending on the level of ability) no longer frightens them. They are now ready to discuss with me how many pages per two-week unit they must hand in for credit. I offer to accept the average number of pages they have completed. They are "entitled" to include material they have written at home, as long as it's focused on topics from my English class. I discourage "Dear Diary" entries and warn students that they may be asked to read aloud in class the ideas they come up with as a result of writing, and that, since I will be reading the journals at intervals, they are expected to stay on the subject. They are also entitled to include lecture notes and reading notes, although I refer to them as "ideas" or "information" they are planning to use in a later composition. Any rough drafts of composition assignments are also acceptable, even if not required. This encourages students to save drafts on which notes from the writing group critique have been recorded, thereby making them more conscious of evaluation's place in writing.

Emphasis on quantity solves several problems. The students who cry, "I hate essays. Can't we do grammar?" or "I don't have nuthin' to write," feel they can achieve only within a rigid structure. Ten years of school has taught them that they can succeed at fill-in-the-blank questions, but would fail to meet standards when they struggled to share their own, sometimes inchoate, thoughts. Their own ideas had become "nuthin'." The journal, however, accepts everything for storage and credit. The student need only generate material. I'm responsible for providing writing-to-learn strategies for selecting, polishing, and publishing their ideas. This structure often unleashes a self that has lots to say.

As they become more fluent writers, students learn to trust the outcome of strategies that at first seem unlikely to produce any "real" writing. I emphasize the importance of recording in their journals personal responses to debates over values, opinions on character motivation, difficulties they had understanding a new concept, all of which may eventually find their way into a composition. Students don't always understand the purpose of some journal topics at first. As one student wrote in her evaluation, "Sometimes I see your reason for the assignment after I've done it." Learning to trust my reason as well as their own is an important stage in our development as a writing community. One day, for example, I asked each student to pick one object from a large group of identical objects and write a description of it. They could have been oranges or pine cones; in this case they were unshelled peanuts. My goal was to help them see how much they could see. Here is one student's response:

> Peanut description
>
> Doesn't talk back
>
> itsy-bitsy head
>
> itsy-bitsy tail (a bunny tail w/7 tiny strands)
>
> 12 strings to hold him together going from mouth to tail
>
> brown patch on his left side
>
> only one peanut inside
>
> Shorty
>
> top of his head is off-center
>
> flatter on the right side
>
> scar on right semi-back
>
> slightly dirty on top of head

Once students had completed the list of characteristics, I collected the peanuts. Then students were to pick their nut out of the larger group of nuts. Nearly all the students remembered what their peanut looked like, except the person who howled: "Someone took my peanut and left this crummy one!" (One or two students still had their peanuts at home at the end of the year. One said, "How can I throw away something I've gotten to know so well?")

Because the peanut exercise helps students recognize their considerable powers of observation, I feel entitled to demand they apply those powers to literature when they write analytical or comparison papers. I can assist in the outcome if I structure the journal topics leading up to the rough draft of the paper. For example, I can ask them to **list,** as they did with the peanut. They may list characteristic sentence structures, typical settings, slang, or frequent themes of various authors. I can ask them to write **dialogues** between two authors exchanging outcomes of their novels in order to prove why the other's conclusion could never work. I can ask them to create a **dramatic scenario** in which they describe one of the novel's characters as one of the FBI's Ten Most Wanted Fugitives, explaining the crime she or he is accused of. After a week of such topics, most students can write an excellent theme comparing the works of two writers. As a matter of fact, many will have trouble discarding the less important material, simply because the ideas belong to them, not a textbook. ("How can I throw away something I've gotten to know so well?")

Yet students do learn to make hard choices. Paula was searching for a unifying idea for her final paper on characterization in Shakespeare's *Romeo and Juliet* when she developed the following **cluster**.

Paris      Romeo      Mercutio
Tybalt

Her cluster needed only four words to set her off on free writing that focused on the character of Romeo.

> Romeo keeps watching Juliet and Paris looks around but still likes Juliet. Romeo more flirty; just changed loves from Rosaline to Juliet. Act II(?) Romeo was really like a little kid when he was in the Friar's cell like a baby with his new toy taken away. Then in the tomb he was so much more mature, he had everything planned out that if she really was dead he would kill himself with poison.

You can see her mind moving from a topic close to her own social experience, the fluidity of teen pairing structures, to a topic that demands a more objective approach from her, Romeo's character change as exemplified by his priorities. Aware of her audience (me) she chose the second topic. If the composition were intended only for her journal, I believe she would have opted for the first choice. Then she could have played around with a personalized horoscope or advice to the love-lorn column as they would be written to a Romeo or Paris.

When they have written drafts, students are ready for **writing groups**. This means listening to ideas about one's own written work, and listening to others' composition ideas in order to make intelligent comments. As students formulate their criticisms, they are learning about their own writing, as well as about the topic at hand. As others make comments, the student-writers catch the fire of new ideas, some of which may be incorporated into their own work, some of which they may simply admire. Students request writing groups just before big papers come due, even if I haven't scheduled them. Having the writing group encourages many students to produce, without the hint of doom that the teacher's due date provokes.

Students soon realize that the teacher is not the only expert in the class. Other students, struggling with the same assignment, can be sources for help. Some student writers are so eager for other writers' critiques that they will arrange time outside class to share papers, or will ask if they can give up twenty minutes of an in-class reading day in order to read each other's papers and write comments.

At first I ask students to reflect on themselves in their journals and speculate on how their past shapes today's person and tomorrow's. When they have demonstrated fluency in their writing and have learned how writing groups can help them revise, they are ready for new challenges. In particular, I want students to be able to see connections between writing and thinking.

One way students can see this connection is to understand the meaning of common teacher directives such as "list . . ." or "define . . ." To help students perceive the different types of thinking required for different types of questions, I relied on Gene Galleli's *Activity Mind-Set Guide* (Buffalo: D.O.R. Pubs., 1977), which is based on Bloom's taxonomy. First, the class listed questions they would like to argue about, ranging from school issues such as "the right of school-age smokers to pollute a specified outdoor area" to "terrorists' impact on developing nations." Then we divided into groups, each with the same assignment:

> Choose one topic and construct six questions students can write on in their journal, one question for each cognitive level.

Students had in their hands a brief version of Galleli's lists. The level on the left is paired with a list of typical teacher directives on the right.

KNOWLEDGE, level 1 = list, recite, identify

COMPREHENSION, level 2 = reword, define, outline, calculate

APPLICATION, level 3 = solve, relate the problems to a new situation, operate

ANALYSIS, level 4 = take apart, simplify

SYNTHESIS, level 5 = combine, reorder, formulate

EVALUATION, level 6 = appraise, referee, justify, criticize, grade

The groups returned to the blackboard with their six questions which the class used as the basis for debates, very informally correcting each other's misinterpretatons of the directive term. To reinforce students' understanding of the directive, I asked them to write on journal topics which included the same words. They read this writing aloud and received comments on how to align their responses to the "cue" word.

Later, I asked students to develop questions for written exams using these directive words. One group took character development, another, plot, symbols, and so forth. They had to reorganize information in order of importance, establish purpose in order to phrase the question (define or justify, but not both!) which would *they* be able to or like to answer in an hour-long essay test. This process of developing their own uses for terms commonly used by teachers helped students see how writing and the learning they are expected to demonstrate intersect.

Students reading Bronowski's *The Ascent of Man* developed eight questions from the chapter demonstrating how Homo sapiens differed from other mammals: "State Bronowski's criteria used to distinguish man from other primates," "Explain the development of less skin pigmentation in Homo sapiens," and "Evaluate Bronowski's reasons for believing Homo sapiens isn't limited to one environment while animals are fixed in one environment." The first two questions are typical of essay tests. Few teachers move beyond levels one or two in the responses they expect from their classes. Question three, however, evoked a surprising response in my students. Although their knowledge was, at best, limited to the facts Bronowski presented, they wanted to do battle with his beliefs and that question offered them the opportunity. Their writing styles were invigorated by the chance to tilt with theoreticians in the best tradition of any academic seminar.

Not all students will have the capacity or interest to take up the gauntlet offered by such questions. Some prefer to summarize or organize data in historical or significant order, or restate concepts from the new material. In the process of selecting the form their question will take, however, they have to try thought processes new to them. Even this brief test strengthens them for the next, until one day they can use the new mode of thinking with confidence.

To encourage students' awareness of the levels of thought required by specific problems, I often ask them to write about how their minds work. A game such as Mastermind provides opportunities for students to devise and discuss strategies of thinking. Sometimes I give them questions from the PSAT's selection of analogies (either pictorial or verbal), and we discuss how our minds maneuver to solve the problem. Some understand the mode of thinking clearly by watching another student at work; some are better served by playing a challenging game and then writing about it in their journals.

Knowledge of the limitless capacity of their brains for new associations frees students to attempt divergent thinking on paper. Their journals are safe places to test ideas with no fear of recrimination for disagreeing with the teacher or the textbook. I only ask, when the new ideas are to be incorporated into a "reader-based" composition, that the writer support theories with evidence taken from personal experience, research, and quotations from our class texts.

As composition topics focus more narrowly on literature, and some students have difficulty understanding the literature, I devise questions that make the material more comprehensible. In studying character development in *Romeo and Juliet*, for example, I spiced the questions with contemporary flavor: "Have you ever known an embittered or frustrated suburban housewife like Juliet's mother? What contributed to her attitude?" Students respond quickly to such a discussion topic, but could just as quickly lose the brief flash of insight in the crush of crowded halls or in a noisy lunchroom. The journal preserves it for them. Trying to put human relationships into perspective may be the largest task facing adolescents. "Have you ever heard a father react in anger to a son or daughter who threatens to embarrass him or the family? What did he say? Did he follow through?" Ten minutes of journal writing for three days can lead to powerful essays on character and motivation in Shakespeare's play, because, of course, while my test questions ask them to interpret Shakespeare's characters in the light of their own experience, the proof of their interpretations must lie in quotations from the characters' lines.

Students often assume that literature has nothing to do with them. They don't see any connection between their own lives and the reading assigned in class. Thanks to reading aloud their journal responses to *Romeo and Juliet* or whatever the class is reading together, they hear themselves interpreting and analyzing literature. They gain respect for each other's depth of insight and gain an understanding of literary criticism. They're also ready for one of the tools that enlarges their thinking about literature: the analogy. The skill to think through an idea from either end, the general or the particular, is evidence of what Piaget calls "formal operations," a higher level of cognitive function. It involves skill with inferential and educative reasoning, and it leads to effective analogic writing. When we see students using analogy competently we may assume they have made the transition from concrete operations to abstract reasoning.

We build up to analogies by playing with metaphors first. (Robert Frost said, "I have wanted in late years to go further and further in making metaphor the whole of thinking.") Metaphors in a composition infuse the piece with more life and may lead the writer to much deeper understanding of his or her point than when the metaphor first popped onto the journal page. Exploring how far to push a comparison between a concept and its metaphor will eventually lead to untruth, but oh, what truths students have discovered about what they "knew" during the exploration.

To help students learn the feel of using metaphors, I often ask **metaphorical questions** such as asking them to picture the plot as a machine, or label each character as a different flower, or describe the setting as a kind of active chemical. With sketches on the blackboard, labeling parts as we go, students pile one crazy idea on another, until they have more than enough for a journal entry. Students have the option of expanding one analogy of their own. The plot as machine, for example, is a favorite, possibly because of its flexibility. By pouring in Romeo, Juliet, and the preexisting feud, knowing that the lovers' deaths will be squirted out of the spout, students can manipulate different characters in the positions of choppers, mixers, and packers to discover the intricacies of Shakespeare's analysis of Renaissance society and young love.

Student writers are exhilarated by the powers their minds turn on when a whole class starts brainstorming on such a problem. I encourage continued use of the metaphor throughout the remainder of the year, particularly in **admit slips**. Journal topics include at least one opportunity a day to play with such a structure, either asking students to explore another author's use of imagery, or inviting them to invent their own. Metaphor becomes a natural part of the students' thought processes, one they can apply to any writing assignment.

What follows are excerpts from Diane's journal while she worked out an essay on one of Jacob Bronowski's chapters in *The Ascent of Man*. The class was attempting to respond to nonfiction using personal opinion bolstered with proofs (quotations) from Bronowski.

The following list is her personalized, shorthand version of the essay questions which groups had developed and written on the board.

> nomads—any hope? Can develop civilization using animal's power—greater than own
>
> explain/interpret why the nomad culture can exist at the same time the modern nuclear culture exists.
>
> evaluate B's statements that "man, like the wheat, is now fixed in his place." [This entry is circled in red pen.]
>
> Although I may have interpreted B's statement incorrectly, I definitely disagree with him. Our world is not limited, nor is our mind. Examples who are not fixed in agriculture ability to choose.

She has decided to answer the last question. She notes that she may have to reread Bronowski, to check her interpretation. The germ of her theme statement is already there. Her next step is to flesh out her ideas.

Draft one

B has made himself limited; with all of his physical facts and discoveries, he has not taken the time to see what is beyond.

man mind frontiers, changes can be reversible—people (going back to old life) not stuck in agriculture—new ideas?

The mind is an extraordinary thing. Scientists, researchers, doctors, and psychologists know very little about the mind and its extent. [The following three sentences are circled in red.] The mind is never fixed, and if the mind is not, the man is not. The mind is still free to wander. Imprisonment of the mind is only possible when it is self-inflicted.

A man imprisoned in chains is only physically bound. He is mentally free and that is what matters.

boundaries/space beyond

physical/mental chains—2 examples

In draft one, she wrote everything she had thought so far, right or wrong. The first paragraph, which I did not include, was like a dialogue, attacking Bronowski's point. Then she apparently reread what she wrote and began to redefine her ideas, scratching out, reading again, and inserting as she wrote. The last four lines begin to focus on the "chained" metaphor. She's found a unifying analogy for her paper.

Diane is still free to develop her ideas. Even the next draft is not going to be evaluated summatively—just critiqued by members of her writing group who will hear her read it.

What a pleasure to read a set of essays with ideas this vivid, rather than the pallid canned rhetoric of students whose style was bottled up in format. This diversity depends on students having had an opportunity to play with language without fear of judgment at first. Language may constrict our view of the world; culture may prejudice us to expect certain things in what we "see." Every generation then will "see" differently. Since today's teacher is yesterday's learner, we must not limit the creative vision of tomorrow's generation to our metaphorical structures. If I prescribe fill-in-the-blank exercises for my students, I am literally prescribing the form their language may take. I'm delimiting the future of their thinking unless I also give the students chances to opt for questions that challenge them to synthesize new information.

Inventing prose fiction is an experience that can help students get the feel of divergent thinking, similar to that in metaphor. In a unit on mythology, where my point was that every culture perceives the universe in metaphorical terms, students first collected proverbs, recollected fables, and read myths from several cultures. On the board we compared the structural differences of each of the three modes of literature, and the dimensions of the narrative elements.

Rather than dictate a definition of the fairy tale to the class, I asked students to write an account of one particular fairy tale as they remembered it. Some were incredibly complete; some had incorporated Disney's version; most were at least two pages long.

Writing groups met and discussed which elements the tale shared with proverbs, fables, and myths, and to what degree. These were then listed on the board. Missing elements which student writers knew lay in their fairy tales were added.

Students copied only those elements which operate in a myth and went home to write a mythological explanation of some phenomenon in our world, in contemporary terms but following the traditional format of their list. They were asked to imagine how a newcomer to our planet might explain aspects of our life that we take for granted. Secure in their understanding of the formula for a myth, nearly every student produced at least a short composition. An excerpt from Diane's journal records her thinking process.

> Most of my ideas are already down on paper. I did an outline yesterday of some of my ideas. I sat on my bedroom floor trying to think of something (especially modern myths) and then they started coming and they kept coming for 2 hours. It was pretty great. I think it's beginning to come together in my mind and it may be a little (or a lot) wrong, but I'm happy with it. I have to find out how long it should be 'cause I probably could write a whole lot.

Her topic was the source of humanity's quest for knowledge. She told the story from the viewpoint that such a quest is a God-given right, regardless of the price such a quest exacts in pain and responsibility for the consequences of actions. In the excerpt above, the fluency she comments on is well developed and so are her powers of concentration since she is able to write for two hours. Although she's uncertain how nearly her idea meets my requirements, she has the confidence to go ahead on her project because she thinks it's good. Her only concern is keeping it short enough!

The class was excited at getting a chance at "creative writing." ("Creative," I believe, is a misnomer. Does this kind of writing have another side to the coin? Degenerative? Is that why so many essays are deadly?) I was pleased with the evidence in the finished products that students had manipulated concepts in their own writing. They had grappled with plot, character, setting, and theme in the extremely restrictive formula of traditional mythology, and the battle taught them more than any number of vocabulary quizzes. Even if their myths were not great literature, the student writers had learned a great deal about myths.

When students are able to synthesize new information, I ask them to devise a research question that has no single answer locatable in an encyclopedia, plot summary, or *Twentieth-Century Authors*. This assignment requires students to read a novel and write a research paper. They are to research the life of the novel's author and determine the source of his characterization, setting, plot, or theme from his life experiences. Diane has chosen the hardest: theme. Its difficulty lies in the challenge to combine knowledge of the people in the author's life who might have offered models for his or her characters, the settings which might have been part of the author's life, and the events, ranging from the most personal to the most obviously historically prominent, which the author experienced. Diane's journal, excerpted below, records quotations from two typically plagiarized sources, *Encyclopaedia Brittanica* and *Twentieth-Century Authors*. You can see her struggle with the information she has read. Diane has done her homework and is wending her way on paper toward a personal, not plagiarized, understanding of fiction.

> On Pasternak's *Dr. Zhivago*
> Past. could have chosen almost any setting real or imaginary for the love triangle that is the main plot. There must be a reason of some sort behind his choice. Because a lot of the book is not concrete plot, and is devoted to showing the characters' feelings and omniscient expressions, it would seem correct to believe these thoughts are not random and have come as a direct result of that time period and its events. Should the theme that Past. had in mind be a delving into his own thoughts, he would then be questioning the revolution and what it meant. There is no end to what one could imagine that had happened to Past. that makes him write.

Many hours of writing purposefully as well as freely has taught Diane to pay careful attention to the amount of space devoted to action as opposed to rhetoric, and she draws her conclusion. Based on the historical context of the author, she can imagine what his purposes were as he wrote. Her mind will move far, far beyond an "A" on the test over plot, character, and setting. She is using writing-to-learn skills to do a kind of thinking new to her.

The semester's end brings evaluations of the teacher by her students. Some of the comments on the journal include, "the strange topics forced me to search and dig through my mind," "helps us think of things we wouldn't ordinarily think of," and "It doesn't really sound like homework although sometimes it does." Students describe the journal as one of the class activities they enjoyed most. Perhaps they enjoy journal writing because they can see their own learning there. It's an experience most academic activity denies students, except perhaps in discussions where the pot is boiling and time is allowed for each person's mind to taste and add to the mix.

Students also mention thinking processes frequently in their evaluations, and their comments confirm my belief that writing to learn develops their ability to work. Their comments reflect that they see speculation as a human activity of which they are capable. They describe their learning as "finding more questions" and clarifying what they think. They are concerned about consistency of views as well as "knowing the material." In other words, they are well on their way to becoming thinking learners.

# Thirty Aides in Every Classroom

Janet K. West
Bainbridge High School, Bainbridge Island, Washington

Feel free to pick up a pencil and change the title of this article. Raise the number or reduce it to suit. Be sure to use a pencil, though, for the number won't be permanent; it will change with each new term of year because my "thirty" represents the number of students in a class. Whatever your real number, I want to suggest that all students can become aides, assistants in their own education.

The biggest discovery I made when I started to have students evaluate their own work was that often they were the only ones who could do it. To put it another way, I realized I couldn't always teach them because only they could discover what they needed to learn. This revelation came when a writing class of college-bound students was working a painful route through Loren Eisley's *Immense Journey*. I wanted to see how much of the man and his attitudes they'd begun to discover. We had struggled with vocabulary, style, and ideas. I say "we," for I too was struggling to find means to help them cope. They took **dialectic** notes. We had had almost page-by-page oral analysis. They had written **precis.** Nothing broke through the wall of frustration, confusion, misconception, even hostility that grew higher daily. So along about Chapter Five, I turned to an exercise I'd learned to use in literature classes to help students understand the characters—the **biopoem.** This time, though, they were to write one about the author.

The degree of cooperation I received was due, I'm sure, as much to relief at avoiding or postponing another antagonistic class discussion as to desire to understand. Some of it was, perhaps, due to a shift in emphasis from previous concentration on the ideas in the book to the man who wrote it, his point of view, and his purpose. Whatever the cause, cooperation was what I got. I'm convinced that if all I had done was ask them to write the biopoem and hand it in, something would have been gained and we'd have had a pleasantly diverting few minutes. But luckily I did more; I asked them to share their poems, to give and get peer response. Students spent almost half an hour criticizing, applauding, justifying, and challenging each other's adjectives in line two of the poem. Those who'd pulled words out of the air with no concern for meaning or application were felled dramatically by classmates with cracks like "Whaddaya mean, he's superfluous? How can a guy be superfluous? Look it up." The sensitive were encouraged by positive responses to their sometimes unexpected contributions to the lines that begin with "Who fears. . . ." One student wrote, "Who fears a closed mind," and when I collected the papers, I found twelve others in the class had added that to their papers. Another wrote, "Who fears the end of life before we know the beginning?" That idea was recorded by several others. A combination of peer and self-evaluation: Someone else's idea was better, struck a responsive note, and was added to or substituted for a weaker one. We could have reached the same insights by other methods, but what seems to me important was that this particular writing-to-learn technique, the biopoem, forced them to produce a similar body of material which could then be compared and evaluated. Discussion had a focus, the result of shared effort they'd made and considered. They'd been exposed to others' styles of thinking, looked at them analytically, and in some way, if only a small one, become aware that thinking processes can be analyzed.

What did they learn? Lots of things. First, that they held many reactions and insights into Eiseley's book in common. This revelation told them that a thread of meaning, style and point of view was in the book, that it was discoverable, and that they were beginning to discover it. Second, that no one of them had a monopoly on discovery, insight, or understanding. Just about everyone had at least one good contribution to make, and just about everyone had a silly, superficial, or completely off-the-mark comment in his or her poem. Third, that the responses of their peers were both helpful and frank, and in criticizing the words and ideas of their peers they were learning how to criticize the words and ideas of Eiseley.

What did I learn? I learned that I hadn't understood or appreciated either students' misconceptions, or their previously untapped ability to apply their fresh intelligence and reactions to the book I'd worked with so many times. In this instance, my teaching contribution was merely to provide the vehicle for learning; they provided the fuel that ran it. They provided it more quickly and in greater quantity than I could have if I'd worked one-to-one with each of them.

Once the biopoem exercise led them to see the person behind the book, I felt free a few days later to assign an **unsent letter** to Mr. Eiseley. Each was to choose an idea or opinion of Eiseley's she or he objected to, resented, or just simply didn't understand, and tell him why. Look at just one result from a girl who had been in tears a week before. She had understood one of his ideas, specifically pinpointed her objections to it, learned to spot the basic stuff of his style, and expressed something about her own reading and learning difficulties.

> Dear Mr. Eiseley,
>
> I disagree with your approach to presenting the idea that man evolved from the water. I refer to Chapter Two . . . entitled "The Flow of the River."
>
> The chapter begins with an explanation that water is the most basic substance in the planet. The words you choose to define this concept such as "magic" and "charmed fairy circle" offer a poetic story for the reader to imagine. Your adventure floating downstream introduces a dream-like quality when you explain your feelings of being part of the living river. . . .
>
> The poetic concepts at the beginning are suffocated in poetic descriptions of the "wind ripples" and "odorous shadows". . . . Because of the poetic presentation I could not absorb your feelings of being part of the river. Instead of experiencing the thrill of sensing one's origins, I tried to interpret the narration of "sliding down the vast tilted face of the continent" and could not parallel floating down a river with "wearing down the face of time."
>
> My unsuccessful attempt at translating your poetry discouraged sympathetic feelings for your tale of the frozen fish. I was unable to accept the reality of a fish reborn from the ice and to use the story as a representation for the idea that change and evolvement are gambles that men and fish both indulge in. This left me with a blank mind, unable to probe curiously the fact that there is no logical explanation for evolution.
>
> Yours truly,
> Betty Hansen

Subsequent discussion of the book was livelier, more to the point, less of a struggle, and more beneficial once momentum had been started. I didn't get twenty-seven brilliant papers (this is the real world), but neither did I get any disasters. Everyone approached the final assignment with a reasonable interpretation of the book and a sense of what a critical review should be, and traces of tire marks from the biopoem exercise ran through each. Best of all, each paper, good or bad, had an individual tread pattern. Each had made a personal contribution to the class's evaluation of Eiseley's book and had proudly incorporated it into the paper. A big improvement over the past when I'd found, all too often, a parroting of ideas I'd suggested as possibilities.

The practice of having students do work that the teacher may never see or grade presents philosophical hurdles for many of us. At least it did for me in the years before my enlightenment. Somehow I felt that if students were asked to spend their time writing, I owed them my time to read (and grade) their work. My classes seesawed between the only two miserable choices my fears and guilt offered: They either wrote frequently for a much over-worked crank, waiting days for my nonetheless hurried responses to their work, or they wrote too infrequently for a more relaxed teacher who returned graded papers within a day or two. While I kept no record to compare, subsequent reflection leads me to suppose that those students who wrote profusely with delayed feedback must have progressed farther than those who wrote less often and received infrequent tender loving care. In writing, at least, constant practice improves fluency. Whether that principle applies to the content of math, history, science, or any other subject, I'm not prepared to say.

Long discussions with my colleagues left my dilemma unsolved but led to deeper layers of concern. I finally dug through them to the fundamental question of just what it was I thought I was teaching. Or, more aptly phrased, what was it my students were supposed to be learning? Could I pinpoint a particular novel, for instance, that was a necessity for their lives? Which one would it be? Or which two or three or ten? Why had we chosen the ones we teach, out of all the good ones available? Which poems or poets were necessities, ignoring any possible cultural veneer we might give our students? (How many of us, much less of them, have ever made or would make sophisticated small talk about T.S. Eliot at a cocktail party?) Realistically, did our choices of curriculum matter? Assuming selections that represented quality, the answer seemed to be "No," followed by the, to me, inevitable conclusion that I wasn't teaching literature in the sense of specific content. Rather, I was trying to teach how to enjoy, understand, and criticize literature. In a word, process.

Are process skills as necessary to other subjects as they are to writing and literature? I think an argument can be made that they are, at least partially as important. In math, for instance, we don't teach answers, because an infinite number of answers exist for an infinite number of problems. We teach process: how to find an answer. I recognize that there will be a specific answer to a specific problem if the correct process is used, but I also know many math teachers who give partial credit to a student's work when the answer is wrong because of inaccurate computations in a correct process.

What do we really teach in history? Facts? Many of us think so, do so, and bore students, who promptly forget them. But what of permanent value do we really want history students to carry away from the class? Isn't it an ability to take a set of historical facts and from them discover cause and effect? Even more basic, isn't it the ability to distinguish between fact and opinion? In other words, to master processes that enable them to make sense of the events that have shaped their world.

What about one of the practical subjects, like home economics? There, process is all. How ridiculous to think one could possibly anticipate all the recipes or patterns a student would want to use in a lifetime. Many of them don't exist yet. What teachers give their students is knowledge of processes that can be applied, with luck, infinitely. The same holds true for shop courses. Seldom would even a freshman want to duplicate the well-made but bizarrely shaped cutting board that ended up as Mother's Christmas present. She certainly doesn't want another one, and probably no one else in the student's life will ever be so doting as to accept one with good grace.

The essence of art is creativity. That precludes rote repetitions and duplication. The art teacher has no choice but to teach process. Anything else is not art—mass production, maybe, but not art. And I would argue that science education is by and about process. Experiments are processes, most frequently to discover other processes. Experiments rise from questions. The art of devising questions that lead to evocative experiments is a matter of process. And certainly the necessary step of evaluating the experiment depends on a process of further questioning.

My real conviction is that the most valuable thing we can and do give our students in any subject is knowledge of how to learn it. Furthermore, we must make them confident enough of their ability so that they learn and ultimately perform as they choose.

In short, they must be weaned. God forbid that either they or we should remain permanently fixed in the student-teacher roles we have in the classroom. At some point the student will have to decide alone whether the joint really is securely glued in a perfect right angle, whether the tax return is correctly computed, whether the letter of application is impressive enough to earn an interview. If we've taught students to make these decisions, they all will be. The ultimate process, the one on which all others depend is self-evaluation.

Have you ever noticed that often when students are handing in a test or other work they slip their papers somewhere into the middle of the pile? They seem to feel embarrassed or threatened at the thought of having you see their work while they're standing right there, or even sitting in the same room. They *know* you will eventually read it, but somehow they think their direct responsibility for it evaporates when you read it in some remote place like the faculty room or your home. They can put a distance between themselves and those marks or numbers or words they authored; judgment won't take place in their world, only in yours. I can sympathize with that behavior because it was the pattern of most of my education. One of the bravest things I ever did was to turn a term paper in early (out of direct necessity, believe me). I knew it would remain distinctively my work, and for once I couldn't run away from my responsibility of authorship. It was frightening, having judgment passed while I was aware of it. That same fear lay behind my initial reluctance to be thrust into the world of peer evaluation in a writing group. How embarrassing to have to read my words aloud to a live audience. But that's where I learned. First of all, that my peers were more helpful than I'd ever found a teacher to be. Second, that since they didn't, after all, have final judgment, I was free to accept or reject their advice. That led me to making conscious decisions on my own, sometimes to please them, sometimes to impress them, which is what I have to do in my real-life audiences. I'm grateful for the practice. So will your students be.

Look at this familiar scene. One boy leans across the aisle and whispers, "What'd you get for number three?" Is that student cheating? No, not if he already has an answer on his own paper. He's just doing what he most needs to do, getting support from a friend before he dares risk having you judge his work. And what if Mary's answer isn't the same as his? They'll argue, or compare processes, to see which one of them is right. That is, if you don't catch them at it and take their papers away. You probably have to if it's a test, but you shouldn't if it's just class work. You showed them how to do it, but they'll teach each other.

If it's been a test you've monitored so well that no one has had a chance to counsel with another, follow the crowd out the door and listen. Ignore "That was a bitch! I know I flunked!" and "Jeez, how unfair can Mrs. West get?" Catch, instead, things like "What'd you put for that question about style?" or "Were we supposed to apply that latest theorem on the last problem?" They're too impatient to wait to find out what an abstract thinks about it when you grade their papers. They want their fears confirmed or destroyed right then by someone whose opinion really matters: their peers.

Much of this typical activity is bravado, of course. Or consolation, or ritual. It's so pervasive, however, that we ought to take note of it. Obviously, what their peers think matters terribly. Shouldn't we be taking advantage of this? We don't have a monopoly of bright ideas and original thoughts, and our opinions certainly don't command the respect nor carry the value that those of their peers do. Students will accept criticism from their peers they won't take from us (or that we can't say). Let's make that work for us—not to relieve our paper load, but to help them learn. We can use it as the first step in weaning them from dependence on our judgments to confident self-evaluation.

But to make our peer evaluation work for them we have to clearly distinguish for ourselves and them the difference between formative and summative evaluation.

I like the word *formative*. The notion of shaping pleases me. First of all, something is being shaped, is growing, becoming. I can see the blob of dough flattening, stretching, thinning, rounding, sometimes sticking to the rolling pin. I have to scrape it off, sprinkle just a tad more flour onto the emerging crust, push a little chunk into the hole torn out, re-roll the patch. If it's for a bottom crust, I don't care. If it's for the top crust, I devise a pattern of steam-slashes to conceal the error. Or I let it go and say it doesn't affect the taste. At least, that's what I hope my family and guests will say. Besides, if I serve the pie from the kitchen and give the funny piece to myself, no one will ever know. A formative process. Not final, I had choices. I had remedies. I could even have wadded the whole thing up and started over, hoping for perfection the second time. Making my crust, I was my own critic, my own formative evaluator.

Recall a paint job you have done. Most likely you were annoyed when your spouse, friend, neighbor, or roommate called your attention as you worked to a spot you'd missed. But you fixed it, didn't you? Weigh that against your annoyance with yourself or someone else who points out that spot after you've finished, cleaned up, put the furniture back, and the paint has dried. That's summative evaluation in its most discouraging form. And most avoidable.

Students don't know these things consciously or automatically. At the very least their attitude about you and the course will improve if you can outline for them, step by step, all the check points along the way. How often should they step down from their stepladder and back off to get a different perspective on the paint job? From what angles should they look at it to see it in different lights? What brush techniques can they use so that the patch won't show? Would it be efficient and helpful to have someone else do the looking too? Maybe that's the best way to start. It's always easier to examine someone else's work than to examine our own. And once critical of others' mistakes, we're a little more cautious about committing the same ones ourselves. Clever as we may think ourselves, we can't instinctively avoid all possible errors—at least not at one time, on one project. How helpful to be forewarned. How comfortable to know we have a chance to spot and correct them, that we know how to.

Let me give you some examples of formative evaluation from my own classes. The subject is English, of course, but you can translate as you will into social studies, science, or whatever. Because I work in a twelve-week trimester, I don't always have time to develop the sense of community that is so essential to effective **writing groups.** Occasionally the class chemistry is right from the beginning, and students readily read their work in their groups. More often, they are reluctant, as I was. When that happens, I simply photocopy assorted anonymous samples of the drafts during the revision process, give everyone a copy, and have the class follow along as I read aloud. Response is inevitable and highly instructive. A page greeted with dead silence tells the writer worlds about the piece. No one reacted to it. It was dead, pointless. When pressed for reasons for their silence, students will give answers like "I don't get it," "It wasn't interesting," or "Who cares?" I can direct them to specifics by asking what's missing, what, if anything, they've been shown (not told), what they'd say if they'd written the piece. These suggestions and responses are seriously noted and often incorporated into subsequent drafts. Shortcomings of spelling, punctuation, and handwriting are always resented and vociferously pointed out. A display, perhaps, to let me know they know what's correct. When such shortcomings present real handicaps to understanding, I second the motion. Occasionally, a student will ask why his or her paper has never been duplicated, and if, as is usually the case, I say that it was too messy and illegible, you can be sure I get a neater draft the next time.

I'd asked a class at one point in a sequence of writings to write a letter to the school board giving their suggestions for improving the school. Among the usual collections of requests for less homework, better parking space, no attendance rules, and the like, was a model of precision and correctness. The draft began along these lines: "Dear School Board: I think (our school) is a very fine one with an excellent educational program." On it went for a page and a half error-free. My reading of it was greeted with silence, broken finally when an anonymous voice in the back of the room muttered, "It sounds like an advertisement." It did, and I'd been wondering how I could suggest that without destroying all the writer's illusions and securities about correct writing. Other papers had said a few nice things too, but more colorfully with more voice. In the discussion that followed, even the school's critics admitted that some people like the school and have a right to say so. What they objected to in this paper was the formal flattery they heard. The final draft was an improvement—not great, but an improvement.

Positive reinforcement comes just as freely as negative criticism, and more spontaneously. A smothered gasp at an unexpected image, a guffaw at an outrageous point of view, an absolutely rigid silence as everyone reads along, engrossed, tell the writer how well the audience has been captured. Thinly disguised students or teachers who figure in the piece are identified out loud at the clue. I don't have to ask for explanations, although I do, forcing the readers to find the exact words that prompted their reactions, asking them what was unexpected, and so on. They become better critics themselves, knowing precisely what moved them, and the writer learns what it was that worked so well. Highly imitative, they'll pepper the next batch of papers with the kinds of things their peers did successfully this time.

After a few rounds of this kind of critiquing, the number of requests for suggestions for improvement of early drafts increases. Self-evaluation is beginning to operate. Sometimes students compare the present project with an earlier piece of their own; sometimes I get a request for ideas to make it work the way someone else's did. I know that peer evaluation works when they write two- or three-sentence **admit slips,** and I see students passing theirs around before I collect them. They're eager for reaction, and obviously expect an appreciative one or they wouldn't have dared pass it across the aisle. The flow of stupid, obscene, or beside-the-point responses dries quickly to a trickle when the thoughtful, clever, imaginative ones get read, posted, and discussed by students from other classes. As being "published" for their peers' enjoyment and edification becomes important, the quality of work rises.

## Encouraging Thinking

So far I've talked about peer response to performance, a step in the process of production. What I'm also beginning to realize is that peer response can be directed to encourage thinking. Recalling and analyzing class discussions of literature, I realize that they have seldom become much more than arguments. Students weren't generating creative ideas or exploring the possibilities others' ideas open up.

But after I started using some writing-to-learn techniques, I found an explosion of peer interaction and evaluation. The day my sophomore mythology class read, in *The Iliad*, Homer's description of the shield Hephaestus made for Achilles, we spent some time analyzing the various scenes in the five concentric circles of the shield. Then I asked them all to list the scenes that would be on such a shield if it were to be made for an American today. In discussing the wedding picture, we had decided that it was symbolic of a cultural ritual and that the modern shield didn't necessarily have to show a wedding to be analogous. Once the lists had been completed, circle by circle, we started sharing. Contributions flew so fast I soon ran out of blackboard, and I know some great suggestions were lost in the shuffle. Many were greeted with laughter, a few with brief applause and most importantly, were generated after the fact, so stimulating were the responses. A few were challenged.

One memorable one came from two girls who'd spent a large part of the working time in deep cahoots in the back corner. They had a novel idea for the wedding scene and couldn't wait to share it. My astonishment was visible when they announced they'd put a picture of people going to the bank in that section of their shield. What a defense they made for the idea! It was a "ritual" that almost everyone practiced, part of our spending-oriented culture. The class realized that the idea had come from a different application of the word "ritual." The two girls had used it in its meaning of "habitual." Everyone else (and I) had taken the word to mean a "rite," even "celebration." And we were off on word meanings and connotations, with enthusiasm running high.

And at the end of that class, one boy lingered to say what fun all the "off-the-wall ideas" had been. I'd enjoyed it too, obviously, and didn't realize until later what had really happened. I'd been using the class as my guinea pigs to try out the exciting list of writing-to-learn exercises I'd developed into a set of lesson plans in a summer workshop. The class had enjoyed them, and an almost daily question had become, "What off-the-wall thing will we do today?" Biopoems, dialogues, guided imagery, etc., had been as novel to them as to me. But go back to the beginning of this paragraph and read exactly what the boy had said. The fun was no longer in my assignments but in their responses. They'd begun competing and feeding off each others' creative energies.

I found, too, that self-evaluation of learning style, progress, and work habits can be as important to a student as evaluation of work when, halfway through a six-week term paper project I panicked, again from awareness that I didn't know what it was my students needed to know in order to learn the term paper process I was trying to teach them. In a flash of combined inspiration and desperation, one day, I asked the class to take a few minutes and write unsent letters to themselves about their progress: How far along were they? What else did they need to research? When had they last spent serious time on the project? What was worrying them? What didn't they understand? What did they want me to explain again? What a wonderful marriage of writing-to-learn and self-evaluation techniques it proved to be! They seemed delighted with the assignment, and wrote busily for a long time. I neither asked nor expected them to share their letters with each other, and I certainly didn't want or expect to see them. Sharing took place privately, however, and I got instant feedback on what a relief it was to have to pinpoint their individual problems and shortcomings. And I certainly received clear and specific requests for further instruction. A few, amused as well as helped by the exercise, insisted on showing me their letters, and just about everyone thanked me. Most major bottlenecks in term paper production were removed, and I was able to program the next few days of instruction to fit students' needs. Again, I didn't get a brilliant set of final papers, but for the first time ever, all papers were handed in on time, and all had, however imperfectly, followed directions. I had never asked students to evaluate their papers before, and I am convinced that it made the difference.

Admit slips are great for this student review, too. I use them regularly for review before a test. I ask students to write something they don't understand and want explained. Or I ask them to write an essay question they know they couldn't answer. This forces students to confront their own misgivings and problems. And by the time each slip has been read by me and answered by other students (or by me, as a last resort), we've had a full period of thorough review of the things they need to have reviewed. It was their lesson, not mine.

I worry lest a reader see my advocacy of peer and self-evaluation as a thinly-veiled device to shift the burden of paper-grading from me to my students. I certainly didn't intend the title of this to imply that student evaluation was the route to a lighter teaching load. Instead, I see the practice as an integral part of many writing-to-learn activities, done purposely to teach important skills. Students assess their own and others' work as it's developing, helping each other to generate, assimilate, and expand knowledge: to find personal direction in their learning. Formative peer evaluation is reaction and suggestion, not judgment. Evaluators benefit, learning to be constructively critical, to appreciate process. Those being evaluated learn responsibility for their work. When they evaluate themselves, they develop the sense of control over their work that is necessary for pride in it.

Finally, the question of grades, of summative evaluation. It must be done. I belong to that legion who love to lament, "Oh, if only we weren't forced to give good grades! If only school weren't such a competitive system." Phooey! Grades are as realistic as all the other final criteria life imposes on us. We will or won't get the job, the promotion, the girl or boy. Even my pie, the crust so lovingly formed, will or won't be edible. Someone, sometime, will pass judgment on our actions and products. My premise here is that our evaluation as teachers will be more useful, easier, and fairer if what we're grading has first passed muster, as it developed in the eyes of the students themselves. One enormous caveat is essential. Peer and self-evaluation will be meaningless if students themselves have no criteria or standards on which to base them, no yardsticks to measure by; our summative evaluation will be arbitrary if we don't use the same yardsticks. We must supply these measurements, and at the beginning of the process. That's what teaching is. We have to supervise and direct the peer evaluation to see that no one has lost or switched yardsticks along the way. The chances of that happening decrease when we invite our students to help design them, let them help set the standards. Yes, we're obligated to stick to content. Yes, our curriculum represents the wisdom of scholars. But also yes, we can engage students in deciding how they can best learn it, how their performance can best be judged. Peer evaluation shows them and us how they're learning as well as what they're learning.

With so much going for it, I'm embarrassed to think how long it took me to discover peer evaluation. I knew, with a kind of desperation, that my students would be weaned (if only by graduation) and only by happy circumstance would have a college roommate, a secretary, or a spouse to do for them what I'd been doing—showing them the weaknesses and errors in their writing. I also knew I hadn't provided them with enough tools or practice to do the job for themselves, to be their own evaluators. Now I feel more confident that these vital dimensions are being added to their education, largely through use of writing-to-learn exercises, which frequently require sharing and peer response. It has benefits for me, too. I can and do assign more work in smaller chunks, while actually decreasing my paper-grading load, because most of the small assignments lead to formative evaluation. Both my students and I know more clearly what I'm looking for when I grade the final product. I have a much clearer idea of the quality to expect when I read that product. Best of all, they've learned more: about the subject, about themselves, and about learning.

# The Course Journal

Pat Juell
Mountain View High School, Vancouver, Washington

> From a distance the greenhouse dominates the landscape, but
> from closer range its strength diminishes. Wind whistles through
> its unfinished walls, and vacant squares await glass fillings. Inside,
> unopened seed packets and clusters of bulbs huddle next to stacks
> of empty clay pots, and sacks of peat moss sag against the wall.
> Nothing green stretches toward the sun from sawdust; nothing liv-
> ing inhabits this glare. What will it take to turn this structure into
> a productive greenhouse?

For me, the greenhouse image conveys the essence of **journals** in a writing-to-learn class. My students/gardeners use journals to store their
work in progress. Conditions both external (from the teacher) and internal (from the writer) provide the development of thinking. The journal is not a diary or a place to put already formed ideas. Instead, the
journal develops ideas from one nub of growth to a garden of observation, reaction, analysis, and evaluation.

In all my classes the course journal addresses the following
objectives.

> To encourage students to become independent thinkers directly
> involved in and aware of their learning
>
> To encourage students to be creative thinkers who develop new
> connections rather than memorize "facts"
>
> To encourage students to use writing as a process for discovery
> and clarification of ideas
>
> To encourage students to build trust in one another and accept
> and appreciate the differences of opinions
>
> To encourage students to learn that writing is thinking and to ex-
> pose them to the thinking of others through sharing writing orally

Achieving these objectives with a course journal takes time. Students need to learn how to be gardeners and to develop the trust and

respect essential for self-confident writing. From the beginning, students need to know that when they write in their journals, they are actively engaged in cultivation of thought. Throughout the course I continue to refer to the greenhouse, complimenting them on the "seeds" for potential growth and gently admonishing them for a crop of "weeds."

This chapter contains three sections. The first deals with community building to develop trust in the classroom and respect for others' opinions. The second section deals with specific writing-to-learn activities used during the first ten minutes of class, and the third section develops a lesson using a sequence of journal assignments.

When the basic concept of greenhouse/journal has been established, we use the journal daily. Then I introduce this statement from Richard Eastman's *Style:* "Writing is a social act. It is carried on with readers and because of readers. The presence of your reader—possibly an embarrassment at first—can become your greatest stimulus."

Sharing journal entries allows students to learn from one another's perspectives, gives them responsibility for their thinking, allows them to respect each other's ideas, and encourages active involvement in their own learning; they cannot be passive. Even though we discuss these ideas in the beginning, the journal begins to have more relevance as students actually experience their audience. The sense of community that fosters this sharing takes time to establish, and during the first month I emphasize activities and experiences to encourage students' enthusiasm for sharing. (For further discussion of classroom atmosphere, see **community building** in the Glossary.)

As sharing becomes more comfortable, I request students to read from their journals, always with the option that they may "pass." Obviously, passing every day is not acceptable, and students use that privilege only occasionally. I usually do not collect journals but evaluate this oral sharing with a grade in my gradebook.

As students write in their journals, I write in mine and share when they want me to. Usually students are pleased to see me write. "If Mrs. Juell takes time to do this journal writing, then it must have some value for us," commented a student in his own journal. I was made even more aware of the impact of my journal sharing when one of my students at the end of the year recalled my entry on the funeral of one of my former students and my subsequent confrontation with the frailty of life. After hearing my journal, he developed an entry explaining what he considered important in his own life and to whom he needed to be kinder. In recalling this journal entry later in the year, he said, "It was then I knew I couldn't just think of myself anymore. I wonder if this is what it means to grow up." I also know that sharing my journal matters when the description of my first black eye corresponds to many of my students' experiences and they see the universality of childhood wounds and traumas. Consistently I find my own journal sharing makes a difference to my students and to their own understanding.

Another important part of the sharing is to have students hear good examples of a writing-to-learn strategy from their classmates and to realize that variety is not only acceptable but it is encouraged. For many students having the exact answers given to them is comfortable; they can write them down, memorize them, and then recite them on a test or essay, never questioning the material, never thinking about the implications of the information. I want them, instead, to be motivated and excited by the connections they are able to make on their own when they begin to question, evaluate, and resolve.

Also, in journal sharing the audience motivates the writer to think through an idea. In the sample below, Annie Strawn begins her entry addressing a certain reluctance to read because she feels competition to be more entertaining. But in the development of this entry she unexpectedly confronts the questions of writing to express her own thoughts regardless of their entertainment value. Ending the journal entry she clarifies her understanding of the writing process. This analysis began as a tentative series of questions and ended with a clear statement of what she needs to do in order to write well; she must write what she believes and thinks in a style appropriate to her.

> The time has come again when I or we the class must probe our minds to come up with an original journal entry. I read my entry Monday. I didn't want to, but did because I have passed all my chances to read before. I don't like reading my journal entries because I feel they aren't entertaining to my audience. I can't entertain a audience with my writing, or should I say can't? Maybe I can, writing just doesn't come as natural to me as it does to some of them. There are some in my class that have an entertaining "style" to their writing and their audience enjoys listening. They were born with a writing talent. Writing is a talent as is music, but a person tends to believe that writing takes more brain power than music. This is true to me, only because music comes easier to me than writing. But to those that have natural writing talent, do they believe that music takes more will power? What an audience wants to hear and what I want to write are two different things. What does an audience want to hear? If I go about writing to an audience that I don't have anything in common with, I lose my inspiration to write anything, because I don't know them and I'm trying to please their ears. Now, comes the question: What do I want to write? I want to write something that tells me that I have sorted out the

many cobwebs and mazes that lay deep in my mind. I want to express on paper my thoughts that no one else can see in my head. If I write to please an audience, I lack any individual or independent style, because I have not written to please myself, but only to please those who don't know me.

Annie Strawn

After she read this entry, I discussed with the class those factors which made this an excellent example for the journal/greenhouse. Annie had stated her uncertainty and as she wrote, she clarified and justified what she wanted from her own writing. Through this writing she developed a self-confidence which wasn't apparent when she began. The advantage of classroom sharing is that it enables the teacher to point out and support strong examples of writing/thinking.

So far two factors have been established. First, students must be comfortable with the greenhouse/journal concept of using writing as a process and catalyst for thought. Secondly, students must understand the sharing process and be willing to participate. Once those two positions are established, specific writing-to-learn strategies can be introduced and emphasized. Students in my classes write every day for ten minutes at the beginning of the period. Usually I introduce a writing technique (such as **clustering, free writing,** or **lists**) which generates the seed thoughts, provides mulch, and suggests future blossoms. Once they feel comfortable with a strategy by sharing and discussing strong examples, I use that technique as part of the lesson for the day. Other chapters will develop in detail the use of writing to learn with specific course content. What I want to discuss here is sequencing this ten-minute writing and applying it to all stages of the writing process.

*Lists*

Even before they get to class, students are familiar with lists, even though they usually have not been timed or asked to write nonstop. Generating a lot of material enables them to realize one item produces another, and the longer they write the more complex their items become. There are other advantages of beginning with the list as a thinking mode: everyone has success with it; all students are able to acquire a body of material; some of this will contain seeds; some will be weeds. As students go over their lists, they are able to see the distinctions between noteworthy and not so noteworthy elements. In fact, other students in the class will point out particularly special parts of a list that has been read. The self-confidence which emerges from the listing leads students to choose this kind of journal writing when they are given the directions "write for ten minutes."

*Free Writing*

Kim's free writing struggles at first with the blank page, but she pushes herself past the intimidation to develop a list of clichés. Given enough time students are able to pass the "weed" stage in a journal entry to substantial writing with purpose as Kim does by focusing on clichés in language.

> Kim Dunham
> Trying to think of something to write all I see is a blank sheet of note-book paper staring me in the face.
> I know I'll make a list of clichés.
> Oh boy, I can't think of one, maybe if I . . .
> O.K. I've got one.
> Time flies when you're having fun. Before I go on with my list I would just like to say, "I love your hair band Lori, elephants are my favorite!
> Number 2—on, no, I'm stuck again, that's it "stuck"
> He's an old stuck in the mud.
> I'm sorry this is so short and stupid. And yes, Mrs. Juell, I am apologizing! For some reason today feels like a Monday to me.
> Number 3     as quiet as a mouse
>                 go fly a kite
>                 easier said than done
>                 over the hill
>                 what's a nice girl like you doing in a place like this
>                 fat as a cow
>                 I couldnt have done it better myself
>                 skinny as a rail
>                 better late than never, huh Jenny?
>                 stiff as a board

From listing I move to free writing. Some students want to take free writing as an invitation to talk only about the weather, how bored they are with school, or what they are going to do after school. But the potential of the free write is, as Susan Jenkins reveals, the honest and aware sense of what can happen between the writer and the thought.

> My Swedish friend and I sat drinking coffee after the movie. We talked about each other, things that have happened, things we want to happen. It was like one big free write. Fragmented sentences, unfinished thoughts . . . but still each of us knew what the other meant . . . honest, open . . . I guess you would call it aware.

In another version of this free writing Michelle develops a descriptive image out of having to come to school on a dark, miserable winter day but instead of complaining about disliking to get up, she approaches it with descriptive flair using the concepts of making ideas specific, the lesson we had been working on for a week. Here she is able to reconstruct and formulate her experience into a rich descriptive passage.

Michelle Hurst

> The alarm clock ringing loudly against my sleep. The warmth of
> a hot shower pouring over my goose bumps. The soothing liquid
> orange juice melting the crunchy toast in my mouth. The wind and
> rain water blotching the street. Bushes and trees swinging in the
> breeze. Tall shadows of lamp posts beating their light into the ce-
> ment. Fluffly dark clouds churning through the sky . . .
> Screaming bus brakes . . .
> Thudding feet finding room to sit. Steady rumble of motor.
> Screaming bus brakes . . .
> Thudding of feet as they find their way off the bus. More wind.
> The school doors open and out floods the heat of the morning.
> Gone with that terrible wind.

Free writing allows students to choose topics that seem relevant to
them at that moment and many times in addressing that topic, they realize through the writing process that they have solved a problem or
come closer to a solution. Steve Joy begins with the frustration of not
making his time in track. As he explains what has happened, he stops
in the middle by saying "I can't believe I just figured out my problem."
From that point the thinking becomes the solution. The writing process
has allowed him to question, to discover, and to resolve a problem.

> Nice day, says Steve. I am not going to Pasco!! Well I can't say I
> didn't expect it. My consistent 2:09 job is not cutting it. Rob has
> done a 2:07, 2:08, 2:17 for a 2:12 average. I will really have to get mad
> and get my times down. I lost my concentration when Frank passed
> me at the 480m pt. I even forgot that I had planned to pick my pace
> up on that corner. I felt like quitting at the 600m pt. and thought to
> myself, "I can't hold this pace." Well at the 700m pt. I decided I
> wasn't through and decided to kick. This lasted about 10 steps,
> then I realized it wasn't getting me anywhere so I went back to the
> usual. I didn't care about the guys in front of me but instead the
> guys in back of me, which seems to be a totally negative attitude. I
> can't believe I just figured out my problem. I'm a positive person
> with a positive outlook on life and while I've been racing the neg-
> ative side seems to appear. I never knew I had a negative side until
> last week when a guy passed me at the line. I saw my frustrated
> side of my negative side. Yesterday I wasn't frustrated just a bit dis-
> appointed. Well on to a positive thinking for next week's race.

The free write strategy requires enough confidence to let the words and
ideas push their way through the pen onto the paper. "See where the
writing will take you and what you realize when you get there" takes
an adventuresome gardener/journal writer. Many students beginning
the journal need much more direction until they develop a sense of confidence in themselves and what the writing-to-learn strategies can do
for their awareness, concentration, and discipline for thinking. Mike

Getty uses the journal write to develop a rationalization for running out of paper. Even though he discusses his problem, he uses the style and vocabulary of the lawyer/narrator from "Bartleby the Scrivener" by Herman Melville, a story we had just been studying that week. The free write gives him the opportunity to "fool around" with the tone and style of the story.

> I am writing my journal on a 8 1/2" by 11" piece of notebook paper with three holes, 32 vertical blue-green lines and one horizontal red line. The reason why I am doing this is because the journal that I normally write in is full of previous day's scrivenings and thereby has no parchment left to scrawl my thoughts of the day. I should have bought myself a rather well-stocked spiral notebook with many pieces of paper in it because then it would last much longer and I wouldn't be reduced to slouching over and scribbling this unimportant statement on this piece of compressed pulp with my shaft of graphite encased in wood. It is possible if not probable that I will purchase another collection of paper before the morrow. If not, my dwindling supply of paper will be exhausted and I will be reduced to twiddling my thumbs, drawing stupid pictures on my pee-chee, and daydreaming during the first ten minutes of Accelerated Senior English.

This is an exceptional entry in many ways. Mike has listened to the lawyer's voice in his reading of "Bartleby" and developed an obvious sensitivity to the syntax and rhythm of Melville's prose. Faced with the problem of no paper, he begins in his own voice but by the second sentence has slipped into the tone of another character not his own. He continues by parodying the situation knowing that his class audience will appreciate the humor, and gentle but effective way to make fun of the lawyer and the Melville assignment.

Along with free writing and listing opportunities, **focused writing** allows students to focus on one idea and explore its potential for new understandings. Not all focused writing need begin with quotations, but I have found the quotation does give students a point from which they can agree, disagree, or expand. Theodore Roethke's statement "I cannot be human; I haven't the time" is a striking example. In eight words, he condenses what it means to be inhuman and by implication what it takes to be humane. Bob Flick reacts by confronting the effects of not taking the time to give. His last statement reveals newfound maturity. His writing/thinking process involves a recollection of the past and a resolution for the future.

> "I cannot be human; I haven't the time." I feel like this applies to me sometimes. Sometimes I have so many things going and so get involved in certain things that I forget or neglect to do the little things that are important to me. I remember last spring when I was

involved in three different plays at once. I had one rehearsal in the
morning before, one during third period, and one at night. At the
same time I was seeing my adopted grandmother, but as I got more
exhausted I visited her less and less. When I found out that she
died, I had to reevaluate what I wanted out of life and what was
important to me.

**Free association** is another writing-to-learn strategy important for
helping students to make connections. They begin with one word and
see where that word takes them. The pleasure of this associative thinking is the element of surprise; when students begin writing, they do not
have any idea where they will go. After journals are written, sharing
increases the students' appreciation for the variety of possibilities with
just four words, because each student makes a totally different set of
connections. Given four words, students are to use all of them in a narrative; if students want to write a poem or develop exposition, they
may, but I encourage them to try narration when they begin this strategy. Most writing that students do in their classes is confined to expository prose; free association gives them an opportunity to make
different connections with ideas and increases their ability to see new
relationships. Marian has taken the four words/phrases, I put on the
board: fork, one kernel of popcorn, shower curtain, and *Elements of
Style*, to deal with the universal frustration of having "the munchies"
with nothing in the house to satisfy this hunger.

> I got hungry last night and decided to find me some grub to eat. I
> get that way you know. So I checked in the kitchen to find nothing
> there. I searched through the cupboards and cabinets but there
> was only air and a couple of dirty forks. This was not a joyful sight
> for me. My tummy was growling and I was missing "Hill Street
> Blues." Frantically I tore into the miscellaneous drawer. The only
> food in there was one kernel of popcorn, green and moldy. I re-
> membered that Mom put the left over Halloween candy in a sack
> above the fridge. Someone has swiped it all and left nothing but an
> overused copy of *Elements of Style*. I could hear the end of the com-
> mercial and the show starting. I screamed and grabbed a knife. I
> flung myself into the bathroom and tore down the shower curtain.
> I shoved this into the microwave with some floor tile and made
> some nachos.

Free association promotes the use of voice and sense of pacing. With
practice, students avoid squeezing all four words into the first paragraph; instead they develop a feeling for timing of characters and conflict. Marian establishes her character's voice in the first sentence and
maintains it through to the last line.

Throughout the first few months of the semester I introduce additional writing-to-learn strategies which students have an opportunity

to practice during the first ten minutes of class. As they share, I am able to comment on qualities which show thought. Steve's entry, written in response to a **guided imagery** where the directions were to "imagine yourself in this seat in another place," develops an image of being in the cockpit of the airplane. He carefully constructs an event, distilling important elements in preparation for takeoff. As he continues to write, he presents problems in vibration which he solves by adjusting the throttle. In just a short amount of time he is able to select and emphasize cause and effect relationships.

> Steve Arbaugh
>
> The seat is comfortable, not the recliner at home, but it's okay. Another seat like yours is on your right. First things first—seat belts and shoulder harness. Now we can begin the starting procedures. All electrical systems off, radios off, fuel on left, mixture rich, cut heat off, master on to 'up' prime twice, make sure everyone is clear, and push the starter button. The starter engages, pushing the big engine around slowly at first, then faster. When it catches, the whole frame vibrates. Adjust the throttle so it runs a little smoother. Oil pressure is in the green, oil temp is moving up, switch mags to both, the battery is charging. The sound of supersonic gyros just starting to spin fills the cabin. Turn on one of the radios to warm it up. Checking wing clearance, we begin to taxi.

Another writing-to-learn strategy used during the ten-minute journal writing is the **creative definition**. This activity asks students to invent definitions for words unknown to them.

In the following example Susan begins with a definition, develops its supposed etymology, and formulates other grammatical forms of the word, and ends with a form that has restricted meaning.

Susan Jenkins

> Jicama: (pronounced hic'-a-ma)
>
> A word of exclamation used to tell your mother you disapprove of a food, job or curfew.
>
> Once three separate words "jic", meaning a show of disgust, and "a Ma", as in "ah, ma, why do I have to do this?"
>
> Jicama should be spoken in a distasteful tone, and is only used properly by a Mexican child.
>
> It originated when an Aztec boy first tasted chocolate unadulterated by sugar. The bitter taste made him exclaim "jic . . . ah ma, do I have to eat it?" and this contraction was now in existence.
>
> Since then, all signs of contractions have been disposed of, and it has become a word accepted by authors, professors, scholars and poets alike. Especially those authors specializing in Hispanic literature and dialect.

Other forms:

Jicamed—what a mother has been after being faced with "jic . . . a ma!"

jicamaly—other phrases of complaint can be done this way.

jicamation—the act of "jicaming."

Slang—just a jic-a-man, used in New York, Los Angeles, and Dallas. Street lingo usually used against the police.

Students do not know the dictionary definition of the word. After finding out that jicama is a crunchy white root vegetable, they are disappointed. Their definitions, based on the sound and structure of the word, formed elaborate connections not inherent in a vegetable definition.

Another writing strategy, the **metaphorical question,** is one of the most difficult for students because it requires them to make unusual connections between two seemingly unrelated elements. It is a strategy that needs more practice than others, and I begin with a simple relationship—"if you were a breakfast cereal, what would you be and why?" This helps students think in comparative terms with familiar subjects. Later they use metaphorical questioning for evaluation. When students were two weeks away from their research paper deadline, I asked them to develop a ten-minute journal entry on "if your research paper were an animal, what would it be?" Kendall's comparison evaluates her writing. In comparing the erratic actions of the rabbit and her own work, she realizes she needs to work for depth and substance to eliminate "bugs and dirt."

Kendall Couch

If my research paper were an animal, it would be a hare. It is similar because the rabbit took off in his race against the tortoise, but did not finish in time. My paper started with a large acceleration, but stopped in the middle to take a break. Like the hare, my paper took too long of a break and did not finish in time. It is also similar in that when a rabbit runs, his legs appear to be a blur. My ideas were a blur when I started. Also a rabbit hops. My paper also was composed in a hopping pattern. I would find one significant idea and then find one unimportant idea. Another way that my paper is similar to a hare is that when a rabbit eats, he quickly devours the food, then later digests it. At first I too grabbed lots of information, then I later digested it. The appearance of a rabbit is similar to my paper. At first glance it looks smooth and calm, but underneath there are bugs and dirt.

Two more strategies introduced for the ten-minute journal are: **role playing,** a method for students to understand ideas from another viewpoint; and the **unsent letter,** which gives students an opportunity to classify ideas by advising a specific audience. In the following unsent letter, Lynn writes to Jason in *Medea*. He has left his wife and children for a younger and wealthier woman; in revenge Medea kills her children knowing Jason's anguish will be unbearable. Lynn speculates on who is to blame and what each character could have done differently. She takes a stand in Medea's behalf, then suddenly realizes Jason might have had reason. Her third sentence considers the harm Jason did when he left Medea, then moves into consoling Jason with a final admonition of not "screwing up the next marriage."

> Jason:
> You really shouldn't have left your wife and family for the princess. But, then again maybe it turned out for the best because you saw what an evil woman Medea was. Maybe none of this would have happened if you hadn't left her. I know people like you. I kind of think maybe it is better this way because what if you never fell in love with the princess, you could have come home later for dinner; or maybe you wouldn't like her dinner sometimes, and being the evil woman she is, she could have zapped you right then and there. So, I hope you try and forget her, and I also hope you find a decent lady to marry. And if you do, don't screw up the marriage; for God's sake, make it last. Oh, and if and when you ever do find this new lady, consult your nearest god, and make sure she's right for you.

The unsent letter enables students to make their feelings conscious, particularly with material that arouses emotional response; in the case of *Medea*, students wonder why characters took such extreme actions and for Lynn, the unsent letter was a clarification and definition of the characters and their motivation.

After using the unsent letters and practicing with a defined audience, students are ready for the more complex relationship of the **dialogue.** In role-playing another voice, writers must synthesize what they know already about the other voice in the dialogue and apply it to the question/answer exchange. Dialogue is most useful, I find, when students are having difficulty delineating arguments or issues from their reading. While reading Mortimer Adler's *How to Read a Book*, students found the language tedious and felt insulted by the title; after all, they felt they knew how to read. The dialogue with Adler forces them to be Adler and clarify and justify his book to the student writer, thereby enabling the student to understand Adler's thesis.

In the following student dialogue *A* stands for Adler while *M* stands for me, the student's identification.

*A:* I hear you are studying my book.

*M:* Yes, but not enjoying it; Mrs. Juell is forcing us to read it. You know you've brought a lot of pain and agony to me and the class—this is a real bitch.

*A:* Why do you think Juell has forced you to read my book?

*M:* She enjoys watching us suffer.

*A:* Besides that, why do you think it's important to spend all this time on suffering through the book?

*M:* She says it will help us read more intelligently and carefully when we are forced to read difficult material—she's getting us ready for college!

*A:* What do *you* think?

*M:* Well, I guess I have to answer this—you do seem to have a system; in fact, now that I think about it your organization looks like an essay.

*A:* What do you mean?

*M:* Well, you seem to introduce your main ideas for the chapter, then explain them, then you give a summary. Don't tell Juell but sometimes I've just read the summary.

*A:* Did you feel that was enough?

*M:* It was for a while, but then Juell seemed to ask questions that I couldn't answer with just the summary.

*A:* Give an example.

*M:* Well, your chapter on philosophy was boring; I really didn't know what it was, but when Juell asked us to develop questions based on our understanding of the chapter, I didn't know what to write so I went back and had to read the chapter.

*A:* What did you find out?

*M:* Well, I found out what philosophy was, that writers raise questions about why we exist and why it is important. I guess that's important because we think we know the answers but maybe when we get to be adults we see things differently, maybe because then we have more experience.

*A:* Is it important to know the questions?

*M:* No, I really don't think so because once you decide what you're going to be, then you set your goals and work toward them—well, maybe it is important now that I think about it. Sometimes you begin to wonder if your choices are right and if you'll be happy—I guess philosophers even ask what happiness means.

*A:* How does this all relate to reading the chapter on philosophy?

*M:* I guess by giving us areas to look at and different categoies of questions asked then we might understand what the philosopher is saying—maybe even disagree with his view if we wanted to.

In writing this ten-minute journal entry, the student begins disgruntled with me for even assigning Adler, but, as the dialogue develops, we see the writer finding reasons for reading and even coming to conclusions about the meaning of philosophy, a term he was vague about when he began the dialogue.

Students are pleasantly surprised at the outcome of dialogues; they say it clarifies their thought. I have found, however, when I get impatient and do not allow much time (dialogue seem to take more than ten minutes), students are not able to get past the basic amenities of opening conversation.

By writing in their journals ten minutes a day, students develop a sense of audience, and learn to appreciate the variety of thinking offered by the other students in class. But the greenhouse will not produce if the gardener spends time only on mulching, watering, and tending plants daily. There has to be a time when the gardener selects, prunes, and transplants developing ideas outside the greenhouse. The last section of this chapter develops a sequence of journal entries that make the roots nurtured in sawdust independent ideas strong enough to stand on their own outside the journal.

As part of the Renaissance unit in Humanities, students become personally involved with one of the "greats" of the period. They begin this project by choosing one person to research and become apprenticed to: a scientist, artist, musician, mathematician, or philosopher. After spending two days in the library completing the research, students write **first thoughts** in their journals about the "master" on whom they did research. What is their emotional reaction to this person? Wendy, who had researched Johannes Kepler, reveals in her journal: "I like him; he is independent, a rebel; he made people question tradition. . . . He is going to be difficult to work with. He seemed moody, preoccupied." Here Wendy not only makes an emotional connection with Kepler, she also understands qualities necessary as catalysts for cultural and scientific change.

The second stage of this role-playing sequence helps students generate enough material for the final stage of their research project, the **biopoem.** The biopoem assignment focuses on the student's relationship as an apprentice to his Renaissance master. Most students have difficulty leaping from research to writing the biopoem because the structure calls for perceptive thinking about the essence of the "master." A biopoem which only states facts does not reflect the potential for evaluation and synthesis so necessary to the success of the biopoem. Therefore, I take the students through two more journal stages before the final biopoem.

After the research in the library and writing first thoughts, students list or cluster at least twenty things important about their "master." Here students are able to develop a cache of important information. When they complete the list or cluster, they are ready to write the unsent letter to their master explaining why they feel it would be an honor to work with him. Before they write, I suggest they consider what their master needs, what he feels, what causes him to worry. They have twenty minutes to complete this part of the sequence in their journals.

Up to this point, ideas in each stage are being selected, formulated, clarified. In the final biopoem stage, students need to synthesize. Since this is a summative assignment, students have overnight to complete the biopoem in their journals to be ready to share with the class the following day.

Wendy's example below makes Kepler more than just an historical figure. She explores his frailty, his sorrow, his humanity while clarifying his contributions to humankind.

Wendy
Motivated, inquisitive, enterprising, but moody
Protege of Johannes Kepler
Who developed the three laws of planetary motion, the first
    nonmystical explanation of planetary attraction, the
    foundations for Isaac Newton's theories.
Who feels Copernicus' astronomical system is valid, Euclid's
    geometry is the image of perfection, and Renaissance man's
    reason must triumph over superstition.
Who needs the friendship of scientists like Galileo, the support of
    his petulant wife, and the instruction of a speech teacher.
Who gives amazingly accurate astrological forecasts, unbelievable
    meaning to the word "persistence," and incredibly complex
    lectures.
Who fears that God has forsaken him, that he will never attain
    salvation, that he contributed to the arrest of his mother as a
    witch.
Who would like to see an end to religious fanaticism, an end to
    war, and an end to famine.
Who lived in the cities of Graz, Prague, and Linz under the rule
    of Rudolf II.
Pare.

Sharing their biopoems allowed students in the class an in-depth view of approximately thirty Renaissance masters. The class took notes and asked questions about each of the biopoems read. After accumulating that information, students were ready for a test on those masters.

I was delighted by the quality of thinking evident in this sequence. Again, knowing it would be presented orally to the class motivated students to work harder on the project. As they worked on polishing the biopoem for structure and parallel construction to enhance rhythms and sound, students gained control in their thinking. They appreciated the structure of this research project because it gave them the freedom to make decisions about what was important but offered the control of writing within the stylized biopoem structure. Finally this journal sequence engaged students in inquiry where the questions were as important as the answers.

The course journal offers students opportunity to understand the function and importance of their intellects. They are no longer bent on asking for "the answer"; they know how to search it out on their own. They no longer wait for someone else to provide an answer; they are enthusiastic about the vitality of their own speculation, reflection, and resolution. They understand that the seed of an idea can be transplanted to a larger assignment, perhaps a research paper, perhaps a test, but all the essential material has begun in their journals. Here a student evaluates the progress of a paper after using the journal to clarify her writing process.

> Once I received the assignment, I did a free write as a journal entry on numbers. In this journal entry I came to a conclusion and listed the importance of numbers. After realizing that the idea of classifying numbers was not a unique idea, I started looking at music and especially Bach's music because I play it so often. The first thing I did was list different terms of music and ideas that I had about music. Once I completed the list, I grouped them into three categories. Again this was not a unique idea so I dropped it. I then found three unique ideas about Bach's music and listed them as the titles to three groups. Under these I listed what, how and why these unique ideas should be played. At this time I could not form a thesis so I just started writing. Finally on my second draft I formed a thesis, but I did not feel it fit my purpose, but I kept it anyway. In my revision I tried to get my paragraphs parallel and make the sentences flow smoothly by taking out fat and putting in more support; I then typed out my paper.

The course journal/greenhouse has been a source of pride for me and my students. Their comments "I didn't realize I knew so much" or "I have grown to respect others' ideas" or "I understand better when I write in my journal" all contribute to enthusiastic learning. But as with the greenhouse, the journal requires patience and commitment from the writer as well as the teacher. Given that attention, the journal can give life to the roots in the sawdust.

# An Impartial Observer's View of Write-to-Learn Classes

Barbara Bronson
University of Washington, Seattle

As reader-instructor in the English and Slavic Departments of the University of Washington, I am concerned with students' writing. As I read and grade papers, I find that many students' formulations of thoughts do not always reveal an idea at work or learning taking place. Thoughts that merit attention are not developed, or there is no focus to an essay. Often there is a confusion or profusion of ideas, and no attempt is made to clarify. Since there is little time at the university level to retrace the steps that should have been taken at the secondary level to correct these problems, or to teach students how to help themselves, I welcomed my assignment to interview teachers and students involved with the writing-to-learn program. These conversations and observations gave me an opportunity to hear and, in some instances, to see what is being done and to evaluate the results of the process in a variety of classroom situations. Here I will describe four representative classes in the program, classes which I visited as an outsider the way a parent or any interested citizen might.

## Special Education in the Suburbs

My first interview was in a suburban school in a pleasant, secluded, residential area of principally middle-class, moderately well-to-do students. I overhear the students talking of colleges and entrance exams as I wait to be directed to the teacher's room. I am to talk with a teacher of special education. We meet during the lunch period in a small, private cubicle. My first question is how she uses the writing-to-learn processes and second, what are the results. She explains that her students have different problems and that she works with them individually and in small groups of three or four, using the free-write, journal, and discussion strategies. She is careful to observe their responses and helps them develop positive efforts wherever possible. The free write is a struggle for many. The journals are not always clear, but the discussion groups help the student who has difficulty with writing by providing an opportunity to correct and explain.

She is particularly enthusiatic about the success of a dyslexic student. In the course of almost a school year, he has been able to make enough progress to graduate with his class. This is a breakthrough she had not expected, and she attributes this student's success to two vital factors inherent in the program. The first is that in the free write and in the journal there is no one right or wrong answer; the fear of being wrong is not present. The student's experience is valid. What he or she sees, feels, thinks, how she or he examines an idea are important. This is a beginning. This validity makes completion and comparison less the issues and creates a climate for learning that frees the student and contributes to self-worth.

She works primarily in reading and selects literature that will elicit a response. She is granted some liberty in this respect as the desire to learn is of prime importance in special education situations. She takes time to comment on the journal entries, though they are jumbled in the beginning. Every step of progress is there for the student to see, and she reinforces these positives. The opportunity to explore an idea, to discover, and to communicate are ventures the student must take, necessarily, at an individual pace.

Dyslexic students often are very bright and sometimes very articulate but unable to incorporate these abilities and talents into their learning. While listening, I am aware that the teacher is patient and persistent and the student determined and persevering. I am disappointed not to meet with the student and hear his response. I had hoped for more change, more improvement or success for many students. Yet the fact remains that, as this student succeeds, the incentive will be there for the teacher and other students. The fact that this student is a senior, that the problem has been with him for so long and yet is being conquered is heartening. This teacher is working with groups that need intense supervision and direction; yet she is discovering that writing to learn can help them to exercise more responsibility in helping each other. This is a discovery for her.

## Literature in a Large City

My next visit is to a school on the outskirts of a large city. The area is densely populated, and the noise and distractions of traffic and the bustle and busyness of the street are constant reminders of the tensions of city life. The building is old, revitalized with vivid paint on overhead structural supports. The pods of classrooms and the teachers' office-desk areas are separated by partitions. Several students wait outside the principal's office talking about the probability of readmission slips. The student body is predominantly black and I, an older white woman, am conspicuous.

The teacher arrives and tells me that many of her students have difficulty with reading and writing in literature classes, and her first experience with the free write proved less than successful. However, one day she asked her students to start a character sketch: "Write about someone you know, add to it each day for a week." Not only did she have some interesting and provocative sketches, but in the small discussion groups the students selected several to be read in class. Their interest in literature was considerably heightened. They began to observe how authors developed characters; how background, setting, speech, and attire contributed to the portrayal of character. She finds that these students' efforts at writing help them to develop critical ability: to compare and to evaluate differences in style and technique that give them the ability to appreciate a wider range of literary experience. She stresses to her students that differences in perception and experience enrich our understanding. Writing to learn is leading students toward a greater interest in literature, and these students are developing, from all reports, an interest in sharing and communicating. They have been issued a challenge and have accepted it. They are writing to learn.

## Humanities in the Country

The third interview is in a school in a lovely rural area not far from one of the shopping-center cities strung along the freeways. The building is a modern cement complex, so recently constructed that the landscaping isn't finished. The teacher of the humanities class is enthusiastic about the high level of interest writing to learn evokes and introduces me to the class as "one of us—another learner—as we all are in this creative program." He directs the class to begin their assignment, and we talk quietly as students write (or ponder what to write). They are completing an assignment on their outside reading. Everyone has selected from a suggested reading list and is writing a summary as preparation for an essay. This is the first time students have been asked to write without the preliminary discussion. The teacher is trying to discover how much of the high-level thinking evidenced in the discussion groups is carried over and how well students can apply the analysis and organization strategies on their own. He explains the free write, the journal, and the discussion procedures he follows and remarks how these have given him a new concept of teaching—creative in the best possible way, using the basic material (literature) as a tool for learning rather than feeding the material and hoping it will be ingested. He collects the papers and asks for response to the experiment. There are groans of "not enough time." Other than that, the general consensus is that this writing was easier than it had been previously. The teacher asks how many are willing to share their notes. Most consent and the few who demur are to stay after class. He has five volunteers who meet with me after class. The young men want to talk first as they have to leave shortly.

One tells me this class has helped him realize school "isn't a bust." He didn't like free writing and journals originally. They seemed "kid stuff." However he discovered that this is what he liked to do. For the first time he felt free to write what he thought, how he felt, and he wasn't "shot down for it." He worked out some frustrations and difficulties in writing about literature. "Once I get into a character, I can be me and the character." He can't yet understand why writing works when he is analyzing a character or a book, but he manages to get in a lot of what he sees and the work itself becomes exciting and rewarding to him. He likes the exchange in the discussion groups and finds others often agree with him, "even if I'm far out." (I later learn this student had behavior problems and, formerly, was more often in the principal's office than in class). He is discovering he has values, and writing in the journal helps him express them. One of the girls suggested he is more "straight" than he likes to admit. This brought a laugh, and he remarked that he did like to turn out a good piece of writing. While he is not a model student, by his own admission, he now is more perceptive and is willing to discipline his thoughts and feelings to a higher purpose than "letting it all out." He hopes to write for the school paper.

The other young man entered the class reluctantly, but felt "it would be good for me." The free write is not his favorite part of the day but the journal has become a habit he enjoys. "I don't mind putting myself on paper. It helps with other classes because I put down questions I don't want to ask in class." He does not say so but it is apparent that he is gaining confidence in putting himself on paper and that he is thoughtfully responding to assignments. He is learning to defend his positions and to respond to others.

The young women are enthusiastic for different reasons. One has gained confidence in expressing her own opinions. She is learning to apply logic: to organize her thoughts. "I used to say what I thought and

expect people to agree without clearly considering the power and persuasion of words." Another adds, "This is like a game. I can find clues
in reading that help me. When a character does something foolish or
threatening, I can remember being that dumb or daredevil. I want to
say, 'Hey, wait a minute.'" She is beginning to relate cause and effect:
to connect experiences. The third young woman feels she is taking a
risk every time she puts herself on paper. She risks change and growth.
"I find I am thinking, not just mouthing what I last heard. I see myself
growing when I look back in my journal at what I wrote in September."

For all of these young people there is a sense of accomplishment and
reward. They are learning to deal with ideas, with concepts. There is a
one-to-one relationship as they work with the material. They analyze
and evaluate on their own.

I return to the classroom to inquire about the students who have had
trouble with the summary. The teacher explains that, for the most part,
these students have reading problems. He talks with each student to
determine where he or she is in relation to the story and asks that each
begin there, with the known, the central characters, a central idea. If
this still presents difficulties, he asks them to consider a poem or a
short story with which they are familiar, to write their first quick
thoughts then to use the journal for further thought and comment. This
return to basics usually solves the problem.

Here the writing-to-learn skills are being used well and effectively.
Students are contributing creatively and developing perceptive sensi-
bilities. I am, however, concerned that they are not moving from the
personal to the concept of broader issues. There is a lack of direction,
lack of effort to see more objectively and widely, a lack of attempt to see
how words can lead to actions. This may be taking place, but it was not
evident in our conversations and my observations. There is an evident
success with these beginning steps of the writing-to-learn process, but,
also, a resulting homogeneity. The teacher is aware of this and plans to
direct further literary reading to an appreciation of differences in human experience, behavior, cultures, and an involvement with a larger
world in considering social and political injustices and human rights.

### Literature in the Country

The final interview is in a school some distance from the city. The
school sprawls over an extensive area, surrounded by small farms and
garden plots. I am directed to the teacher's room and arrive minutes before the class is to start. The teacher informs me they will begin with a
free write and some readings from those writings. I sit to one side and

observe. The room is windowless, bleak but for the attractive posters and the small signs posted randomly. Three particularly catch my eye.

"Learning improves the quality of the mind."

"Writing is the act of discovery."

"Creativity: the ability to make connections."

These will come to life as I listen and talk with the teacher and members of this class. There is an unexpected vitality for this last period of the day as thirty students file in, some nodding or speaking as they pass me. Every seat is taken, the desks arranged in a semi-circle with the teacher's desk centered against a wall. Everyone seems to be talking at once, to his neighbor or addressing the teacher, yet it is an orderly confusion with which they appear comfortable. The general hubbub subsides when the teacher says, "All right. Take up pencils and journals. Free write." I learn later, in the interview, the five-minute interval before writing is a brain-airing session. The students are accustomed to this exchange—a chance to gear up for the fifteen-minute writing period that is to follow. The teacher writes with them. As one of her confidence- and trust-building techniques, she shares her writing with them from time to time. This group has been together almost a full school year and has developed a routine and an art in working together. Students listen to each other. What captures the eye and warms the heart is their evident enjoyment of what they are doing. When the fifteen-minute writing sprint is completed, there are more volunteers willing to share their writing than there is time. The teacher selects three who reveal very dissimilar styles and subjects. The first is pure fantasy—a Walter Mitty type of experience, resembling a dream, with one quick final sentence to bring us back to reality, the reality of the schoolroom. The second, an experience of racism that proves later (in the student interviews) to be autobiographical. The third, a comment on war. None of these is polished in the accepted sense of that word, but each reveals something of the identity of the writer and a freedom of expression that speaks well for the ability to grasp an idea or a subject and to present a thoughtful consideration of it. (I heard from the teachers themselves, earlier, how the free write can inspire and refine one's thinking. The teachers have had this experience in their own training workshop. This is the first time I have seen it work so effectively in a classroom.) An interview after class gives students an opportunity to say what their experience has meant.

I talk with seven of the students from this class. More volunteered. The teacher selected these as representative of different viewpoints. I ask, "What have you learned from this approach to literature?" The answers are varied. "How to think about connections—cause and effect," "how to read for ideas," "a love for words and their meanings," "self-worth," "concentration and organization of my thoughts." Each has taken a turn in this response but two opt to speak later. No criticism is given, no comment made. Their choice is tacitly acceptable to all. There is respect for others in this group. When one student has not spoken for a time, someone will ask him or her "What do you think?" I remark about this, and they tell me that in the discussion groups they try for full participation. "Everyone has something to offer. She or he may dispute or confirm, but we learn from each other."

They agree they were not enthusiastic about journals in the beginning. One member felt it would be "an invasion of privacy." He was reassured by the teacher that his personal life was not the purpose of the journal. Some personal revelation may be there from time to time, but the purpose is to encourage objective thinking. Personal gripes and difficulties may often be used as a catharsis, a clearing of the air before thinking (like the five-minute period before free write in class) but are not the primary considerations or the goals. (The teacher informed me later that she assigns a writing project when a student has a problem with writing only to gripe. A focus is often the necessary antidote.)

The journal has been helpful to more than one student. It is a record of comments and analyses and helps toward a more objective and thoughtfully critical viewpoint. One student in this group became interested in a summer writing seminar and gives the writing-to-learn process credit for his increased interest in his studies in general and an improvement in attitude and gradepoint average. Another is writing poetry, a venture he had always wanted to try, but he was afraid of being thought "sappy." The introduction of contemporary poets in the reading assignments has given him courage to try. One of his poems has now been published. Another has found he enjoys reading for the pleasure it affords. "I've read what I had to, but choosing to read is something else." He explains that he has a job that requires his presence but not his constant attention. He is a watchman and reading "good books" is not only recreation but gives him "the chance to make connections." He has begun to be discriminating in his choices and asks that literature give him more than a cursory look at life.

The two who chose to speak later have more detailed and personal perceptions. One of the class assignments was to chart a family tree consulting family members as available. For this student it meant contacting family members in other parts of the country. In one instance his letter effected a family reconciliation. For him the family tree became not a list of the dead but a communication with the living. Writing to learn has been purposeful in a concrete manner he had not imagined. He thinks there is "magic in words" that can make reconciliation possible. He is beginning to see how diplomatic relations can hinge on the word and thinks he may make a study of languages.

This class is composed of students of different racial and cultural backgrounds, and, in the discussions of the family tree, students became aware that differences in race and culture do not always mean differences in customs and traditions. There was more than one laugh shared over an idiosyncratic aunt or uncle or an arch-conservative grandparent. The concept of family takes on new meaning as they realize the differences that exist in families who manage to exist together tolerantly if not amicably. "Democracy seems possible" as one student remarked.

The other delayed student response concerns a paper on rape that led its author into questions of responsibility and victimization. From a fear of being victimized, she worked toward possible alternatives in prevention (eye and groin defense tactics) and a concern for rape victims.

> "I did not come up with anything new. TV shows it all, but I found it out for myself and learned a lot about how to protect myself. I learned how to present what I wanted to say and convinced myself that I am interested in psychological research."

These students commented particularly on the positive effect of having the teacher participate in the free write. The trust that is established contributes to the student's ability to share and to the interest and enthusiasm of the class. In "laying herself on the line" she establishes a climate for trust. It is evident that as entries in the journal are discussed in the small peer groups, there is a rapport that develops and the fear of differing with each other or speaking out gradually dissipates and a concern for others supplants it. A black student can learn of the bias and racism that Asian Americans suffer. All the comments are valid in discussion groups, and often personal attitudes are changed. Students learn to be constructively critical of themselves and others without being thought vindictive or stupid. This is a new concept for many students.

Differences in opinion can be instructive and revealing and the freedom to develop in thinking and writing helps to create responsibility. Identity is growing as standards, ideas, and value judgments are examined and questioned or supported. As perceptions grow, the students are increasingly aware of the elements of literature, or differences in style, in genre, and the character and quality of specific works. For those fortunate enough to be in a multi-racial, multi-cultural classroom there is an opportunity to find a common ground, a common study of differences and similarities where there are not divisive factors. This may not make for an orderly or quiet classroom at times, but the students see education as a fresh and creative possibility that creates an atmosphere where learning is taking place, where new avenues and approaches to old problems give some insight that is revealing and rewarding. These ideas, sparked by the combination of literature and a lively response can produce the kind of paper I will look forward to reading.

As an observer I find that students experience frustrations, initially, in this writing-to-learn process. Accountability is uncomfortable. Yet students say writing to learn develops "a clarification of self." Because writing requires engagement, students overcome passivity and begin to connect experiences. Consequently they begin to think more deeply. Writing helps them to define what they know and what they need to know and to clarify concepts. Students learn self-discipline, open-mindedness, and an ability to find central ideas. They become better readers, better listeners, and they develop confidence in their learning ability.

Writing to learn forces teachers to reexamine their concepts of learning. They lead the students into doing the exploring, into making discoveries for themselves. The process changes the nature of study questions and analysis, and as the students' creative energies are channeled into useful skills, the dialogue and exchange that occur vitalize both teachers and students.

Most importantly, writing to learn educates the students into the kind and quality of work that utilizes their experiences, their creative abilities, to evaluate what they study. Not only does their writing improve, but they develop skills which they can use in other areas of their lives.

# Writing and Learning: What the Students Say

Ralph S. Stevens III
Coppin State College, Baltimore, Maryland

What students say about writing to learn is not always what teachers most want to hear. One, for instance, said he wanted to drop his English class. Yet when his counselor asked him why, he unintentionally revealed his teacher's success with writing-to-learn strategies: "She makes us think too much."

By now, the reader is familiar with writing-to-learn strategies and knows one of their primary functions is to stimulate thought. Writing and thinking may be hard work, but I've talked with many students who accept the challenge: "How can you learn if you don't write?" was one student's comment. She was hardly alone in her opinion, yet her rhetorical question is worth noting because of who she is: not an honors, or college prep, or even an average student, but one labeled "alternative," her school's euphemism for students who are unable to succeed in advanced or average classes. Writing to learn is democratic and does not discriminate on the basis of ability. Students from a variety of backgrounds, students good, mediocre, and poor, those who resist learning as well as those who don't, can all respect teaching which challenges them to think about and respond to their school subjects, and which encourages them to express themselves.

In the course of talking with eighty high school students from twenty writing-to-learn classes, I heard this theme often. Students appreciate teachers who assume the best about them and respect what they have on their minds. Said one group about the duo which taught their two-segment humanities course: "They trust us. Other teachers expect you can't handle it, but [these two] don't treat us like kids." That students can willingly accept the challenge of learning is strongly implied by these words spoken by a senior in a psychology class: "Writing makes you commit yourself more than talking does. If you write it down, you're committing yourself; there's more pressure to tell the

truth." When students speak of committing themselves and of responding to the "pressure to tell the truth," they are in effect voicing
their openness to the kind of teaching and learning espoused in this
book, the kind that, as one student put it, "gets students to think, as
opposed to having the book do it for them."

My object in this chapter is to discuss the results of interviews I conducted with nineteen groups of students from twenty classrooms in
which writing-to-learn techniques were being used. The subject of the
interviews was writing and learning, and my hope is that hearing what
they have to say on that subject will help teachers understand students'
educational values. This book is written by teachers and represents
their beliefs and hopes, their goals and ideals. But this is only one point
of view, one already well-represented in the popular and professional
press. Students, too, respond to and think about school and learning.
They have their own opinions, beliefs, and values. Though these may
not be as well-articulated as those of teachers, they deserve a hearing.
This chapter attempts to provide that hearing and in so doing to open
the book's perspective to include both sides of the teaching-learning
process.

Ranging in size from three to eight, most groups I interviewed con-
sisted of three or four students. All had experience with the techniques
described throughout this book. They were selected for the interviews
by their teachers, the chief criterion for selection being willingness to
talk; I wanted no one in an interview who didn't want to be there. All
groups included male and female students, and most had representa-
tives of low, average, and high ability levels. It is not only the successful
or able student who speaks here. One teacher, for instance, requested
participation from a senior who knew he wasn't going to graduate but
who was willing to discuss his writing.

My initial object in conducting the interviews was to determine how
successfully the writing-to-learn pedagogy was being implemented in
high school courses, and thus my chief questions had to do with what
strategies were being used on a regular basis and whether students had
any difficulty with them. But I soon discovered implementation to be a
minor question; in fact, there was ultimately little question at all: as students talked about their writing, it became evident that writing to learn
was being widely used. At the end of the chapter I have listed, for those
interested, the interview questions, with my reasons for using them.
But, as in most successful interviews, the questions served mainly as a
starting point, prompting students to disclose their perceptions of the
value and purpose of writing and learning and teaching. For this reason, I am presenting the interview data in terms of the topics which

dominated the responses, rather than classifying it according to the questions themselves.

Over thirty topics were raised during the interviews, but these can be arranged in three general categories:

1. The teacher and teaching
2. Writing and learning
3. The learner

### The Teacher and Teaching

Students talked about their teachers primarily in response to the question, "Is there anything unusual or different about this class?" although the topic came up throughout the interviews. Eleven of the nineteen groups mentioned teaching methods as one respect in which writing-to-learn classes are different from traditional courses, and most groups made some reference to teachers' attitudes, personalities, and styles. It should come as no surprise that students feel the teacher exerts considerable influence on writing and learning. One group from a junior English class made this clear in a discussion of two contrasting kinds of writing, used in the course: the traditional "theme" and the less traditional "course journal." The teacher imposed fairly strict criteria of correctness on the theme, and a paper weak in organization or argument would be returned "with a big *REJECT* stamped on it." Though they felt such methods helped them improve their writing skills, they made it clear that the authoritarian approach inhibited thinking and learning. In the less traditional journal writing, however, with the teacher maintaining a benign distance, students actually felt encouraged to think.

This group also felt that, in general and in spite of his *REJECT* stamp, their teacher was "more relaxed" than most, "easier to talk to, to learn from, open to [our] ideas." And they were obviously impressed by his being "willing to change his mind." The effect, they explained, was more open discussion, which they felt gave students the chance to "get their own say." As will become apparent, students felt considerable freedom of expression in writing-to-learn courses, their unprompted testimony suggesting the value they give this. In nine of the interviews, the teacher's attitude was cited as one of the factors contributing to self-expression. One group, for instance, claimed that their teacher's willingness to share his own opinions and recount his own experiences encouraged expression. For another group, the teacher's encouragement and acceptance of all response stimulated open and imaginative writing.

It was not only the ability to encourage expression that gave the teacher prominence in students' comments. Several groups mentioned that their teachers were able to "come down to [the students'] level." What was meant by this was not condescension, but the teacher's ability to understand the student's point of view when faced with an unfamiliar or difficult assignment. Greatly appreciated were teachers who could see what the assignment required and give adequate directions. Of their sophomore English class, one group said, "It's harder, but the way [the teacher] explains it makes it easier," and "She's down with us kids." As one member of the group put it, "Other teachers don't explain the assignment if I can't do it, but she really helps you do it."

In their comments on teachers, then, students value teachers who encourage them to speak their minds and then listen when they do so. What this suggests, of course, is what will become even more apparent when we consider the learner. In valuing the freedom to express themselves, students imply a willingness to respond to what they're studying and engage in a learning process which demands they be more than passive recipients of another's knowledge.

## Writing and Learning

Writing was the subject of four of the interview questions, and thus quite naturally the most frequent subject of student responses. All groups mentioned two or more of the writing-to-learn techniques as typical of the writing they did in class, and most referred to the techniques as one way in which the class was unusual or different. But this is hardly surprising. More significant is what students had to say about the purposes of writing, and how these relate to learning.

The major tenet of the lessons and techniques described in this book is by now familiar to the reader: Writing is not simply a form of communicating the known but of exploring and learning about the unknown. Students' perceptions of the purpose of writing are obviously important in determining whether this principle bears fruit in the classroom. It speaks well for teachers and students that all the groups interviewed mentioned some aspect of learning as a major purpose for writing. And most of them did so unprompted, in response to being asked "why are you doing all this writing?" In only four interviews was the subject of writing as learning first mentioned by the interviewer. Students themselves usually initiated the subject.

Several aspects of learning were mentioned in the interviews. Fourteen groups indicated that it facilitates thinking; five spoke of its power as a memory aid; and several referred to the greater intensity of learning through writing. For many students, writing meant that learning took on an affective aspect: they became more personally involved in and affected by what they studied, finding themselves able to sympathize with other points of view and to "form relationships with" characters in the literature they were reading.

In reference to "writing as thinking," student comments ranged from the simple and direct—"writing makes you think"—to the more subtle and analytical—"[writing helps you learn] because of the questioning process during the writing process and after." "You have all these ideas in your head," commented one student, "but you're not aware of them until you write them down." "If you can write it, you can understand it," said a student from another class. In general, most students revealed a well-articulated experience of writing as a form of thinking. As one student put it, "some people don't even know what they think until they write."

Students seemed aware of writing as a process that both generates and shapes thought. It gets us thinking about the subjects," was one student's way of putting it. Said another, in reference to the topic of a particular lesson, "writing helps you form your opinion of capital punishment."

Other students were aware of the mnemonic function of writing: "If you write about it, you remember it better," suggested one. For students in a foreign language class, writing was a way of using, and through use, of remembering, what they'd learned: "It sinks in a lot better—as long as I put what I'm learning to use, I'll remember it." For another group, writing was a lot of work, but worth it because "we don't forget anything this way."

Students in eight of the nineteen groups were conscious of a learning process that, because of writing, was more intense than in more conventional classes. "I really got into it in detail," was one remark that typified this perception of writing as a more intense form of learning. Another comment on the subject was more graphic: the writing, said one student in a literary origins class, "makes imprints in your brain about the story." Said a student in another group, "It makes you think about [the book], and go into it in depth."

"Learning in depth" was a theme touched on by one group in contrasting writing to learn with traditional composition. A girl in a philosophy elective told how free writing led her to a "deeper level" of thought, where she found that she was "not just exposing truths but finding them." The formal demands of traditional writing, however, because it made it "harder to structure" ideas, inhibited such depth of thought. A classmate shed light on this predicament when she explained that she finds herself "leaving out lots of ideas" because of the demands of form, and that the results, to her mind, are thus more superficial than those of free writing.

Another group, this one from a junior English class, spoke of the same difference between traditional writing and the more flexible writing-to-learn techniques. One student claimed that because of the formulaic quality of traditional composition, there is relatively little thinking involved; he said he could "dash off an *A* paper while watching TV," and his tone suggested little respect for the intellectual content of writing so produced. In contrast, he felt he had learned more about say *The Scarlet Letter* through journal writing, which, he said "allows us to get raw ideas down without concern for wording; that way we get better ideas, learn more."

Such comments as these, about the greater depth of learning that can take place through writing, suggest something about why students perceive writing as a mode of learning. They associate "composition" with developing writing ability, not with learning. They have no particular disposition toward seeing themes and essays as having significant intellectual content; they are more concerned with form: with being "correct." They can perceive techniques such as free writing as being connected with learning because when they are not required to be conscious of matters of form or usage they are more conscious of what is going on in their own heads. This, it might be hypothesized, is in part what creates the sensation of "learning in depth." Another factor is certainly the freedom to express one's own ideas and opinions which writing to learn imparts. Students seem less likely to be conscious of "learning" when they are simply repeating ideas dictated by teacher or text. When expressing their own ideas, they seem more aware of the intellectual process. One group mentioned that writing "makes you a part" of what is being studied, and that they learn by being able to express the subject in their own terms.

Most groups, then, saw writing to learn as concerned primarily with learning rather than with developing writing skill. It should be pointed out that nothing in what students said indicated any consciousness that writing was being used in their courses deliberately as a mode of learning. While they were often conscious of their own learning processes, learning theory, in any formal sense, seemed to have no bearing on their comments. Although one student did mention that the kind of writing they'd been doing taps the right side of the brain, such sophistication was largely absent. The phrase "writing-to-learn" was mentioned in none of the interviews. I bring this up to forestall any conclusion that the reason students spoke so often of writing in terms of learning was simply because the connection is suggested by the terminology. Writing-to-learn terminology was as absent from student's vocabularies as it was from the interviews themselves.

Not all students see learning as the primary function of writing. Two groups said that improving writing ability was the chief function, and two others mentioned this as at least one function of writing. But altogether it might be concluded that these groups are the exceptions that prove the rule. And all groups agreed that writing enhances learning.

In this connection, it is worth noting that only two groups mentioned any difficulty with the writing they were asked to do, and in both cases the comments concerned only one assignment. In general, all groups indicated that they had no difficulty with the required writing.

## The Learner

Students spoke of many different things during the interviews, but in nearly everything they said, one theme was prominent: themselves as learners. Although I have separated "The Learner" as a topic of student response, during the interviews there was no such separation. Students did not talk about themselves as a topic other than writing or learning or teaching. Rather, their awareness of themselves, of their role in the classroom, was apparent in the remarks on these other subjects.

I include the learner as a separate category for the following reason: Writing-to-learn strategies implicitly place the student at the center of the teaching-learning process. This does not mean that writing to learn is student-centered, and I came to think a better term might be "response-centered": students are required to respond frequently (in writing, primarily, but also in discussion groups and other classroom activities) to the subject being taught. These responses become, ideally, the focus of instruction. James Britton says that an essential part of the writing process is "explaining the matter to oneself." In writing-to-learn classes the same can be said of learning, that an essential part of the learning process is "explaining the matter to oneself." And this is what students are doing when they respond in nontraditional ways to course topics.

Furthermore, explaining the matter to oneself encourages the student to make connections between the subject and her or his own life.

Piaget claims that learning takes place only in relation to the learner's environment, for it is this environment which provides a web of meaning in which new information can be caught and digested.

The process this implies requires the student to participate more actively in education than when he or she is merely required to listen to lectures and discussion, read books, and repeat on tests the information so acquired. It demands, first of all, that students be self-conscious about their learning, aware of their responses to new material, and of how it relates to what they already know. And it requires that they be willing to express those responses.

I asked no question directly related to the learner as the center of this pedagogy. But as I talked with students, I saw that many of them were responding willingly, even enthusiastically, to the role outlined above. This was clear, for instance, in their comments about teachers encouraging them to speak their minds and respecting them for doing so. A remark recorded earlier suggests an awareness of the importance of student response. Speaking of ways in which her philosophy class was unusual, one student said of her teacher that she "tries to get students to think, instead of getting the book to do it for them." Of the same teacher another student said that "you can say anything you want, though she won't necessarily agree." And a third student in the same group mentioned the attribute of "openness: there are no value judgments."

In citing these qualities as differences between the writing-to-learn classes and more traditional courses, these students recognize the role imposed on them by "response-centered" instruction. And another comment from the same group shows the way that role fosters learning through the inner dialogue of "explaining the matter to oneself": "when I read [something I've written] and run into something negative, I'll question it."

Thirteen of the nineteen groups made some reference to being allowed or encouraged to express themselves (and by "express" I mean not "repeat information learned," but expressing one's own feelings and opinions). It is difficult to document, or "prove," student's attitudes toward this freedom, since none of the questions dealt directly with this subject. However, inasmuch as the tone of the comment means anything, this interviewer heard considerable enthusiasm for the opportunity to respond openly. One group spoke of enjoying the writing because "we can use our imagination, and we don't have to put down just what someone tells us to." Another group mentioned journal writing as "writing down what you think is important," and "what you need to know." With this kind of learning, they said, "it's all yours—nothing that's ever been done before."

The remarks recorded earlier under "Writing and Learning" show students aware of the learning process, conscious of "explaining the matter to themselves," responding favorably to the process. That they willingly accept the responsibility, and work, of responding frequently, is apparent in the tone of the additional comments quoted above. That tone was occasionally so obvious it could be recorded on paper: "When [the writing] is fun you remember better," and "when it's fun, you're more interested in the subject, and it's easier to associate with it." Comments such as these suggest that learners are as much a factor in the writing-to-learn class as they were in the interview responses.

## What the Interviews Suggest

In summary, I would like to point out the implications these interviews have for teachers.

1. Teachers can expect students to respond favorably to a classroom environment which encourages and respects self-expression, and to see this as relevant to learning when such expression is relevant to material being studied. ("Freedom of expression" should not be taken to mean license to say and discuss anything.)
2. Students not only are able to do the writing described in this book, but can enjoy it and find it purposeful.
3. Teachers can expect students to be aware of their own learning processes and to accept responsibility for them.
4. The teacher would do well to run an "active classroom" in which students have many opportunities to interact with each other and the course material. Students respect activities that demand their attention to course material and produce results. Said one student: "Usually when I see a film, I'll just drift off, but when I know I have to write about it, I really pay attention."
5. Students value learning when they can see its relevance to what they already know, and teachers might consider including exploration of such connections as part of instructional units. Testimony to the value of this is given in the remarks of a Washington State History student. Her community had recently been host to Indo-Chinese refugees, and she had heard another student complaining about the number of Cambodians who had recently moved into the neighborhood. She said that she had been studying the attitude of another group of natives (the American Indian) toward another "invasion": the westward expansion of the nineteenth century. She saw the similarity between the two situations

and said this helped her understand the point of view of the Indian then, and of her neighbor now. Thus this student was able to explain what she'd learned in terms of her own life, making the connection with her environment which Piaget claims is essential to learning.

## Conclusion

My concern has been to summarize as accurately as possible what a small group of students had to say about writing and learning. I think we can conclude from what they say that students of all abilities can take responsibility for, and find value in, the learning process. In an era of low test scores, and emphasis on minimum standards for competency, and a fear that students cannot learn "the basics," we are constantly pressured to condescend to our students, to "teach down" to them. The failure of high school students to pass literacy tests leads to "basic skills" English courses in which they read books of little literary value, and the greatest writing challenge is to fill out a job application. Student's failure on math exams leads to courses in which they engage in lessons on balancing a checkbook. Such a curriculum assumes the worst about the student. Yet even "the worst" students say they are capable of accepting greater challenges.

## Description of Interview Questions

1. Each interview began with two questions intended to determine the student's overall perception of the writing-to-learn class: "Is this class unusual in any way?" and "Has your teacher said anything about trying something different in this class?" I wanted to determine whether students saw themselves as being engaged in a learning process significantly different from what they were accustomed to.
2. In order to determine something about the role of writing in the course, I asked, "How often do you write and what kinds of writing do you do?" This not only prompted descriptions of the learning situation, but helped establish a vocabulary about the course which would facilitate the interview itself.
3. The fourth and fifth questions were: "What do you think is the reason for doing all this writing?" and "Do you think writing helps you learn, and why?" As discussed in this chapter, the sec-

ond of these questions was usually answered in response to the first, and often students would touch on the purpose of writing in their answers to the earlier question about the kinds of writing. These questions were intended to determine whether the theory of writing to learn was in any way realized in practice.

4. The last question also related to the learning process, but with the focus more on the writing techniques than on the process as a whole. I wanted to know whether students were being asked to engage in techniques that required unusual or unaccustomed skills, since this would have some bearing on how they would view the learning process. I, therefore, asked "Do you have any trouble doing the writing?" In asking this question, I could draw on the vocabulary established by the earlier questions about kinds of writing, for instance, "Do you have any trouble with this guided imagery?"

# Glossary

Anne Ruggles Gere
University of Washington, Seattle

As might be expected of teachers who worked together for several years, project participants developed a common language. In particular, the group settled on terms to describe various strategies for writing to learn. The following section defines terms, explains the value of the writing that results, and, where possible, credits sources. For a more complete explanation and for examples of variation in implementation, turn to chapters by authors named at the end of each listing.

**Admit slips** are brief written responses (which fit on a half sheet of paper) often collected as tickets of "admission" to class. These are collected and read aloud by the teacher with no indication of the authorship of individual statements. Admit slips are frequently used in community building. Exit slips are a variation.
See Forsman, Juell, Pearse, Schmidt, Yoshida.

**Biopoem** follows this pattern:
Line 1.  First name
Line 2.  Four traits that describe character
Line 3.  Relative ("brother," "sister," "daughter," etc.) of _____
Line 4.  Lover of _____(list three things or people)
Line 5.  Who feels _____(three items)
Line 6.  Who needs _____(three items)
Line 7.  Who fears _____(three items)
Line 8.  Who gives _____(three items)
Line 9.  Who would like to see _____(three items)
Line 10. Resident of _____
Line 11. Last name

Biopoems enable students to synthesize learning because they must select precise language to fit into this form.
See Johnston, Juell, Pearse, Watson, West, Yoshida.

**Brainstorming** collects, in writing, all ideas generated by an individual or group charged with a given topic.
Brainstorming provides students with an abundance of ideas about a given subject, showing them how many perspectives are possible.

See Beaman, Juell, Marik, Peterson, Yoshida.

**Clustering** is a strategy described by Gabriele Rico in her book *Writing the Natural Way: Using Right Brain Techniques to Release Your Expressive Powers.*
Clustering helps arrange ideas that have been generated by writing.

See Beaman, Forsman, Juell, Marik, Peterson, Watson, Zimmerman.

**Community building** is an essential part of writing to learn in any classroom because students need to establish trust before they will be willing to take the risks involved in writing to learn. Many strategies are used to develop community in a classroom and to continue the process throughout the year. Here are a few examples of community building activities.

Have students observe their classmates and then write a list in their journal of all the things they have in common with others in the class. Ask each student to share one thing not previously mentioned by another classmate.

Have each student interview another and then introduce the person they interviewed to the class. After every three or four interviews ask the class to name those students who have just been presented. When all have been interviewed, ask each student to write the names of all students in the class.

Take roll by asking each student to respond to a metaphorical question such as: If you were a dessert (or junk food, or breakfast cereal, or animal, or road sign), what would you be?

Ask students to write an epitaph for themselves. What do they want people to remember about them? Students share in their groups and a group leader shares the results with the class. This can be modified to fit an assignment in math, history, science, art, or any other subject. For example, in history class write an epitaph for a historical character, in math class write the epitaph for a mathematical concept, in art class write one for an artist or art concept.

See Juell, Pearse, Schmidt, Yoshida.

**Completions** ask writers to supply endings to sentence fragments. Writing completions pushes students to focus their thinking.

See Beaman, Juell.

**Creative definitions** resembles the parlor game Dictionary in asking writers to invent definitions for words. This process of inventing stretches the imagination.

See Juell.

**Dialectics** draw on a strategy described by Ann Berthoff in *Forming, Thinking, Writing*. Writers divide a page in half and on the left side record notes from reading and on the right side list comments or questions about the material read. This written interchange leads to the development of new ideas about a subject.

See Arkle, West, Yoshida.

**Dialogues** are a form of role playing in which the writer creates an exchange between two characters being studied.

See Beaman, Forsman, Juell, Pearse, Peterson, Watson, Yoshida, Zimmerman.

**Dictation** asks writers to copy exactly the words that are read aloud to them. The usual procedure is to read the whole selection through once and then repeat in sections.

Dictation helps students absorb new material, and at the same time makes them conscious of how language works.

See Beaman, Peterson, Yoshida.

**Dramatic scenarios** present writers with situations of conflict drawn from subject matter and ask them to respond. By asking students to project themselves into the material, dramatic scenarios increase involvement with what is being studied.

See Beaman, Forsman.

**Exit slips** are usually distributed at the end of class and provide closure for learning by asking students to summarize what has occurred during the preceding class. These slips provide closure for students and, if collected by teachers, indicate what students know and need to know.

See Juell, Yoshida.

**First thoughts** were identified by Peter Elbow in *Writing with Power*. Their immediate written impressions frequently become the basis for further writing. First thoughts provide students a benchmark with which to measure their own learning.

See Arkle, Juell, Marik, Pearse, Peterson.

**Focused writing** invites writers to concentrate on a single topic during nonstop writing of specified duration. Like brainstorming, focused writing enables students to see how much they have to say on a given subject.

See Beaman, Forsman, Juell, Marik, Pearse, Watson, Yoshida, Zimmerman.

**Free writing** emphasizes fluency by asking writers to write continuously for a specified period of time. The fluency induced by free writing makes other forms of writing to learn possible.

See Juell, Zimmerman.

**Guided imagery** is described in Tristine Rainer's *The New Diary.* It combines relaxation techniques with oral narrative to provide writers with an imaginative experience which becomes the basis for writing. Like role playing and dramatic scenarios, guided imagery asks students to become directly involved in what they study, gives them direct instruction in how to proceed.

See Juell, Watson.

**Instant versions** are suggested by Peter Elbow in *Writing with Power.* They ask writers to pretend that they are actually composing a final draft long before they are ready to actually complete such a task. The instant version helps writers focus and clarify ideas. Like first thoughts, instant versions give writers a benchmark for measuring their own progress, and they also push writers to generate a great deal of material quickly.

See Arkle.

**Journals** are, as Roethke says, greenhouses in which ideas grow. Journals provide a place to keep many of the writings described in this list and are central to writing to learn. Without journals, writing to learn loses its effectiveness because students have no way to preserve evidence of their learning.

See Arkle, Beaman, Forsman, Juell, Johnston, Marik, Pearse, Peterson, Watson, Yoshida.

The following are ideas to get students writing in their journals:

List the smells you like.

List the famous people you would invite to a party you were giving.

Write a letter to someone in class you don't know very well explaining why you would like to know him or her.

Write a response to something you read in the paper last night or watched on television.

Write a dialogue between you and your pen exploring the obligations you have to one another and your responsibilities to each other.

Begin your entry with "What if. . . ."

Begin your entry with "I wonder. . . ."

Begin your entry with "I remember when. . . ."

Begin your entry with "The field trip I would like to take with this class would be to _____ because. . . ."

Begin with "Before I was five, I. . . ."

Describe a wound you got as a child.

Write a letter to your future child or grandchild.

Write a letter to your hair, your feet, or some other body part.

Write a letter to a particular trait or ambition.

Assume you are a rock. Write a monologue telling us your history. Select a particular rock and set up its environment.

React, comment on, explain, defend, or argue with one of the following quotations.

"I can't be human. I haven't the time" (Theodore Roethke).
"There are worse words than cuss words; there are words that hurt" (Tillie Olsen).
"It is impossible to persuade a man who does not disagree but smiles" (Muriel Sparks).
"I expect you to be human beings. Don't laugh—that's already an incredible assumption: they're a disappearing species" (Theodore Roethke).
Write a narration that contains each of the following words: quarter, Bahamas, staple, ruffles.
Make a list of your important possessions.
Speculate on where you will be and what you'll be doing on this date next year.

See Beaman, Forsman, Juell, Marik, Peterson, Watson, Yoshida, Zimmerman.

**Lists** invite writers to generate information for further examination. Listing provides students a shorthand form for recording many ideas.

See Beaman, Foresman, Juell, Marik, Peterson, Watson, Yoshida, Zimmerman.

**Metaphorical questions** draw on Peter Elbow's discussion of metaphor in *Writing with Power.* They invite writers to think in analogous terms. Metaphorical questions lead to metaphorical thinking, a form essential to cognitive development.

See Arkle, Foresman, Juell, Pearse, Yoshida.

**Nutshelling** is described by Linda Flower in *A Problem-Solving Approach to Writing* and asks the writer to identify central ideas in information. This process enables writers to begin the process of selection essential to critical thinking.

See Pearse, Watson.

**Question of the day** invites writers to describe themselves or others within a specified category. Responses to this question open the way to metaphorical thinking.

See Juell.

**Role-playing** invites writers to participate imaginatively in material being studied. Like other forms of imaginative projection, role-playing fosters learning through involvement.

See Forsman, Johnston, Juell, Marik, Peterson, Yoshida.

**Treeing** as described by Linda Flower in *A Problem-Solving Approach to Writing* organizes bits of information into forms that show their relationship.
Like nutshelling, this strategy leads to evaluative thinking.

See Marik, Pearse.

**Unsent letters** are a form of role-playing that asks writers to draft letters in response to material being studied. They are described in Tristine Rainer's *The New Diary.*
Like other forms of role playing, unsent letters require imaginative involvement with material studied.

See Beaman, Juell, Pearse, Watson, West.

**Writing Groups** provide writers with peer response to work in progress. Procedures for groups vary, but the following set of directives draws on Peter Elbow's *Writing without Teachers.*

> *Each member is allocated an equal portion of the available time.* Groups designate a timekeeper and divide the time available by the number of people present. It is the timekeeper's responsibility to be sure the group stays on schedule, allowing an equal amount of time for each member.

*Each member's allocated time is divided into half for reading and half for group response.*

The timekeeper stops the reading if it goes too long. If an individual has a total of thirty minutes, no more than fifteen minutes should be spent reading.

*Work in progress is read aloud once, the author pauses long enough for group members to write initial responses, then the author reads the writing a second time. During the second reading, group members take detailed notes on their responses to what they hear.*

Oral rather than written versions of work in progress are presented to writing groups because hearing rather than seeing work prevents fussing with small features on the page and keeps attention focused on the larger effects of writing. Group members take no notes during the first reading, but before the second, they record general impression responses. During the second reading, group members take careful notes so that they may refer the author to specific passages.

*Group members give oral responses to the author immediately after the second reading.*

Each member speaks in turn with no comment from anyone else in the group. Usually responses begin with "After the first reading I felt/thought . . ." and then proceed to the list of responses collected during the second reading.

*Oral responses are from the perspective of the audience: they do not offer advice.* Rewriting is the author's job. Members of the writing group are responsible for telling the author what they hear and how they respond.

*The author remains silent as group members respond and writes all comments for future reference.*

During the meeting of the writing group, the author's job is to collect as much information as possible about the effect of the piece just read, not to defend or explain the writing.

See Forsman, Pearse, West.

# Bibliography

Linda J. Clifton
University of Washington, Seattle

Barr, Mary, Pat D'Arcy, and Mary Healy, eds. *What's Going On? Language Learning Episodes in British and American Classrooms, Grades 4–13.* Montclair, N.J.: Boynton/Cook, 1981.
Personal accounts by thirteen teachers in Britain and the U.S. describing the ways in which language functions in their individual classrooms to help students discover as well as report their learning.

Barrel, J. "Reflections on Critical Thinking in Secondary Schools." *Educational Leadership*, March 1983, 45–49.
Gives examples of student behavior which seem merely playful but which develop imagination, invention, and critical thinking, then draws conclusions about the cognitive, affective, and moral development taking place and about implications for curriculum.

Berthoff, Ann E. *Forming-Thinking-Writing: The Composing Imagination.* Montclair, N.J.: Boynton/Cook, 1982.
A college text meant to teach students how to get started writing, how to get past writing barriers, how to control effects, how to define, limit, expand, subordinate, coordinate, recapitulate, how to know when to stop. Combines theory and practice. Lots of examples of writing and exercises which draw on both sides of the brain.

Bloom, Benjamin S., et al. *A Taxonomy of Educational Objectives: Handbook 1: Cognitive Domain.* New York: Longman, 1977.
Part I of Bloom's classification system of educational objectives. Classifies the cognitive domain into the hierarchy of knowledge, comprehension, application, analysis, synthesis, and evaluation, subdivides each class, and gives examples of each. Useful for identifying learning goals and behaviors that demonstrate higher level thinking.

Britton, James. *Language and Learning.* New York: Penguin Books, 1972.
Explores the relationship of speaking and writing to learning. Develops the concept of expressive language as the foundation of all other types of language. This idea of expressive language is central to thinking about writing as a way of learning.

_____,et al. *The Development of Writing Abilities (11–18)*. London: MacMillan, 1975.

Britton's report on his investigation of student writing in the school situation. Lays out his methodology, definitions, the special demands and limits of writing in a school setting. Creates the term "transactional," "poetic," and "expressive" as descriptions of the principal functions of writing utterances and defines each. Presents results of the study, its implications, and directions for further research. A fundamental resource for considering the problems and possibilities in fostering writing development in students in the schools.

Draper, Virginia. *Formative Writing: Writing to Assist Learning*. Berkeley: Bay Area Writing Project, 1979.

Discusses a variety of techniques for stimulating and utilizing writing done to assist and refine the process of learning. Includes examples from student work.

Elbow, Peter. *Writing with Power: Techniques for Mastering the Writing Process*. New York: Oxford, 1981.

Descriptions of many writing techniques that can be adapted to complement any subject: free writing, direct writing, open-ended and loop processes, revising methods, approaches to audience, criterion-based and reader-based feedback, development of voice. Includes annotated bibliography on self-publishing writing.

Emig, Janet. *The Composing Processes of Twelfth Graders*. Urbana, Ill.: NCTE, 1971.

An NCTE research report of case studies on how twelfth graders compose; includes a review of the literature on creative process and rhetoric, a detailed profile of a twelfth-grade writer, and sketches of seven other twelfth graders. Distinguishes between "reflexive" and "extensive" writing (similar to Britton's "expressive" and "transactional" writing) and analyzes components of the composing process for each. Suggests directions for further research.

_____."Writing as a Mode of Learning." *College Composition and Communication* 28 (May 1977): 122–28.

Discusses why writing is a powerful tool for learning: "If the most efficacious learning occurs when learning is reinforced, then writing through its inherent re-inforcing cycle involving hand (enactive learning), eye (iconic learning), and brain (symbolic learning) makes a uniquely powerful multirepresentational mode for learning." Points out that writing involves both sides of the brain, that it integrates past, present, and future to make meaning, that it involves both analysis and synthesis, and that it provides a record of the process of learning as well as its product.

Executive Committee of the National Council of Teachers of English. "Essentials of English: A Document for Reflection and Dialogue." *English Journal* 72 (February 1983): 51–53.

A position statement, approved in October 1982, by the Executive Committee of the National Council of Teachers of English, identifying the "focus, balance and purpose" of an appropriate program in English language arts. Encourages emphasis on writing as a process in which students discover what they have to say.

Freisinger, Randell. "Cross-Disciplinary Writing Workshops: Theory and Practice." *College English* 42 (October 1980): 154–66.
Distinguishes language for learning from language for informing; declares that excessive emphasis in schools on writing to inform may seriously impair cognitive development for many students. Addresses the problem of helping students move to Piaget's formal operations stage, a transaction that up to 50 percent of our adolescents fail to make before reaching college age.

Fulwiler, Toby. "Journals across the Disciplines." *English Journal* 69 (December 1980): 14–19.
Discusses the reasons and methods for incorporating journal writing into classroom activity and describes the writing-across-the-curriculum program in the Humanities division at Michigan Technological University.

Fulwiler, Toby, and Art Young, eds. *Language Connections: Writing and Reading across the Curriculum.* Urbana, Ill.: NCTE, 1982.
A collection of articles about the various functions of expressive, transactional, and poetic writing across the curriculum, about the significance of reading research for all teachers, and about ways to respond to writing. Annotated bibliography.

Hays, Janice N., et al., eds. *The Writer's Mind: Writing as a Mode of Thinking.* Urbana, Ill.: NCTE, 1983.
A collection of articles which consider new information, cognitive development, pedagogy, and brain research in relation to the composing process. Uses many ideas from classical rhetoric and attempts to integrate these with an approach that sees writing as a process rather than a product and that regards writing as a means of fostering cognitive development.

Herrington, Anne J. "Writing to Learn: Writing across the Disciplines." *College English* 43 (April 1981): 379–87.
Suggests several writing assignments useful for facilitating learning in social studies courses and methods for presenting those assignments, and presents a rationale for using writing as a means for learning in all disciplines.

Hillocks, George, Jr. "Inquiry and the Composing Process: Theory and Research." *College English* 44 (November 1982): 659–73.
Points out that writing skills alone are insufficient for producing excellent analytic writing, that the writer must understand as well as know how to analyze the data to be discussed. Identifies various strategies of inquiry usable in a variety of unrelated disciplines: observation, description, generalization, comparison, contrast, definition, hypothesis, and test. Constructs a model demonstrating the relationship of these strategies to levels of cognitive development. Shows that student writing improved when materials and activities were designed by the following process: (1) identify the strategy to

be taught, (2) identify characteristics of the written product indicating use of the strategy, (3) identify tasks for the writer which implement the strategy, (4) order the tasks from least to most difficult. Gives numerous examples from classrooms. Concludes that involving students in practice of strategies improves writing more than does imitation of models, though both methods result in improvement.

Johnson, Sabina Thorne. "The Ant and the Grasshopper: Some Reflections on Prewriting." *College English* 43 (March 1981): 232–41.

Compares recent theoretical approaches to prewriting, which Johnson calls "intuitional," and with classical rhetoric and heuristics, which she calls "intellectual." Says classical rhetoric requires the writer to move from data to thesis while more recent approaches seek to force the writer to discover questions and connections among data by unearthing these from the subconscious. Questions both approaches for their usefulness in training students to think or write with facility.

Kirby, Dan and Tom Liner. *Inside Out: Developmental Strategies for Teaching Writing.* Montclair, N.J.: Boynton/Cook, 1981.

Two classroom teachers present a compendium of their strategies for encouraging students to discover and develop their own linguistic resources. Emphasizes the writing process: "getting started, getting down, getting it right, checking it out." Stresses the importance of making the classroom a community of writers, with the teacher as colleague. Discusses the theory behind their work, the writing process, the classroom environment, the journal, evaluating and responding to writing, audience and voice, revision, publication, specific modes of writing; gives numerous exercises and examples for implementation day by day in the classroom. Includes useful list of resources on theory and methods, films, poetry, publishing.

Knoblauch, C.H. and Lil Brannon. "Writing as Learning through the Curriculum." *College English* 45 (September 1983): 465–74.

Emphasizes the importance of regarding writing as a means of "finding and conveying meanings, " a heuristic for understanding any of the disciplines. Defines knowledge as a constant process of refining patterns of relationships, so that writing becomes integral to learning since its very nature forces the learner to discover those relationships in order to state them. Criticizes the work of Maimon, Berthoff, and Herrington. Gives specific examples for incorporating writing as heuristic into classroom activity.

Macrorie, Ken. *Telling Writing.* 2d ed. Rochelle Park, N.J.: Hayden, 1976.

Begins by indicting the category of transactional writing called "theme-writing," written only as a school exercise and not for real communication, and labels it "Engfish." Begins with exercises to encourage what Britton calls expressive writing—writing the truth for ourselves about our experiences—and moves on to revision, precision, irony, dialog, and a variety of other writing strategies.

Uses examples from student writing and from literature to illustrate and analyze the qualities of good writing.

Maimon, Elaine P., et al. *Writing in the Arts and Sciences.* Cambridge, Mass. Winthrop, 1981.

A textbook designed for the college English composition course, based on the assumptions that writing is a process, a way to learn as well as to communicate, and, in any discipline, "a form of social behavior in that discipline." The first section demonstrates use of writing to learn, the second, use of writing to communicate in each of several disciplines. Uses extensive examples of student writing. Supplies a variety of ways to generate and organize ideas.

Martin, Nancy, P. D'Arcy, B. Newton, and R. Parker. *Writing and Learning across the Curriculum 11–16.* London: Ward Lock, 1976.

A follow-up to Britton's *Development of Writing Abilities (11–18)*, using Britton's system of classification, and presenting numerous examples of student response. Encourages teachers to provide a variety of audiences and a range of purposes both for student writing and talking. Illustrates extensively how children can understand new material by using the information in expressive writing, by writing for other audiences than "teacher-as-examiner." Concludes that a shift to cooperative learning between students and between teachers and students, to education as a dialogue, to a view of the learner as someone in transition, to progress as "the ability to use language more widely rather than more 'correctly,'" will foster creativity and thinking and that such a shift may be necessary to change opportunities for learning writing.

Mayher, John S., Nancy Lester, and Gordon Pradl. *Learning to Write—Writing to Learn.* Montclair, N.J.: Boynton/Cook, 1983.

A very readable introduction to its subject, this book draws on the work of James Britton, Donald Graves, Janet Emig, Linda Flower, Sondra Perl, and others to make its points that one learns to write by writing and that writing provides a means of learning. Summarizes recent research findings, provides numerous extensive examples of student and teacher responses, supplies exercises to encourage the reader to experiment with the issues raised by writing. Discusses the writing process, grammar, vocabulary study, the research paper. Includes concrete suggestions for using writing to learn, K–14, and for helping colleagues in other disciplines to use student writing as a teaching tool.

Miles, Josephine. *Working Out Ideas: Predication and Other Uses of Language.* Berkeley: Bay Area Writing Project, 1979.

Analyzes problems in student writing as failures to form clear predications and build detail upon those. Suggests methods for helping students to develop their rational abilities by using such patterning. Discusses styles in composition with examples from a range of British and American writers from the sixteenth to the twentieth century. Demonstrates how creation of an initial predication affects the grammatical constructions as well as the content that will follow.

Moffett, James. *Teaching the Universe of Discourse*. Boston: Houghton Mifflin, 1968.

A companion to and rationale for Moffett's student-centered curriculum. Proposes that English, like mathematics, is a symbol system, and "when a student 'learns' one of these systems, he learns how to operate it," and therefore the student should use his time manipulating the system "in every realistic way it can be used" rather than in studying it as an object. Relates what is known about cognition development to a proposed curriculum sequence. Argues that teaching about a subject (e.g., Christensen's generative rhetoric of the sentence) is a less powerful teaching tool than providing opportunities for practice of that subject (e.g., consideration in context of the effectiveness of differently organized sentences). Argues that students should learn to write by writing.

——————————. *Active Voice: A Writing Program across the Curriculum*. Montclair: N.J.: Boynton/Cook, 1981.

Describes a writing curriculum which works as a spiraling "accumulating repertory" from speech to private writing to public writing, from intimate to remote audiences, from recording to theorizing. Outlines and analyzes thirty-one specific assignments.

Piaget, Jean. *The Language and Thought of the Child*. trans. M. Gabain. London: Routledge & Kegan Paul, 1959.

Piaget's classic study from 1921–22 of the stages of cognitive development in children begins by asking "What are the needs which a child tends to satisfy when he talks?" Classifies child language by purpose and structure, characterizes stages of development for ages four to eleven as revealed in language use, and cites extensive examples drawn from observation. Points out the importance in development of noncommunicating, or egocentric language.

Progoff, Ira. *At a Journal Workshop: The Basic Text and Guide for Using the Intensive Journal Process*. New York: Dialogue House Library, 1975.

Proposes that certain principles and disciplines must govern the use of journals if they are to be effective in promoting personal growth, and that various types of journals may serve in helping writers discover new meanings in their lives. Leads the reader through various kinds of journal writing.

Rainer, Tristine. *The New Diary*. New York: St. Martin's Press, 1979.

Shows how journal writing can be a tool for personal growth. Includes a wide variety of exercises to stimulate such writing. The diary is "the only form of writing that encourages total freedom of expression, . . . immune to any formal rules of content, structure, or style" and thus becomes a powerful tool for self-discovery, for writing to learn.

Rico, Gabriele L. *Writing the Natural Way: Using Right-Brain Techniques to Release Your Expressive Powers*. Los Angeles: Tarcher, 1983.

Discusses the theory of hemisphericity, argues for nonlinear approaches to generating writing, presents numerous examples for stimulating written expression, many of these being variations on clustering technique.

Rosenblatt, Louise M. *Literature as Exploration*. 3d ed. New York: Noble and Noble, 1976.
  Discusses a range of possible student responses to literature and strategies for eliciting such responses. While she does not deal with writing as such, her perceptions and strategies are useful in an approach to teaching literature in which students write to learn.

Sampson, Gloria Paulik, and Nancy Carlman. "A Hierarchy of Student Responses to Literature." *English Journal* 71 (January 1982): 54–57.
  Demonstrates through examples how students can be helped to move through identification, disassociation, and evaluation to develop their responses to literature. Includes bibliography of research and teaching material.

Tchudi, Stephen. *Writing in the Content Areas: The NEA Inservice Training Program*. West Haven, Conn.: National Education Association, 1984.
  This package, written by a former president of NCTE, includes forty specific resources to help teachers of all subjects at all grade levels with practical techniques of teaching writing while teaching other subject matter. Filmstrips, audiotapes, monographs, and reproducible handouts accompany this program.

Vygotsky, Lev S. *Thought and Language*. Ed. Gertrude Vakar, trans. Eugenia Hanfmann. Cambridge, Mass.: MIT Press, 1962.
  Important discussion of the relationship between development of speech and development of thought. Takes the point of view that thought and speech have different hereditary roots and follow independent developmental lines but that in humans the two lines of development interact, foster each other, and the connection itself continues to develop. Challenges Piaget's concept of intellectual development. Description of "inner speech" parallels Britton's ideas concerning the function of "expressive writing."

Wolfe, Denny, and Robert Reising. *Writing for Learning in the Content Areas*. Portland, Maine: J. Weston Walch, 1983.
  A practical compendium of specific lessons involving writing in a variety of disciplines including math, social studies, and the sciences.

Wotring, Anne Miller, and Robert Tierney. *Two Studies of Writing in High School Science*. Berkeley: Bay Area Writing Project, 1981.
  Specific, detailed description of the experience of two students and of the researcher using writing to think about chemistry. Discusses how the writing process developed, how it made the writers feel, what problems were encountered. Draws conclusions about the experience of these writers and of the other 26 writers in the chemistry class. Gives specific suggestions to teachers for encouraging writing to think. Second half of the book discusses the use of expressive writing to teach biology, describes a controlled experiment involving 136 students explaining the variety of writing used. Finds that use of expressive writing as a learning tool increases retention of what students have learned.

# Contributors

**Stephen Arkle** has taught English for eleven years. He is presently teaching in the Lake Washington School District. Stephen is department chairman and teaches both regular and intensive or honors classes. The class referred to in his chapter is called "senior English studies" which is designed to take students to self-directed study. The chapter explains how writing-to-learn strategies have affected his students' ability to not only write better but to think better.

**Bruce Beaman** has taught for fifteen years at Mountlake Terrace High School, one of five high schools in the Edmonds School District about ten miles north of Seattle. Bruce teaches psychology, sociology, contemporary problems, and psychology of self-esteem. In his chapter he explains how he uses writing to help his students become involved and learn more effectively in these classes.

**Barbara Bronson** has been part-time reader/instructor in the English and Slavic Departments at the University of Washington for the past ten years. Because she was not directly involved in the Writing-in-the-Humanities program, she was assigned the project of interviewing teachers and students in the program and observing classroom techniques. The interviews and observations covered a three-month period in the spring of 1982.

**Linda J. Clifton** is the Assistant Director of the Puget Sound Writing Program at the University of Washington, and an English teacher at the Woodinville High School in Woodinville, Washington. She is the editor of the *Crab Creek Review* and has written and presented workshops on a variety of English education issues.

**Syrene Forsman** has taught sophomore English, humanities, and junior creative writing for ten years at Roosevelt High School in Seattle. The study body numbers 1600 students of every ethnic background from Asian to Scandinavian. In her chapter Syrene explains that writing to learn in her classroom means learning to think and discusses strategies for and results of using writing to develop thinking.

**Anne Ruggles Gere** teaches English at the University of Washington and directs the Puget Sound Writing Program. In addition, she directed the Writing-to-Learn project sponsored by the National Endowment for the Humanities. In the introduction, she traces the principles that underlie writing to learn.

236

**Patricia Johnston** has taught science in grades seven through twelve for over twenty years. She is currently teaching general chemistry, honors chemistry, and physics at Shorecrest High School in the Shoreline School District, a suburban area immediately north of the Seattle city limits. In her chapter she explains how she uses writing to help her students learn more about life science, biology, zoology, chemistry, and physics.

**Pat Juell** has taught for over twenty years in California and Washington public high schools. Currently she teaches at Mountain View High School (Evergreen School District) in Vancouver, Washington, where her classes include basic composition, creative writing, humanities, college prep writing, and accelerated senior English. In her chapter Pat discusses the basic function of the course journal in the writing-to-learn process. She covers methods to get the teacher started, ways to solve problems that might occur, and provides sample lessons using a sequence of journal-writing strategies.

**Ray Marik** has taught special education and regular classes in the Seattle School District for twenty years. He teaches special education classes in language arts, math, U.S. history, and world history. His students have learning and language disabilities, behavioral disabilities, mental handicaps, and neurological impairments. They are all educated in the same class, but are grouped according to class standings, e.g. sophomores for world history; juniors for U.S. history; other classes are nongraded. Class size averages ten students. In his chapter, Ray describes writing-to-learn strategies that have been successfully used with certain special-education students.

**Steve Pearse** has taught English at Shorewood High School in the Shoreline District, a suburban community just north of Seattle, for nine years. He teaches both regular and honors freshmen as well as regular and advanced sophomores, juniors, and seniors. Courses are one semester in length, and the average class size is twenty-eight. In his chapter, Steve discusses the many advantages a writing-to-learn program offers, from student-teacher relationships to evaluation and student creativity.

**Deborah Peterson** has taught German for two years in the Bethel School District, a semi-rural area south of Tacoma. She teaches first- and second-year students. Her classes have been relatively large: forty in her first-year classes and thirty in her second-year class. In her chapter she explains how writing-to-learn techniques have helped her monitor student progress in these large classes and how these techniques have improved students' organizational skills as well as knowledge of grammar, spoken forms, and cultural concepts.

**Don Schmidt** teaches math at Woodbrook Junior High in the Clover Park School District. Ninety-two percent of the students are from families stationed on nearby military bases, McCord or Fort Lewis. Because of their frequent military-related moving, many Woodbrook students have not kept pace with their less transient peers. Forty percent of the students read below grade level, and a majority are two or more years deficient on math skills measured by standardized tests. In his chapter Don describes his strategies for using writing to help students deal with both affective and cognitive problems in learning math.

**Ralph Stevens** served as Assistant Director of the Puget Sound Writing Program from 1978 to 1983. He was Assistant Director of the NEH-sponsored project on writing to learn. He is currently living in Baltimore, Maryland, where he teaches in an English program for foreign students at Coppin State College.

**Tom Watson** teaches U.S. history to juniors and seniors and Pacific Northwest studies (Washington state history) to freshmen and seniors at Shorecrest High School, located in a suburb north of Seattle. Tom's classes contain students of all ability levels. In his chapter he describes how writing to learn helps his students learn more about history.

**Janet West** has taught elective courses for grades nine through twelve in English literature, mythology, college preparatory expository writing, general composition, journalism, and mass media on Bainbridge Island for fourteen years. In her chapter she explains her conviction that peer evaluation, a natural corollary to writing-to-learn techniques, is an essential dimension of every student's education.

**Jessie Yoshida** has taught English at Inglemoor High School in Bothell, a north Seattle suburb, since 1968. She teaches literature and composition to sophomores and juniors as well as philosophy and personal communications electives to juniors and seniors. While students are grouped into honors, regulars, and alternative English classes, electives draw from all three groups. In her chapter, Jessie describes how writing to learn helped students understand difficult texts and concepts in a philosophy elective.

**Priscilla Zimmerman** has taught art electives at the high school level for eight years. Her courses aim at increasing students' appreciation of art as well as developing skills in art production. In her chapter she discusses how the language of art is the vehicle through which students learn to make knowledgeable and sensitive responses to art, and she explains how she uses writing-to-learn strategies to increase students' appreciation of art.